Salem Witchcraft;

COMPRISING

MORE WONDERS OF THE INVISIBLE WORLD.

Collected by ROBERT CALEF;

AND

WONDERS OF THE INVISIBLE WORLD,

BY COTTON MATHER:

TOGETHER WITH

NOTES AND EXPLANATIONS
BY SAMUEL P. FOWLER.

THE LAWBOOK EXCHANGE, LTD.
Clark, New Jersey

ISBN 978-1-58477-462-4 (hardcover)
ISBN 978-1-61619-451-2 (paperback)

Lawbook Exchange edition 2005, 2014

The quality of this reprint is equivalent to the quality of the original work.

THE LAWBOOK EXCHANGE, LTD.
33 Terminal Avenue
Clark, New Jersey 07066-1321

Please see our website for a selection of our other publications and fine facsimile reprints of classic works of legal history:
www.lawbookexchange.com

Library of Congress Cataloging-in-Publication Data

Salem witchcraft : comprising More wonders of the invisible world / collected by Robert Calef. and, Wonders of the invisible world / by Cotton Mather : together with notes and explanations by Samuel P. Fowler.
    p. cm.
Originally published: Salem, Mass. : H.P. Ives and A.A. Smith, 1861.
ISBN 1-58477-462-2 (alk. paper)
   1. Trials (Witchcraft)—Massachusetts. 2. Massachusetts—History—Colonial
period, ca. 1600-1775. I. Fowler, Samuel Page, 1800-1888. II. Calef, Robert, 1648-1719. More wonders of the invisible world. III. Mather, Cotton, 1663-1728. Wonders of the invisible world.

KFM2478.8.W5S23 2005
133.4'3'097445—dc22   2004050906

Printed in the United States of America on acid-free paper

Salem Witchcraft;

COMPRISING

MORE WONDERS OF THE INVISIBLE WORLD.

Collected by ROBERT CALEF;

AND

WONDERS OF THE INVISIBLE WORLD,

BY COTTON MATHER:

TOGETHER WITH

NOTES AND EXPLANATIONS

BY SAMUEL P. FOWLER.

SALEM, Mafs:
H. P. Ives and A. A. Smith,
1861.

Entered according to Act of Congress, in the year 1860, by
H. P. IVES AND A. A. SMITH,
In the Clerk's Office of the District Court of the District of
Massachusetts.

Riverside, Cambridge:
Stereotyped and Printed by
H. O. HOUGHTON.

MORE WONDERS
OF THE
INVISIBLE WORLD,
OR
THE WONDERS
OF
THE INVISIBLE WORLD
DISPLAYED.

IN FIVE PARTS.

PART I.—An Account of the Sufferings of Margaret Rule, written by the Rev. Cotton Mather.

PART II.—Several Letters to the Author, &c. and his Reply relating to Witchcraft.

PART III.—The Differences between the Inhabitants of Salem Village, and Mr. Parris, their Minister, in New-England.

PART IV.—Letters of a Gentleman uninterested, endeavouring to prove the received opinions about Witchcraft to be Orthodox. With short Essays to their Answers.

PART V.—A short Historical Account of Matters of Fact in that Affair.

TO WHICH IS ADDED

A POSTCRIPT,

RELATING TO A BOOK ENTITLED "THE LIFE OF SIR WM. PHIPS."

COLLECTED BY

ROBERT CALEF,

Merchant, of Boston, in New-England.

PRINTED IN LONDON, A. D. 1700, AND IN 1796.
RE-PRINTED IN SALEM, IN 1823.
IN BOSTON, 1828.

PREFACE.

OBERT CALEF was a merchant in Boſton, and died in 1720. His "More Wonders of the Inviſible World" was firſt publiſhed in London, in a ſmall quarto volume, in 1700, and reprinted at Salem in 1796 and in 1823; another edition was iſſued in Boston in 1828. It is thought by ſome, that it was publiſhed in England on account of the unwillingneſs of publiſhers in Boſton to incur the wrath of the Mathers. But this is doubtful, as it was a common thing for authors to ſend over their manuſcripts to England to be publiſhed. Cotton Mather, in his diary,—alluding to the publiſhing of Calef's "More Wonders of the Inviſible World,"—ſays: "He ſent this vile volume to London to be publiſhed, and the book is printed, and the impreſſion is this

week arrived here. The books that I have sent over into England, with a design to glorify the Lord Jesus Christ, are not published, but strangely delayed; and the books that are sent over to vilify me, and render me incapable to glorify the Lord Jesus Christ, — these are published. I set myself to humble myself before the Lord under these humbling and wondrous dispensations, and obtain the pardon of my sins, that have rendered me worthy of such dispensations." Dr. Elliot informs us that Dr. Increase Mather — who was then president of Harvard College — ordered the wicked book of Calef to be burnt in the college-yard, and that "It is worthy of observation, that Hutchinson — who was nearly related to the Mather family — speaks of R. Calef as a man of a fair mind, who substantiated his facts."

THE EPISTLE TO THE READER,

AND MORE ESPECIALLY TO THE NOBLE BARONS OF THIS AGE, WHEREVER RESIDING.

GENTLEMEN,

OU, that are freed from the flavery of a corrupt education; and that, in fpite of human precepts, example, and precedents, can hearken to the dictates of fcripture and reafon; for your fakes I am content that thefe collections of mine, as alfo my fentiments, fhould be expofed to public view; in hopes that, having well confidered and compared them with fcripture, you will fee reafon, as I do, to queftion a belief fo prevalent as that here treated of, as alfo the practice flowing from thence; they ftanding as nearly connected as caufe and effect; it being found wholly impracticable to extirpate the latter, without firft curing the former. And if the buffoon or fatirical will be exercifing their talents, or if the bigots wilfully and blindly reject the teftimonies of their own reafon, and more

sure word, it is no more than what I expected from them. But you, gentlemen, I doubt not, are willing to distinguish between truth and error; and if this may be any furtherance to you herein, I shall not miss my aim. But if you find the contrary, and that my belief herein is any way heterodox, I shall be thankful for the information to any learned or reverend person, or others, that shall take that pains to inform me better, by scripture or sound reason; which is what I have been long seeking for, in this country, in vain.

In a time when not only England in particular, but almost all Europe, had been labouring against the usurpations of tyranny and slavery, the English America has not been behind in a share of the common calamities; more especially, New England has met not only with such calamities as are common to the rest, but with several aggravations enhancing such afflictions, by the devastations and cruelties of the barbarous Indians in their eastern borders, &c. But this is not all; they have been harast (on many accounts) by a more dreadful enemy, as will herein appear to the considerate.

Were it, as we are told in *Wonders of the Invisible World*, "that the devils were walking about our streets with lengthened chains, making a dreadful noise in our ears; and brimstone (even without a metaphor) was making a horrid and hellish stench in our nostrils;" and, "that the devil, exhibiting himself ordinarily as a black man, had decoyed a fearful knot of proud, froward, ignorant, envious and malicious creatures, to lift themselves in his horrid service, by entering their names in a book tendered unto them; and that they have had their meetings and sacraments, and associated themselves to destroy the kingdom of our Lord Jesus Christ, in these parts of the world; having each of them their spectres, or devils, commissioned by them, and representing of them to be the engines of their malice, by these wicked spectres seizing poor people about the country, with various and bloody torments, and of those evidently preternatural torments some have died; and that they have bewitched some even so far as to make them self-destroyers, and others in many towns here and there languished under their evil hands— the people, thus afflicted, miserably scratched and bitten; and that the same invisible furies did stick pins in them, and scald them, distort and disjoint them, with a thousand other plagues; and sometimes drag them out of their chambers, and carry them over trees and hills, miles together, many of them being tempted to sign the devil's laws "—" those furies, whereof several have killed more people perhaps than would

serve to make a village "—If this be the true
state of the afflictions of this country, it is very
deplorable, and beyond all other outward calamities miserable. But if, on the other side, the
matter be, as others do understand it, that the
devil has been too hard for us by his temptations, signs, and lying wonders, with the help of
pernicious notions, formerly imbibed and professed; together with the accusations of a parcel
of possessed, distracted or lying wenches,* accusing their innocent neighbours, pretending
they see their spectres, i. e. devils in their likeness, afflicting of them; and that God in righteous judgment (after men had ascribed his power
to witches, of commissioning devils to do these
things) may have given them over to strong delusions to believe lies, &c., and to let loose the
devils of envy, hatred, pride, cruelty and malice
against each other, yet still disguised under the
mask of zeal for God, and left them to the
branding one another with the odious name of
witch; and upon the accusation of those above
mentioned, brother to accuse and prosecute
brother, children their parents, pastors and
teachers their immediate flock, unto death;
shepherds becoming wolves; wise men infatu-
ated; people hauled to prisons; with a bloody

---

* The circle of accusing girls at Salem Village.

noise pursuing to, and insulting over the (true) sufferers at, execution; while some are fleeing from that called justice, justice itself fleeing before such accusations, when once it did but begin to refrain further proceedings; and, to question such practices, some making their escape out of prisons, rather than by an obstinate defence of their innocency to run so apparent hazard of their lives; estates seized, families of children and others left to the mercy of the wilderness (not to mention here the numbers proscribed, dead in prisons or executed, &c.)—All which tragedies, though begun in one town, or rather by one parish, has plague-like spread more than through that country, and by its echo giving a brand of infamy to this whole country throughout the world :—If this were the miserable case of this country in the time thereof, and that the devil had so far prevailed upon us, in our sentiments and actions, as to draw us from so much as looking into the scriptures for our guidance in these pretended intricacies; leading us to a trusting in blind guides, such as the corrupt practices of some other countries, or the bloody experiments of Bodin,* and such other authors; — then, though our case be most miserable, yet

---

* John Bodin was a Frenchman, and the author of " Demonomania." Dr. Harsenet, Archbishop of York, informs us " that his Brain was the Theatre and Sport-House for the Devils to dance

it muſt be ſaid of New-England, thou haſt deſtroyed thyſelf, and brought this greateſt of miſeries upon thee.

And now, whether the witches (ſuch as have made a compact by explicit covenant with the devil, having thereby obtained a power to commiſſion him,) have been the cauſe of our miſeries; or whether a zeal, governed by blindneſs and paſſion and led by precedent, has not herein precipitated us into far greater wickedneſs (if not witchcrafts) than any have yet been proved againſt thoſe that ſuffered:—to be able to diſtinguiſh aright in this matter, to which of theſe two to refer our miſeries, is the deſign of the preſent work.

As to the former, I know of no ſober man, much leſs reverend chriſtian, that, being aſked, dares affirm, and abide by it, that witches have that power, viz. to commiſſion devils to kill and deſtroy; and as to the latter, it were well if there were not too much of truth in it, which remains to be demonſtrated.

iii. That he believed that a Witch, by Ointment and Charms, may transform herſelf into the ſhape of any Beaſt, Bird or Fiſh.— And that Bodin relates a ſtory of an Egg, which a Witch ſold to an Engliſhman, and by the ſame transformed him into an Aſs, and made him her Market-Mule three years, to ride on to buy Butter; and how at laſt ſhe remorphized him into the Native Shape of a Man again." This experiment of the witch in furniſhing herſelf with a market beaſt is certainly novel and queer, and has not been attained as yet by any ſpiritual manifeſtation of the preſent day.

But here it will be said, What need of raking in the coals that lay buried in oblivion? We cannot recal those to life again, that have suffered, supposing it were unjustly; it tends but to the exposing the actors, as if they had proceeded irregularly.

Truly I take this to be just as the devil would have it, so much to fear disobliging men, as not to endeavour to detect his wiles, that so he may the sooner, and with the greater advantages, set the same on foot again (either here or elsewhere), so dragging us through the pond twice by the same cat. And, if reports do not herein deceive us, much the same has been acting this present year in Scotland. And what kingdom or country is it, that has not had their bloody fits and turns at it? And if this is such a catching disease and so universal, I presume I need make no apology for my endeavours to prevent, as far as in my power, any more such bloody victims or sacrifices; though indeed I had rather any other would have undertaken so offensive, though necessary, a task; yet, all things weighed, I had rather thus expose myself to censure, than that it should be wholly omitted. Were the notions in question innocent and harmless, respecting the glory of God, and well-being of men, I should not have engaged in them; but finding them, in my esteem, so intolerably destructive of both, this, together with my being by warrant called before the justices, in my own just vindication I took it to be a call from God, to my power, to vindicate his truths, against the pagan and popish assertions which are so prevalent; for though christians in general do own the scriptures to be their only rule of faith and doctrine, yet these notions will tell us, that the scriptures have not sufficiently, nor at all described the crime of witchcraft, whereby the culpable might be detected, though it be positive in the command to punish it by death; hence the world has been from time to time perplexed, in the prosecution of the several diabolical mediums of heathenish and popish invention to detect an imaginary crime (not but that there are witches such as the law of God describes) which has produced a deluge of blood; hereby rendering the commands of God not only void but dangerous.

So also they own God's providence and government of the world; and that tempests and storms, afflictions and diseases, are of his sending; yet these notions tell us, that the devil has the power of all these, and can perform them when commissioned by a witch thereto; and that he has a power, at the witch's call, to act and do, without and against the course of nature, and all natural causes, in afflicting and killing of innocents; and this it is that so many have died for.

Alfo it is generally believed, that if any man has ſtrength, it is from God the Almighty Being: but theſe notions will tell us, that the devil can make one man as ſtrong as many; which was one of the beſt proofs, as it was counted, againſt Mr. Burroughs the miniſter; though his contemporaries in the ſchools, during his minority, could have teſtified, that his ſtrength was then as much ſuperior to theirs as ever (ſetting aſide incredible romances) it was diſcovered to be ſince: thus rendering the power of God, and his providence, of none effect.

Theſe are ſome of the deſtructive notions of this age; and however the aſſerters of them ſeem ſometimes to value themſelves much upon ſheltering their neighbours from ſpectral accuſations, they may deſerve as much thanks as that tyrant, that, having induſtriouſly obtained an unintelligible charge againſt his ſubjects, in matters wherein it was impoſſible they ſhould be guilty, having thereby their lives in his power, yet ſuffers them of his mere grace to live, and will be called gracious lord.

It were too Icarian a taſk for one, unfurniſhed with neceſſary learning, and library, to give any juſt account from whence ſo great deluſions have ſprung, and ſo long continued. Yet, as an eſſay from thoſe ſcraps of reading that I have had opportunity of, it will be no great venture to say, that signs and lying wonders have been one principal cause.

It is written of Justin Martyr, who lived in the second century, that he was before his conversion a great philosopher; first in the way of the stoicks, and after, of the peripateticks, after that of the pythagorean, and after that of the platonist, sects; and after all proved of eminent use in the church of Christ: yet a certain author, speaking of one Apollonius Tyaneus, has these words: "That the most orthodox themselves began to deem him vested with power sufficient for a deity; which occasioned that so strange a doubt from Justin Martyr, as cited by the learned Gregory, fol. 37: If God be the creator and lord of the world, how comes it to pass that Apollonius his telisms have so much over-ruled the course of things? for we see that they also have stilled the waves of the sea, and the raging of the winds, and prevailed against the noisome flies, and incursions of wild beasts, &c." If so eminent and early a christian were by these false shews in such doubt, it is the less wonder, in our depraved times, to meet with what is equivalent thereto. Besides this, a certain author informs me, that Julian (afterwards called the apostate) being instructed in the philosophy and disciplines of the heathen, by Libarius his tutor, by this means he came to love philosophy better than the gofpel, and fo by degrees turned from chriftianity to heathenifm."

This fame Julian did, when apoftate, forbid that chriftians fhould be inftructed in the difcipline of the gentiles; which, it feems, Socrates, a writer of the ecclefiaftical hiftory, does acknowledge to be by the fingular providence of God; chriftians having then begun to degenerate from the gofpel, and to betake themfelves to heathenifh learning. And in the Mercury for the month of February, 1695, there is this account, "That the chriftian doctors, converfing much with the writings of the heathen, for the gaining of eloquence, a council was held at Carthage, which forbad the reading of the books of the gentiles."

From all which it may be eafily perceived, that in the primitive times of chriftianity, when not only many heathen of the vulgar, but alfo many learned men and philofophers, had embraced the chriftian faith, they ftill retained a love to their heathen learning; which, as one obferves, being tranfplanted into a chriftian foil, foon proved productive of pernicious weeds, which overran the face of the church; hence it was fo deformed, as the reformation found it.

Among other pernicious weeds arifing from this root, the doctrine of the power of devils, and witchcraft, as it is now and long has been underftood, is not the leaft: the fables of Homer, Virgil, Horace and Ovid, &c. being for the elegancy of their language retained then (and fo are to this day) in the fchools, have not only introduced, but eftablifhed, fuch doctrines, to the poifoning the chriftian world. A certain author expreffes it thus: "That as the chriftian fchools at firft brought men from heathenifm to the gofpel, fo thefe fchools carry men from the gofpel to heathenifm, as to their great perfection." And Mr. I. M. in his *Remarkable Providences*, gives an account, that (as he calls it) an old council did anathematize all thofe that believed fuch power of the devils, accounting it a damnable doctrine. But as other evils did afterwards increafe in the church (partly by fuch education) fo this infenfibly grew up with them, though not to that degree as that any council, I have ever heard or read of, has to this day taken off thofe anathemas; yet after this the church fo far declined that witchcraft became a principal ecclefiaftical engine (as alfo that of herefy was) to root up all that ftood in their way; and befides the ways of trial that we have ftill in practice, they invented fome which were peculiar to themfelves; which, whenever they were minded to improve againft any orthodox believer, they could eafily make effectual. That deluge of blood, which that Scarlet Whore has to anfwer for, fhed under this notion, how amazing is it!

The firft in England, that I have read of, of any note, fince the reformation, that afferts this doctrine, is the famous Mr. Perkins: he, as alfo Mr. Gaul, Mr. Bernard, &c. feem all of them to have undertaken one tafk; taking notice of the multiplicity of irregular ways to try them by, invented by heathen and papifts, they made it their bufinefs, and main work, herein to oppofe fuch as they faw to be pernicious. And if they did not look more narrowly into it, but followed the firft, viz. Mr. Perkins, whofe education (as theirs alfo) had foreftalled him into fuch belief, whom they readily followed, it cannot be wondered at. And that they were men liable to err, and fo not to be trufted to as perfect guides, will manifeftly appear to him that fhall fee their feveral receipts laid down to detect them, by their prefumptive and pofitive ones; and confider how few of either have any foundation in fcripture, or reafon; and how vaftly they differ from each other in both; each having his art by himfelf, which forty or an hundred more may as well imitate, and give theirs, *ad infinitum*, being without all manner of proof. But though this be their main defign, to take off people from thofe evil and bloody ways of trial, which they fpeak fo much againft; yet this does not hinder, to this day, but the same evil ways, or as bad, are still used to detect them by, and that even among protestants; and are so far justified, that a reverend person has said lately here, How else shall we detect witches? And another, being urged to prove by scripture such a sort of witch as has power to send devils to kill men, replied, that he did as firmly believe it, as any article of his faith; and that he (the inquirer) did not go to the scriptures to learn the mysteries of his trade or art. What can be said more to establish their heathenish notions, and to vilify the scriptures, our only rule? and that, after we have seen such dire effects thereof, as has threatened the utter extirpation of this whole country.

And as to most of the actors in these tragedies, though they are so far from defending their actions, that they will readily own that undue steps have been taken, &c. yet it seems they choose that the same should be acted over again, enforced by their example, rather than it should remain as a warning to posterity, as herein they have mist it. So far are they from giving glory to God, and taking the due shame to themselves.

And now, to sum up all in a few words, we have seen a bigoted zeal stirring up a blind and most bloody rage, not against enemies, or irreligious, profligate persons; but (in judgment of

TO THE READER.

charity, and to view) againſt as virtuous and religious as any they have left behind them in this country, which have ſuffered as evil doers (with the utmoſt extent of rigour, not that ſo high a character is due to all that ſuffered) and this by the teſtimony of vile varlets,* as not only were known before, but have been further apparent ſince, by their manifeſt lives, whoredoms, inceſt, &c. The accuſations of theſe, from their ſpectral ſight, being the chief evidence againſt thoſe that ſuffered; in which accuſations they were upheld by both magiſtrates and miniſters, ſo long as they apprehended themſelves in no danger.

And then, though they could defend neither the doctrine nor the practice, yet none of them have, in ſuch a public manner as the caſe requires, teſtified againſt either; though at the ſame time they could not but be ſenſible what a ſtain and laſting infamy they have brought upon the whole country, to the endangering the future welfare not only of this but of other places, induced by their example; if not to an entailing the guilt of all the righteous blood that has been by the ſame means ſhed, by heathen or

---

* In the Act to reverſe the Attainders of Geo. Burroughs, paſſed in 1711, it is ſaid "that ſome of the principal accuſers and witneſſes in the dark and ſevere proſecutions of 1692, have ſince diſcovered themſelves to be perſons of profligate and vicious converſation."

papifts, &c. upon themfelves, whofe deeds they have fo far juftified, occafioning the great difhonour and blafphemy of the name of God, fcandalizing the heathen, hardening of enemies; and, as a natural effect thereof, to the great increafe of atheifm.

I fhall conclude, only with acquainting the reader, that of thefe collections, the firft, containing More Wonders of the Invifible World,*

* The Proceedings of the Maffachufetts Hiftorical Society, in their 1ft vol., page 288, inform us that " Calef was furnifhed with materials for his work by Mr. Brattle of Cambridge and his brother of Bofton, and other gentlemen who were oppofed to the *Salem* proceedings." That the judges fought the advice and countenance of the leading minifters we have fufficient proof; alfo that the principal examining magiftrates, John Hathorne and Jonathan Corwin, when faltering in their courfe at the multiplicity of the complaints from diftreffed perfons, occafioned by fuppofed witchcraft, were cheered on in their profecutions by receiving fueh letters of commendation from the principal inhabitants of Salem Village as the following : —

Thefe to the Honered John

Hathorne and Jonathan Corwin Efquires —

Lieuing at Salem prefent.

Salem Village this 21ft of
April 1692 —

Much Honered — After moft humble and hearty thanks prefented to your Honrs. for the great care and paines you have already taken for us, for which you know we are never able to make you Recompence, and we believe you do not expect it of us, therefore a full reward be given you of the Lord God of Ifrael, whofe caufe and intereft you have efpoufed, and we truft this fhall add to your Crown of Glory in the day of the Lord Jefus — And we beholding continually the tremendious works of Divine Providence, not only every

I received of a gentleman, who had it of the author, and communicated it to ufe, with his exprefs confent, of which this is a true copy. As to the letters, they are, for fubftance, the fame I fent, though with fome fmall variation, or addition. Touching the two letters from a gentleman, at his requeft I have forborn naming him. It is great pity that the matters of fact, and indeed the whole, had not been done by fome abler hand, better accomplifhed, and with the advantages of both natural and acquired judgment; but others not appearing, I have enforced myfelf to do what is done; my other occafions will not admit any further fcrutiny therein. R. C.

Auguft 11, 1697.

day but every hour; thought it our duty to Inform your Honors of that we conceive you have not heard, which are high and dreadful, of a wheel within a wheel, at which our ears do tingle — Humbly craving continually your prayers and help in this diftrefled cafe; So praying Almighty God continually to prepare you, that you may be a terror to evil doers, and a praife to them that do well — We remain yours to ferve in what we are able

THOMAS PUTNAM —

The author of the above letter is the worthy parifh clerk of Salem Village; and what probably caufed his ears to tingle, was the fufpicion which began to be entertained againft George Burroughs, his former minifter, of being a wizard. Nine days after the date of his letter, April 30, 1692, Jonathan Walcott and Thomas Putnam made complaint againft Burroughs to the Salem magiftrates.

PART I.

ACCOUNT OF THE SUFFERINGS

OF

MARGARET RULE.

SIR,

NOW lay before you a very entertaining ſtory — a ſtory which relates yet more Wonders of the Inviſible World — a ſtory which tells the remarkable afflictions and deliverance of one that had been prodigiouſly handled by the Evil Angels. I was myſelf a daily eye-witneſs to a large part of theſe occurrences, and there may be produced ſcores of ſubſtantial witneſſes to the moſt of them; yea, I know not of any one paſſage of the ſtory but what may be ſufficiently atteſted. I do not

write it with a defign of throwing it prefently into the prefs, but only to preferve the memory of fuch memorable things, the forgetting whereof would neither be pleafing to God, nor ufeful to men; as alfo to give you, with fome others of peculiar and obliging friends, a fight of fome curiofities. And I hope this apology will ferve to excufe me, if I mention, as perhaps I may, when I come to a tenth paragraph in my writing, fome things which I would have omitted in a farther publication.

COTTON MATHER.

ANOTHER BRAND

PLUCKT OUT OF THE BURNING,

OR

MORE WONDERS OF THE INVISIBLE WORLD.

ECT. 1. Within thefe few years, there died in the fouthern parts, a chriftian Indian, who, notwithftanding fome of his Indian weaknefs, had fomething of a better character, of virtue and goodnefs, than many of our people can allow to moft of their countrymen, that profefs the chriftian religion. He had been a zealous preacher of the gofpel to his neighbourhood, and a fort of overfeer or officer, to whofe conduct was owing very much of what good order was maintained among thefe profelyted favages. This man, returning home from the funeral of his fon, was complimented by an Englifhman, expreffing forrow for his lofs. Now, though the Indians ufed upon the death of relations to be the moft paffionate and outrageous creatures

in the world, yet this converted Indian handsomely and cheerfully replied, Truly I am sorry, and I am not sorry: I am sorry that I have buried a dear son; but I am not sorry that the will of God is done: I know that without the will of God my son could not have died; and I know that the will of God is always just and good, and so I am satisfied. Immediately upon this, even within a few hours, he fell himself sick, of a disease that quickly killed him; in the time of which disease, he called his folks about him, earnestly persuading them to be sincere in their praying unto God, and to beware of the drunkenness, the idleness, the lying, whereby so many of that nation disgraced their profession of christianity; adding, that he was ashamed, when he thought how little service he had hitherto done for God; and, that if God would prolong his life, he would labour to do better service; but that he was fully sure he was now going to the Lord Jesus Christ, who had bought him with his precious blood; and for his part, he longed to die, that he might be with his glorious Lord; and, in the midst of such passages, he gave up the ghost; but in such repute, that the English people, of good fashion, did not think much of travelling a great way to his interment. Lest my reader do wonder why I have related this piece of a story, I will now hasten to abate that wonder, by telling that whereto this was intended but for an introduction. Know then, that this remarkable Indian being, a little before he died, at work in the wood, making of tar, there appeared unto him a black man, of a terrible afpect, and more than human dimenfions, threatening bitterly to kill him, if he would not promife to leave off preaching, as he did, to his countrymen, and promife particularly, that if he preached any more, he would fay nothing of Jefus Chrift unto them. The Indian was amazed, yet had the courage to anfwer, I will, in fpite of you, go on to preach Chrift, more than ever I did; and the God whom I ferve will keep me, that you fhall never hurt me. Hereupon the apparition, abating fomewhat of his fiercenefs, offered to the Indian a book of a confiderable thicknefs, and a pen and ink, and faid, that if he would now fet his hand unto that book, he would require nothing further of him; but the man refufed the motion with indignation, and fell down upon his knees into a fervent and pious prayer unto God, for help againft the tempter; whereupon the demon vanifhed.

This is a ftory which I would never have tendered unto my reader, if I had not received it from an honeft and ufeful Englifhman, who is at this time a preacher of the gofpel to the Indians; nor would the probable truth of it have encouraged me to have tendered it, if this alfo had not been a fit introduction unto a yet further narrative.

SECT. 2. It was not much above a year or two after this accident (of which no manner of noife has been made) that there was a prodigious defcent of devils upon divers places near the centre of this province; wherein fome fcores of miferable people were troubled by horrible appearances of a black man, accompanied with fpectres, wearing thefe and thofe human fhapes, who offered them a book to be by them figned, in token of their being lifted for the fervice of the devil; and, upon their denying to do it, they were dragooned with a thoufand preternatural torments, which gave no little terror to the beholders of thefe unhappy people. There was one in the north part of Bofton feized by the evil angels many months after the general ftorm of the late enchantments was over, and when the country had long lain very quiet, both as to moleftations and accufations from the invifible world: her name was Margaret Rule, a young woman: fhe was born of fober and honeft parents, yet living; but what her own character was before her vifitation I can fpeak with the lefs confidence of exactnefs, becaufe I obferve that wherever the devils have been let loofe, to worry any poor creature among us, a great part of the neighbourhood prefently fet themfelves to inquire, and relate all the little vanities of their childhood, with fuch unequal exaggerations, as to make them appear greater finners than any whom the pilot of hell has not yet preyed upon. But it is affirmed, that, for about half a year before her vifitation, fhe was obfervably improved in the hopeful fymptoms of a new creature; fhe was become ferioufly concerned for the everlafting falvation of her foul, and careful to avoid the fnares of evil company. This young woman had never feen the afflictions of Mercy Short, whereof a narrative has been already given; and yet, about half a year after the glorious and fignal deliverance of that poor damfel, this Margaret fell into an affliction, marvellous, refembling hers in almoft all the circumftances of it; indeed the afflictions were fo much alike, that the relation I have given of the one, would almoft ferve as the full hiftory of the other; this was to that little more than the fecond part of the fame tune; indeed Margaret's cafe was in feveral points lefs remarkable than Mercy's, and in fome other things the entertainment did a little vary.

SECT. 3. It was upon the Lord's day, the 10th of September, in the year 1693, that Margaret Rule, after fome hours of previous difturbance in the public affembly, fell into odd fits, which caufed her friends to carry her home, where her fits in a few hours grew into a figure that fatisfied the fpectators of their being preternatural. Some of the neighbours were forward enough to fufpect the rife of this mifchief in an houfe hard by, where lived a miferable woman, who had been formerly imprifoned, on the fufpicion of witchcraft, and who had frequently cured very painful hurts, by muttering over them certain charms, which I fhall not endanger the poifoning of my reader by repeating. This woman had, the evening before Margaret fell into her calamities, very bitterly treated her, and threatened her; but the hazard of hurting a poor woman, that might be innocent, notwithftanding furmifes that might have been more ftrongly grounded than thofe, caufed the pious people in the vicinity to try, rather, whether inceffant fupplication to God alone might not procure a quicker and fafer eafe to the afflicted, than hafty profecution of any fuppofed criminal; and accordingly that unexceptionable courfe was all that was ever followed; yea, which I looked on as a token for good, the afflicted family was as averfe, as any of us, to entertain thoughts of any other courfe.

SECT. 4. The young woman was affaulted by eight cruel fpectres, whereof fhe imagined that fhe knew three or four; but the reft came ſtill with their faces covered, ſo that ſhe could never have a diſtinguiſhed view of the countenance of thoſe whom ſhe thought ſhe knew; ſhe was very careful of my reiterated charges, to forbear blazing their names, leſt any good perſon ſhould come to ſuffer any blaſt of reputation, through the cunning malice of the great accuſer; nevertheleſs, having ſince privately named them to myſelf, I will venture to ſay this of them, that they are a ſort of wretches, who for theſe many years have gone under as violent preſumptions of witchcraft, as perhaps any creatures yet living upon earth; although I am far from thinking that the viſions of this young woman were evidence enough to prove them ſo. Theſe curſed ſpectres now brought unto her a book about a cubit long—a book red and thick, but not very broad; and they demanded of her, that ſhe would ſet her hand to that book, or touch it at leaſt with her hand, as a ſign of her becoming a ſervant of the devil. Upon her peremptory refuſal to do what they aſked, they did not after renew the proffers of the book unto her, but inſtead thereof they fell to tormenting of her in a manner too helliſh to be ſufficiently deſcribed — in thoſe torments confining her to her bed for juſt ſix weeks together.

SECT. 5. Sometimes, but not always, together with the spectres, there looked in upon the young woman (according to her account) a short and a black man, whom they called their master — a white, exactly of the same dimensions and complexion and voice, with the devil that has exhibited himself unto other infested people, not only in other parts of this country, but also in other countries, even of the European world, as the relation of the enchantments there informs us. They all profess themselves vassals of this devil, and in obedience unto him they addressed themselves unto various ways of torturing her. Accordingly she was cruelly pinched with invisible hands, very often in a day, and the black and blue marks of the pinches became immediately visible unto the standers by. Besides this, when her attendants had left her without so much as one pin about her, that so they might prevent some feared inconveniences, yet she would every now and then be miserably hurt with pins, which were found stuck into her neck, back and arms; however, the wounds made by the pins would in a few minutes ordinarily be cured; she would also be strangely distorted in her joints, and thrown into such exorbitant convulsions as were astonishing unto the spectators in general. They that could behold the doleful condition of the poor family without sensible compassions, might have entrails indeed; but I am sure they could have no true bowels in them.

Sect. 6. It were a most unchristian and uncivil, yea, a most unreasonable thing, to imagine, that the fits of the young woman were but mere impostures; and I believe scarce any but people of a particular dirtiness will harbour such an uncharitable censure. However, because I know not how far the devil may drive the imagination of poor creatures, when he has possession of them, that at another time, when they are themselves, would scorn to dissemble any thing, I shall now confine my narrative unto passages wherein there could be no room left for any dissimulation. Of these, the first that I'll mention shall be this: From the time that Margaret Rule first found herself to be formally besieged by the spectres, until the ninth day following, namely, from the 10th of September to the 18th, she kept an entire fast, and yet she was unto all appearance as fresh, as lively, as hearty, at the nine days end, as before they began; in all this time, though she had a very eager hunger upon her stomach, yet, if any refreshment were brought unto her, her teeth would be set, and she would be thrown into many miseries; indeed once or twice or so in all this time, her tormentors permitted her to swallow a mouthful of somewhat that might increase her miseries, whereof a spoonful of rum was the most considerable; but otherwise, as I said, her fast unto the ninth day was very extreme and rigid: however, afterwards there scarce passed a day wherein she had not liberty to take something or other for her sustentation. And I must add this, further, that this business of her fast was carried so, that it was impossible to be dissembled without a combination of multitudes of people, unacquainted with one another, to support the juggle; but he that can imagine such a thing of a neighbourhood, so filled with virtuous people, is a base man — I cannot call him any other.

SECT. 7. But if the sufferings of this young woman were not imposture, yet might they not be pure distemper? I will not here inquire of our sadducees, what sort of a distemper it is, that shall stick the body full of pins without any hand that could be seen to stick them; or whether all the pin-makers in the world would be willing to be evaporated into certain ill habits of body, producing a distemper; but of the distemper my reader shall be judge, when I have told him something further of those unusual sufferings. I do believe that the evil angels do often take advantage, from natural distempers in the children of men, to annoy them with such further mischiefs, as we call preternatural. The malignant vapours and humours of our diseased bodies may be used by devils, thereinto insinuating as engines of the execution of their malice upon those bodies; and perhaps, for this reason, one sex may suffer more troubles of some kinds from the invisible world than the other; as well as for that reason, for which the old serpent made, where he did, his first address. But I pray, what will you say to this? Margaret Rule would sometimes have her jaws forcibly pulled open, whereupon something invisible would be poured down her throat; we all saw her swallow, and yet we saw her try all she could, by spitting, coughing and shrieking, that she might not swallow; but one time the standers-by plainly saw something of that odd liquor itself on the outside of her neck: she cried out of it, as of scalding brimstone poured into her, and the whole house would immediately scent so hot of brimstone that we were scarce able to endure it — whereof there are scores of witnesses; but the young woman herself would be so monstrously inflamed, that it would have broke a heart of stone to have seen her agonies. This was a thing that several times happened; and several times, when her mouth was thus pulled open, the standers-by clapping their hands close thereupon, the distresses that otherwise followed would be diverted. Moreover there was a whitish powder, to us invisible, sometimes cast upon the eyes of this young woman, whereby her eyes would be extremely incommoded; but one time some of this powder was fallen actually visible upon her cheek, from whence the people in the room wiped it with their handkerchiefs; and sometimes the young woman would also be so bitterly scorched with the unseen sulphur thrown upon her, that very sensible blisters would be raised upon her skin, whereto her friends found it necessary to apply the oils proper for common burnings; but the most of these hurts would be cured in two or three days at farthest. I think I may without vanity pretend to have read not a few of the best systems of physick that have been yet seen in these American regions, but I must confess that I have never yet learned the name of the natural distemper whereto these odd symptoms do belong: however, I might suggest perhaps many a natural medicine which would be of singular use against many of them.

Sect. 8. But there fell out some other matters far beyond the reach of natural distemper. This Margaret Rule once in the middle of the night lamented sadly that the spectres threatened the drowning of a young man in the neighbourhood, whom she named unto the company: well, it was afterwards found that at that very time this young man, having been prest on board a man of war, then in the harbour, was out of some dissatisfaction attempting to swim ashore, and he had been drowned in the attempt, if a boat had not seasonably taken him up; it was by computation a minute or two after the young woman's discourse of the drowning, that the young man took the water. At another time she told us, that the spectres bragged and laughed in her hearing about an exploit they had lately done, by stealing from a gentleman his will soon after he had written it; and within a few hours after she had spoken this, there came to me a gentleman with a private complaint, that having written his will, it was unaccountably gone out of the way; how, or where, he could not imagine; and besides all this, there were wonderful noises every now and then made about the room, which our people could ascribe to no other authors but the spectres; yea, the watchers affirm, that they heard those fiends clapping their hands together with an audibleness wherein they could not be imposed upon; and once her tormentors pulled her up to the ceiling of the chamber, and held her there, before a very numerous company of spectators, who found it as much as they could all do to pull her down again. There was also another very surprising circumstance about her, agreeable to what we have not only read in several histories concerning the imps that have been employed in witchcraft, but also known in some of our own afflicted: we once thought we perceived something stir upon her pillow at a little distance from her; whereupon one present laying his hand there, he to his horror apprehended that he felt, though none could see it, a living creature not altogether unlike a rat, which nimbly escaped from him; and there were divers other persons who were thrown into a great consternation by feeling, as they judged, at other times, the same invisible animal.

Sect. 9. As it has been with a thousand other enchanted people, so it was with Margaret Rule in this particular, that there were several words which her tormentors would not let her hear, especially the words Pray or Prayer, and yet she could so hear the letters of those words distinctly mentioned as to know what they meant. The standers-by were forced sometimes thus in discourse to spell a word to her; but because there were some so ridiculous as to count it a sort of spell or a charm for any thus to accommodate themselves to the capacity of the sufferer, little of this kind was done. But that which was more singular in this matter was, that she could not use these words in those penetrating discourses wherewith she would sometimes address the spectres that were about her. She would sometimes for a long while together apply herself to the spectres, whom she supposed the witches, with such exhortations to repentance as would have melted an heart of adamant to have heard them; her strains of expression and argument were truly extraordinary; persons perhaps of the best education and experience, and of attainments much beyond hers, could not have exceeded them; nevertheless, when she came to these words, God, Lord, Christ, Good, Repent, and some other such, her mouth could not utter them; whereupon she would sometimes, in an angry parenthesis, complain of their wickedness in stopping that word, but she would then go on with some other terms that would serve to tell what she meant. And I believe that if the most suspicious person in the world had beheld all the circumstances of this matter, he would have said it could not have been dissembled.

SECT. 10. Not only in the Swedish, but also in the Salem witchcraft, the enchanted people have talked much of a white spirit, from whence they received marvellous assistances in their miseries. What lately befel Mercy Short, from the communications of such a spirit, hath been the just wonder of us all; but by such a spirit was Margaret Rule now also visited. She says that she could never see his face; but that she had a frequent view of his bright, fhining and glorious garments; he ftood by her bed-fide continually, heartening and comforting her, and counfelling her to maintain her faith and hope in God, and never comply with the temptations of her adverfaries. She fays he told her, that God had permitted her afflictions to befal her for the everlafting and unfpeakable good of her own foul, and for the good of many others, and for his own immortal glory; and that fhe fhould therefore be of good cheer, and be affured of a fpeedy deliverance; and the wonderful refolution of mind wherewith fhe encountered her afflictions was but agreeable to fuch expectations. Moreover, a minifter having one day with fome importunity prayed for the deliverance of this young woman, and pleaded that as fhe belonged to his flock and charge, he had fo far a right unto her as that he was to do the part of a minifter of our Lord for the bringing of her home unto God, only now the devil hindered him in doing that which he had a right thus to do; and whereas he had a better title unto her to bring her home to God, than the devil could have unto her to carry her away from the Lord, he therefore humbly applied himfelf unto God, who alone could right this matter, with a fuit that fhe might be refcued out of Satan's hands. Immediately upon this, though fhe heard nothing of this tranfaction, fhe began to call that minifter her father, and that was the name whereby fhe every day before all forts of people diftinguifhed him. The occafion of it fhe fays was this: the white fpirit prefently upon this tranfaction did after this manner fpeak to her: Margaret, you now are to take notice that fuch a man is your father; God has given you to him; do you from this time look upon him as your father, obey him, regard him, as your father; follow his counfels, and you fhall do well. And though there was one paffage more, which I do as little know what to make of as any of the reft, I am now going to relate it: more than three times have I feen it fulfilled in the deliverance of enchanted and poffeft perfons, whom the providence of God has caft into my way, that their deliverance could not be obtained before the third faft kept for them, and the third day ftill obtained the deliverance; although I have thought of befeeching of the Lord thrice, when buffeted by Satan: yet I muft earneftly entreat all my readers to beware of any fuperftitious conceits upon the number *three*; if our God will hear us upon once praying and fafting before him, it is well; and if he will not vouchfafe his mercy upon our thrice doing fo, yet we muft not be fo difcouraged as to throw by our devotion; but if the fovereign grace of our God will in any particular inſtances count our patience enough tried when we have ſolemnly waited upon him for any determinate number of times, who ſhall ſay to him, What doeſt thou? And if there ſhall be any number of inſtances wherein this grace of our God has exactly holden the ſame courſe, it may have a room in our humble obſervations, I hope, without any ſuperſtition. I ſay then that after Margaret Rule had been more than five weeks in her miſeries, this white ſpirit ſaid unto her, "Well, this day ſuch a man (whom he named) has kept a third day for your deliverance; now be of good cheer, you ſhall ſpeedily be delivered." I inquired whether what had been ſaid of that man was true, and I gained exact and certain information that it was preciſely ſo; but I doubt left in relating this paſſage that I have uſed more openneſs than a friend ſhould be treated with, and for that cauſe I have concealed ſeveral of the moſt memorable things that have occurred, not only in this but in ſome former hiſtories, although indeed I am not ſo well ſatisfied about the true nature of this white ſpirit, as to count that I can do a friend much honour by reporting what notice this white ſpirit may have thus taken of him.

SECT. 11. On the laſt day of the week her tormentors (as ſhe thought and ſaid) approaching towards her, would be forced ſtill to recoil and retire as unaccountably, unable to meddle with her; and they would retire to the fire ſide with their poppets; but going to ſtick pins into thoſe poppets, they could not (according to their viſions) make the pins to enter. She inſulted over them with a very proper deriſion, daring them now to do their worſt, whilſt ſhe had the ſatisfaction to ſee their black maſter ſtrike them and kick them, like an overſeer of ſo many negroes, to make them to do their work, and renew the marks of his vengeance on them when they failed of doing it. At laſt, being as it were tired with their ineffectual attempts to mortify her, they furiouſly ſaid, " Well, you ſhan't be the laſt." And after a pauſe they added, " Go, and the devil go with you, we can do no more ; " whereupon they flew out of the room, and ſhe, returning perfectly to herſelf, moſt affectionately gave thanks to God for her deliverance. Her tormentors left her extremely weak and faint, and overwhelmed with vapours, which would not only cauſe her ſometimes to ſwoon away, but alſo now and then for a little while diſcompoſe the reaſonableneſs of her thoughts. Nevertheleſs, her former troubles returned not; but we are now waiting to ſee the good effects of thoſe troubles upon the ſouls of all concerned. And now I ſuppoſe that ſome of our learned witlings of the coffee-houfe, for fear left thefe proofs of an invifible world fhould fpoil fome of their fport, will endeavour to turn them all into fport; for which buffoonery their only pretence will be, " They can't underftand how fuch things as thefe could be done; " whereas indeed he that is but philofopher enough to have read but one little treatife, publifhed in the year 1656, by no other man than the chirurgeon of an army, or but one chapter of Helmont, which I will not quote at this time too particularly, may give a far more intelligible account of thefe appearances than moft of thefe blades can give why and how their tobacco makes them fpit, or which way the flame of their candle becomes illuminating. As for that cavil, " The world would be undone if the devils could have fuch power as they feem to have in feveral of our ftories," it may be anfwered, that as to many things, the lying devils have only known them to be done, and then pretended unto the doing of thofe things; but the true and beft anfwer is, that by thefe things we only fee what the devils could have power to do, if the great God fhould give them that power; whereas now our hiftories afford a glorious evidence for the being of a God. The world would indeed be undone, and horribly undone, if thefe devils, who now and then get liberty to play fome very mifchievous pranks, were not under a daily restraint of some Almighty Superior from doing more of such mischiefs. Wherefore, instead of all apish shouts and jeers at histories which have such undoubted confirmation, as that no man that has breeding enough to regard the common laws of human society, will offer to doubt of them, it becomes us rather to adore the goodness of God, who does not permit such things every day to befal us all, as he sometimes did permit to befal some few of our miserable neighbours.

SECT. 12. And why, after all my unwearied cares and pains to rescue the miserable from the lions and bears of hell, which had seized them, and after all my studies to disappoint the devils in their designs to confound my neighbourhood, must I be driven to the necessity of an apology? Truly the hard representations wherewith some ill men have reviled my conduct, and the countenance which other men have given to these representations, oblige me to give mankind some account of my behaviour. No christian can (I say none but evil workers can) criminate my visiting such of my poor flock as have at any time fallen under the terrible and sensible molestations of evil angels: let their afflictions have been what they will, I could not have answered it unto my glorious Lord, if I had withheld my just counsels and comforts from them; and if I have also with some exactness observed the methods of the invisible world, when they have thus become observable, I have been but a servant of mankind in doing so; yea, no less a person than the venerable Baxter has more than once or twice in the most publick manner invited mankind to thank me for that service. I have not been insensible of a greater danger attending me in this fulfilment of my ministry, than if I had been to take ten thousand steps over a rocky mountain filled with rattle-snakes; but I have considered, he that is wise will observe things; and the surprising explication and confirmation of the biggest part of the bible, which I have seen given in these things, has abundantly paid me for observing them. Now, in my visiting of the miserable, I was always of this opinion, that we were ignorant of what power the devils might have to do their mischiefs in the shapes of some that had never been explicitly engaged in diabolical confederacies, and that therefore, though many witchcrafts had been fairly detected on inquiries provoked and begun by spectral exhibitions, yet we could not easily be too jealous of the snares laid for us in the devices of Satan. The world knows how many pages I have composed and published, and particular gentlemen in the government know how many letters I have written, to prevent the exceffive credit of fpectral accufations; wherefore I have ftill charged the afflicted that they fhould cry out of nobody for afflicting of them; but that, if this might be any advantage, they might privately tell their minds to fome one perfon of difcretion enough to make no ill ufe of their communications; accordingly there has been this effect of it, that the name of no one good perfon in the world ever came under any blemifh by means of an afflicted perfon that fell under my particular cognizance; yea, no one man, woman or child ever came into any trouble for the fake of any that were afflicted, after I had once begun to look after them. How often have I had this thrown into my difh, "that many years ago I had an opportunity to have brought forth fuch people as have in the late ftorm of witchcraft been complained of, but that I fmothered all; and after that ftorm was raifed at Salem, I did myfelf offer to provide meat, drink and lodging for no lefs than fix of the afflicted, that fo an experiment might be made, whether prayer with fafting, upon the removal of the diftreffed, might not put a period to the trouble then rifing, without giving the civil authority the trouble of profecuting thofe things which nothing but a confcientious regard unto the cries of miferable families could have overcome the reluctancies of the honourable judges to meddle with." In short, I do humbly but freely affirm it, that there is not a man living in this world who has been more desirous than the poor man I to shelter my neighbours from the inconveniences of spectral outcries; yea, I am very jealous I have done so much that way, as to sin in what I have done; such have been the cowardice and fearfulness whereunto my regard unto the dissatisfaction of other people has precipitated me. I know a man in the world, who has thought he has been able to convict some such witches as ought to die; but his respect unto the publick peace has caused him rather to try whether he could not renew them by repentance; and as I have been studious to defeat the devils of their expectations to set people together by the ears thus, I have also checked and quelled those forbidden curiosities which would have given the devil an invitation to have tarried amongst us, when I have seen wonderful snares laid for curious people, by the secret and future things discovered from the mouths of damsels possest with a spirit of divination. Indeed I can recollect but one thing wherein there could be given so much as a shadow of reason for exceptions, and that is, my allowing of so many to come and see those that were afflicted. Now for that I have this to say, that I have almost a thousand times entreated the friends of the miserable, that they would not permit the intrusion of any company, but such as by prayers or other ways might be helpful to them; nevertheless I have not absolutely forbid all company from coming to your haunted chambers; partly because the calamities of the families were such as required the assistance of many friends; partly because I have been willing that there should be disinterested witnesses of all sorts, to confute the calumnies of such as would say all was but imposture; and partly because I saw God had sanctified the spectacle of the miseries on the afflicted unto the souls of many that were spectators; and it is a very glorious thing that I have now to mention: The devils have with most horrid operations broke in upon our neighbourhood, and God has at such a rate overruled all the fury and malice of those devils, that all the afflicted have not only been delivered, but I hope also savingly brought home unto God, and the reputation of no one good person in the world has been damaged; but instead thereof the souls of many, especially of the rising generation, have been thereby awakened unto some acquaintance with religion; our young people, who belonged unto the praying meetings, of both sexes, apart, would ordinarily spend whole nights by whole weeks together in prayers and psalms upon these occasions, in which devotions the devils could get nothing, but, like fools, a scourge for their own backs; and some scores of other young people, who were strangers to real piety, were now struck with the lively demonstrations of hell evidently set forth before their eyes, when they saw persons cruelly frighted, wounded and starved by devils, and scalded with burning brimstone; and yet so preserved in this tortured state, as that, at the end of one month's wretchedness, they were as able still to undergo another; so that of these also it might now be said, "Behold they pray." In the whole — the devil got just nothing — but God got praises, Christ got subjects, the Holy Spirit got temples, the church got addition, and the souls of men got everlasting benefits.* I am not so vain as to say that any wisdom or virtue of mine did contribute unto this good order of things; but I am so just as to say, I did not hinder this good. When therefore there have been those that picked up little incoherent scraps and bits of

* The estimated value of the tragedy of 1692 by Dr. Mather, in a moral and religious point of view, has not as yet been seen or experienced. We are certainly better able to judge of the effect produced by the delusion from our stand-point in 1860, than was Mather from his in 1693. While we are certain that virtue has received no aid from the transaction, it is not so apparent as he supposed " that the devil got just nothing." It has its use, however, as a beacon to warn us from too near an approach to such delusions, or those similar to them of the present day.

my discourses in this fruitful discharge of my ministry, and so travestied them in their abusive pamphlets as to persuade the town that I was their common enemy in those very points, wherein, if in any one thing whatsoever, I have sensibly approved myself as true a servant unto them as possibly I could, though my life and soul had been at stake for it — yea to do like satan himself, by sly, base, unpretending insinuations, as if I wore not the modesty and gravity which became a minister of the gospel — I could not but think myself unkindly dealt withal, and the neglect of others to do me justice in this affair has caused me to conclude this narrative with complaints in another hearing of such monstrous injuries.

PART II.

SEVERAL LETTERS, &c.

Boston, Jan. 11, 1693.

Mr. Cotton Mather,
Reverend Sir,

INDING it needful on many accounts, I here present you with the copy of that paper which has been so much misrepresented, to the end that what shall be found defective or not fairly represented (if any such shall appear) they may be set right, — which runs thus:

September the 13*th*, 1693. In the evening, when the sun was withdrawn, giving place to darkness to succeed, I with some others were drawn by curiosity to see Margaret Rule, and so much the rather, because it was reported Mr. M—— would be there that night. Being come to her father's house, into the chamber wherein she was in bed, I found her of a healthy countenance, of about seventeen years old, lying very still, and speaking very little; what she did say seemed as if she were light-headed. Then Mr. M—— (father and son) came up, and others with them; in the whole there were about thirty or forty persons; they being set, the father on a stool, and the son upon the bed-side by her, the son began to question her:

Margaret Rule, how do you do? then a pause without any answer.

Question, What! do there a great many witches sit upon you? *Answer*, Yes.

Question, Do you not know that there is a hard master? Then she was in a fit. He laid his hand upon her face and nose, but as he said without perceiving breath; then he brushed her on the face with his glove, and rubbed her stomach (her breast not being covered with the bed-clothes) and bid others do so too, and said it eased her — then she revived.

Q. Don't you know there is a hard master?
A. Yes.

Reply, Don't serve that hard master — you know who.

Q. Do you believe? Then again she was in a fit, and he again rubbed her breast, &c.

About this time, Margaret Perd, an attendant, assisted him in rubbing her. The afflicted spake angrily to her, saying, Don't you meddle with me — and haftily put away her hand. He then wrought his fingers before her eyes, and afked her if fhe faw the witches? *A.* No.

Q. Do you believe? *A.* Yes.

Q. Do you believe in you know who?— *A.* Yes.

Q. Would you have other people do fo too — to believe in you know who? *A.* Yes.

Q. Who is it that afflicts you? *A.* I know not, there is a great many of them.

About this time the father queftioned, if fhe knew the fpectres. An attendant faid, if fhe did fhe would not tell. The fon proceeded:

Q. You have feen the black man, have you not? *A.* No.

Reply, I hope you never will.

Q. You have had a book offered you, have you not? *A.* No.

Q. The brufhing of you gives you eafe, don't it? *A.* Yes. She turned herfelf, and a little groaned.

Q. Now the witches fcratch you, and pinch you, and bite you, don't they? *A.* Yes.

Then he put his hand upon her breaft and belly, viz. on the clothes over her, and felt a living thing, as he faid; which moved the father alfo to feel, and fome others.

Q. Don't you feel the *live thing* in the bed? *A.* No.

Reply, That is only fancy.

Q. The great company of people increafe your torment, don't they? *A.* Yes.

The people about were defired to withdraw. One woman faid, I am fure I am no witch, I will not go; fo others; fo none withdrew.

Q. Shall we go to prayers? Then fhe lay in a fit as before. But this time, to revive her, they waved a hat, and brufhed her head and pillow therewith.

Q. Shall we go to prayer, &c. fpelling the word. *A.* Yes.

The father went to prayer for perhaps half an hour, chiefly againft the power of the devil and witchcraft, and that God would bring out the afflicters. During prayer-time, the fon ftood by, and when they thought fhe was in a fit, rubbed her and brufhed her as before, and beckoned to others to do the like. After prayer he proceeded:

Q. You did not hear when we were at prayer, did you? *A.* Yes.

Q. You don't hear always — you did not hear for fome time paft, a word or two, did you? *A.* No.

Then turning him about, faid, this is juft another Mercy Short. Margaret Perd replied, fhe was not like her in her fits.

Q. What does she eat or drink? *A.* She does not eat at all, but drinks *rum.**

Then he admonished the young people to take warning, &c. saying it was a sad thing to be so tormented by the devil and his instruments. A young man present, in the habit of a seaman, replied, "*This is the Devil all over.*" Then the ministers withdrew. Soon after they were gone the afflicted desired the *women* to be gone, saying, that the company of the *men* was not offensive to her; and having hold of the hand of a young man, said to have been her sweetheart formerly, who was withdrawing, she pulled him again into his seat, saying, he should not go to-night.

September the 19*th*, 1693. This night I renewed my visit, and found her rather of a

---

* The affliction of Margaret Rule, like that of the Surrey Demoniac, Richard Dugdale of England, was nothing more than a bad case of delirium tremens. Richard was singularly tossed and buffeted by Satan, when nine ministers undertook to exorcise him, by many months of continued prayer and fasting, and happily succeeded on the 24th of March, 1689. The record of the event informs us, when Satan finally left Richard, he had a terrible fit and vomited, whereon the devil, when he could no longer withstand the ministers, with singular impudence cried, "Now, Dickey, I must leave thee, and must afflict thee no more." It is probable that the success in this famous case of the Surrey Demoniac occurred to the mind of Dr. Mather, when he offered to provide meat, drink, and lodging for no less than six of the possessed of Salem Village, that "the *possessed* might be scattered sunder," so that an experiment might be made, whether prayer with fasting, upon the removal of the accused, might not put a period to the rising trouble.

fresher countenance than before. About eight persons were present with her. She was in a fit, screaming and making a noise. Three or four persons rubbed and brushed her with their hands: they said that the brushing did put them away, if they brushed or rubbed in the *right place;* therefore they brushed and rubbed in several places, and said that when they did it in the *right place* she could fetch her breath, and by that they knew. She being come to herself was soon in a merry talking fit. A young man came in, and asked her how she did. She answered, very bad, but at present a little better.

He soon told her he must be gone, and bid her good-night; at which she seemed troubled, saying that she liked his company, and said she would not have him go till she was well; adding, for I shall die when you are gone. Then she complained they did not put her on a clean cap, but let her lie so like a beast, saying she should lose all her fellows. She said she wondered any people should be so wicked as to think she was not afflicted, but to think she dissembled. A young woman answered, Yes, if they were to see you in this merry fit, they would say you dissembled indeed. She replied, Mr. M—— said this was her laughing time, she must laugh now. She said Mr. M—— had been there this evening, and she enquired how long he had been gone. She said he stayed alone with her in the room half an hour, and said that he told her there were some that came for spies, and to report about town that she was not afflicted; that during the said time she had no fit; that he asked her if she knew how many times he had prayed for her to-day; and that she answered, that she could not tell; and that he replied, he had prayed for her nine times to-day. The attendants said that she was sometimes in a fit, that none could open her joints, and that there came an old *iron-jawed* woman and tried, but could not do it; they likewise said, that her head could not be moved from the pillow. I tried to move her head, and found no more difficulty than another person (and so did others) but was not willing to offend by lifting it up, once being reproved for endeavouring it; they saying angrily, you will break her neck. The attendants said Mr. M―― would not go to prayer with her when people were in the room, as they did one night — that night he felt the *live creature*. Margaret Perd and another said they smelt brimstone. I and others said we did not smell any; then they said they did not know what it was. This Margaret said she wished she had been here when Mr. M―― was here. Another attendant said, If you had been here, you might not have been permitted in, for her own mother was not suffered to be present.

Sir, after the sorest affliction and greatest blemish to religion that ever befel this country, and after most men began to fear that some undue steps had been taken, and after his excellency (with their Majesties' approbation as is said) had put a stop to executions, and men began to hope there would never be a return of the like; finding these accounts to contain in them something extraordinary, I writ them down the same nights, in order to attain the certainty of them, and soon found them so confirmed that I have (besides other demonstrations) the whole under the hands of two persons who are ready to attest the truth of it; but not satisfied herewith, I shewed them to some of your particular friends, that so I might have the greater certainty; but was much surprised with the message you sent me, that I should be arrested for slander, and at your calling me one of the worst of liars, making it pulpit news, with the name of pernicious libels, &c. This occasioned my first letter: [as followeth.]

September the 29*th*, 1693.
Reverend Sir,

I having written from the mouths of several persons, who affirm they were present with Margaret Rule the 13th inftant, her anfwers and behaviour, &c., and having fhewed it to feveral of my friends, as alfo yours, and underftanding you are offended at it, this is to acquaint you that if you and any one particular friend will pleafe to meet me and fome other indifferent perfon with me at Mr. Wilkins's, or at Benj. Harris's, you intimating the time, I fhall be ready there to read it to you, as alfo a further account of proceedings the 19th inftant, which may be needful to prevent groundlefs prejudices, and let deferved blame be caft where it ought. From, fir, yours, in what I may, R. C.

The effects of which, fir, (not to mention that long letter only once read to me,) was, you fent me word you would meet me at Mr. Wilkins's; but, before that anfwer, at yours and your father's complaint, I was brought before their majefties' juftice, by warrant, for fcandalous libels againft yourfelf, and was bound over to anfwer at feffions. I do not remember you then objected againft the truth of what I had wrote, but afferted it was wronged by omiffions; which, if it were fo, was paft any power of mine to remedy, having given a faithful account of all that came to my knowledge: and, fir, that you might not be without fome cognizance of the reafons why I took fo much pains in it, as alfo for my own information, (if it might have been) I wrote to you my second letter to this effect:

November the 24*th,* 1693.

Reverend Sir,

Having expected some weeks your meeting me at Mr. Wilkins's, according to what you intimated to me, and the time drawing near for our meeting elsewhere, I thought it not amiss to give you a summary of my thoughts in the great concern, which, as you say, has been agitated with so much heat. That there are witches is not the doubt; the scriptures else were vain, which assign their punishment to be by death; but what this witchcraft is, or wherein it does consist, seems to be the whole difficulty: and as it may be easily demonstrated, that all that bear that name cannot be justly so accounted; so that some things and actions, not so esteemed by the most, yet upon due examination will be found to merit no better character.

In your late book you lay down a brief synopsis of what has been written on that subject, by a triumvirate of as eminent men as ever handled it (as you are pleased to call them) viz. Mr. Perkins, Gaule and Bernard, consisting of about thirty tokens to know them by, many of them distinct from, if not thwarting, each other: among all of which I can find but one decisive, viz. that of Mr. Gaule, head iv. and runs thus: "Among the moſt unhappy circumſtances to convict a witch, one is a maligning and oppugning the word, work or worſhip of God, and by any extraordinary ſign ſeeking to ſeduce any from it. See Deut. xiii. 1, 2. Matt. xxiv. 24. Acts xiii. 8. 10. 2 Tim. iii. 8. Do but mark well the places; and for this very property, of thus oppoſing and perverting, they are all there concluded arrant and abſolute witches."

This head, as here laid down and inſerted by you, either is a truth or not; if not, why is it here inſerted from one of the triumvirate? If it be a truth, as the ſcriptures quoted will abundantly teſtify, whence is it that it is ſo little regarded, though it be the only head well proved by ſcripture, or that the reſt of the triumvirate ſhould ſo far forget their work as not to mention it? It were to be unjuſt to the memory of thoſe otherwiſe wiſe men, to ſuppoſe them to have any ſiniſter deſign; but perhaps the force of a prevailing opinion, together with an education thereto ſuited, might overſhadow their judgments, as being wont to be but too prevalent in many other caſes. But if the above be truth, then the ſcripture is full and plain, what is witchcraft. And if ſo, what need of his next head of hanging people without as full and clear evidence as in other caſes? Or what need of the rest of the receipts of the triumvirate? What need of praying that the afflicted may be able to discover who it is that afflicts them? or what need of searching for teats for the devil to suck, in his old age; or the experiment of saying the Lord's prayer, &c. with a multitude more, practised in some places superstitiously inclined? Other actions have been practised for easing the afflicted, less justifiable, if not strongly favouring of witchcraft itself, viz. fondly imagining by the hand, &c. to drive off spectres, or to knock off invisible chains, or by striking in the air to wound either the afflicted or others, &c. I write not this to accuse any, but that all may beware; believing that the devil's bounds are set, which he cannot pass; that devils are so full of malice, that it cannot be added to by mankind; that where he hath power he neither can nor will omit executing it; that it is only the Almighty that sets bounds to his rage, and that only can commissionate him to hurt or destroy any.

These last, sir, are such foundations of truth, in my esteem, that I cannot but own it to be my duty to assert them, when called, though with the hazard of my all; and consequently to detest such as these, that a witch can commissionate devils to afflict mortals; that he can, at his or the witch's pleasure, assume any shape;

that hanging or drowning of witches can leſſen his power of afflicting, or reſtore thoſe that were at a diſtance tormented, with many others depending on theſe; all tending, in my eſteem, highly to the diſhonour of God, and the endangering the well-being of a people; and do further add, that as the ſcriptures are full that there is witchcraft (ut ſup.) ſo 'tis as plain that there are poſſeſſions, and that the bodies of the poſſeſt have hence been not only afflicted, but ſtrangely agitated, if not their tongues improved to foretel futurities, &c. and why not to accuſe the innocent, as bewitching them? having pretence to divination to gain credence. This being reaſonable to be expected from him who is the father of lies, to the end he may thereby involve a country in blood, malice and evil-ſurmiſing, which he greedily ſeeks after, and ſo finally lead them from their fear and dependence upon God, to fear him and a ſuppoſed witch, thereby attaining his end upon mankind; and not only ſo, but natural diſtempers, as has been frequently obſerved by the judicious, have ſo operated as to deceive more than the vulgar, as is teſtified by many famous phyſicians and others. And as for that proof of multitudes of confeſſions, this country may be by this time thought competent judges what credence we ought to give them, having had such numerous instances, as also how obtained.

And now, sir, if herein be any thing in your esteem valuable, let me entreat you not to account it the worse for coming from so mean a hand; which, however you may have received prejudice, &c. am ready to serve you to my power; but if you judge otherwise hereof, you may take your own methods for my better information. Who am, sir, yours to command, in what I may, R. C.

In answer to this last, sir, you replied to the gentleman that presented it, that you had nothing to prosecute against me; and said, as to your sentiments in your books, you did not bind any to believe them; and then again renewed your promise of meeting me, as before, though not yet performed. Accordingly, though I waited at sessions, there was none to object ought against me, upon which I was dismissed. This gave me some reason to believe that you intended all should have been forgotten; but, instead of that, I find the coals are fresh blown up, I being supposed to be represented, in a late manuscript, *More Wonders of the*, &c. as travestying your discourse in your faithful discharge of your duty, &c. and such as see not with the author's eyes, rendered sadducees and witlings, &c. and the arguments that square not with the sentiments therein contained, buffoonery; rarely, no doubt, agreeing with the spirit of Christ, and his dealings with an unbelieving Thomas, yet whose infidelity was without compare less excusable; but the author having resolved long since to have no more than one single grain of patience with them that deny, &c. the wonder is the less. It must needs be that offences come, but wo to him by whom they come. To vindicate myself therefore from such false imputations, of satan-like insinuations, and misrepresenting your actions, &c. and to vindicate yourself, sir, as much as is in my power, from those suggestions, said to be insinuated, as if you wore not the modesty and gravity that becomes a minister of the gospel; which, it seems, some, that never saw the said narratives, report them to contain; I say, sir, for these reasons, I here present you with the first copy that ever was taken, &c. and purpose for a week's time to be ready, if you shall intimate your pleasure to wait upon me, either at the place formerly appointed, or any other that is indifferent; to the end that, if there shall appear any defects in that narrative, they may be amended.

Thus, sir, I have given you a genuine account of my sentiments and actions in this affair; and do request and pray, that if I err, I may be shewed it from scripture, or found reason, and not by quotations out of Virgil, nor Spanish rhetorick. For I find the witlings mentioned are so far from answering your profound questions, that they cannot so much as pretend to shew a distinction between witchcraft in the common notion of it, and possession; nor so much as to demonstrate that ever the Jews or primitive christians did believe that a witch could send a devil to afflict her neighbours. But to all these, sir, (ye being the salt of the earth, &c.) I have reason to hope for a satisfactory answer to him, who is one that reverences your person and office; and am, sir, yours to command, in what I may, R. C.

Boston, Jan. the 15*th*, 1693.
Mr. R. C.

Whereas you intimate your desires, that what is not fairly (I take it for granted you mean truly also) represented in a paper you lately sent me, containing a pretended narrative of a visit by my father and self to an afflicted young woman, whom we apprehended to be under a diabolical possession, might be rectified; I have this to say, as I have often already said, that I do scarcely find any one thing in the whole paper, whether respecting my father or self, either fairly or truly represented. Nor can I think that any, that know my parent's circumftances, but muft think him deferving a better character by far, than this narrative can be thought to give him. When the main defign we managed, in vifiting the poor afflicted creature, was to prevent the accufations of the neighbourhood, can it be fairly reprefented that our defign was to draw out fuch accufations? which is the reprefentation of the paper. We have teftimonies of the beft witneffes, and in number not a few, that when we afked Rule whether fhe thought fhe knew who tormented her, the queftion was but an introduction to the folemn charges which we then largely gave, that fhe fhould rather die than tell the names of any whom fhe might imagine that fhe knew. Your informers have reported the queftion, and report nothing of what follows, as effential to the giving of that queftion. And can this be termed a piece of fairnefs? Fair it cannot be, that when minifters faithfully and carefully difcharge their duty to the miferable in their flock, little bits, fcraps and fhreds of their difcourfes fhould be tacked together to make them contemptible, when there fhall be no notice of all the neceffary, feafonable and profitable things that occurred in thofe difcourfes; and without which, the occafion of the leffer paffages cannot be underftood: and yet I am furnifhed with abundant evidences, ready to be sworn, that will positively prove this part of unfairness, by the above mentioned narrative, to be done both to my father and self. Again, it seems not fair or reasonable that I should be exposed for that which yourself (not to say some others) might have exposed me for if I had not done, viz. for discouraging so much company from flocking about the possest maid; and yet, as I persuade myself, you cannot but think it to be good advice to keep much company from such haunted chambers. Besides, the unfairness doth more appear, in that I find nothing repeated of what I said about the advantage which the devil takes from too much observation and curiosity.

In that several of the questions in the paper are so worded as to carry in them a presupposal of the things inquired after, to say the best of it, is very unfair. But this is not all; the narrative contains a number of mistakes and falsehoods, which, were they wilful and designed, might justly be termed gross lies. The representations are far from true, when 'tis affirmed my father and self being come into the room, I began the discourse: I hope I understand breeding a little better than so. For proof of this, did occasion serve, sundry can depose the contrary.

'Tis no less untrue, that either my father or self put the question, How many witches sit upon you? We always cautiously avoided that expression, it being contrary to our inward belief. All the standers-by will, I believe, swear they did not hear us use it, (your witnesses excepted) and I tremble to think how hardy those woful creatures must be, to call the Almighty, by an oath, to so false a thing. As false a representation 'tis, that I rubbed Rule's stomach, her breast not being covered. The oath of the nearest spectators, giving a true account of that matter, will prove this to be little less than a gross (if not a doubled) lie; and to be somewhat plainer, it carries the face of a lie contrived on purpose (by them at least to whom you are beholden for the narrative) wickedly and basely to expose me: for you cannot but know how much this representation hath contributed to make people believe a smutty thing of me. I am far from thinking but that in your own conscience you believe, that no indecent action of that nature could then be done by me before such observers, had I been so wicked as to have been inclined to what is base. It looks next to impossible that a reparation should be made me for the wrong done to (I hope, as to any scandal) an unblemished, though weak and small, servant of the church of God. Nor is what follows a less untruth, that it was an attendant and not myself who said, If Rule knows who afflicts her, yet she won't tell. I therefore spoke it that I might encourage her to continue in that concealment of all names whatsoever; to this I am able to furnish myself with the attestation of sufficient oaths. 'Tis as far from true, that my apprehension of the imp, about Rule, was on her belly; for the oaths of the spectators, and even of those that thought they felt it, can testify that it was upon the pillow, at a distance from her body. As untrue a representation is that which follows, viz. that it was said unto her, that her not apprehending of that odd, palpable, though not visible, mover, was from her fancy; for I endeavoured to persuade her that it might be but fancy in others, that there was any such thing at all. Witnesses every way sufficient can be produced for this also. It is falsely represented, that my father felt on the young woman after the appearance mentioned, for his hand was never near her; oath can sufficiently vindicate him. 'Tis very untrue, that my father prayed, for perhaps half an hour, against the power of the devil and witchcraft, and that God would bring out the afflicters: witnesses of the best credit can depose, that his prayer was not a quarter of an hour, and that there was no more than about one

claufe, towards the clofe of the prayer, which
was of this import; and this claufe alfo was
guarded with a fingular warinefs and modefty,
viz. If there were any evil inftruments in this
matter, God would pleafe to difcover them:
and that there was more than common reafon
for that petition, I can fatisfy any one that will
pleafe to inquire of me. And ftrange it is, that
a gentleman that from eighteen to fifty-four hath
been an exemplary minifter of the gofpel; and
that, befides a ftation in the church of God, as
confiderable as any that his own country can
afford, hath for divers years come off with
honour, in his application to three crowned
heads, and the chiefeft nobility of three kingdoms; knows not yet how to make one fhort
prayer of a quarter of an hour, but in New-
England he muft be libelled for it. There are
divers other down-right miftakes, which you
have permitted yourfelf (I would hope not
knowingly and with a malicious defign) to be
receiver or compiler of, which I fhall now forbear to animadvert upon. As for the appendix
of the narrative, I do find myfelf therein injuri-
oufly treated; for the utmoft of your proof, for
what you fay of me, amounts to little more
than this, viz. Some people told you, that
others told them, that fuch and fuch things
did pafs; but you may affure yourfelf, that I

am not unfurnished with witnesses that can convict the same. Whereas you would give me to believe the bottom of these, your methods, to be some dissatisfaction about the commonly received power of devils and witches; I do not only with all freedom offer you the use of any part of my library, which you may see cause to peruse on that subject, but also, if you and any one else, whom you please, will visit me at my study, yea, or meet me at any other place, less inconvenient than those by you proposed, I will with all the fairness and calmness in the world dispute the point. I beg of God that he would bestow as many blessings on you, as ever on myself; and out of a sincere wish that you may be made yet more capable of these blessings, I take this occasion to lay before you the faults (not few nor small ones neither) which the paper contained, you lately sent me, in order to be examined by me. In case you want a true and full narrative of my visit, whereof such an indecent travesty (to say the best) hath been made, I am not unwilling to communicate it; in mean time must take liberty to say, it is scarcely consistent with common civility, much less christian charity, to offer the narrative, now with you, for a true one, till you have a truer; or for a full one, till you have a fuller. Your sincere (though injured) friend and servant,

C. MATHER.

The copy of a paper received with the above letter.

I do testify that I have seen Margaret Rule, in her afflictions from the invisible world, lifted up from her bed, wholly by an invisible force, a great way towards the top of the room where she lay; in her being so lifted, she had no assistance from any use of her own arms or hands, or any other part of her body, not so much as her heels touching her bed, or resting on any support whatsoever. And I have seen her thus lifted, when not only a strong person hath thrown his whole weight across her to pull her down, but several other persons have endeavoured, with all their might, to hinder her from being so raised up; which I suppose that several others will testify as well as myself when called unto it. Witness my hand, SAMUEL AVES.

We can also testify to the substance of what is above written; and have several times seen Margaret Rule so lifted up from her bed, as that she had no use of her own limbs to help her up; but it was the declared apprehension of us, as well as others, that saw it, impossible for any hands, but some of the invisible world, to lift her. ROBERT EARLE,
JOHN WILKINS,
DAN. WILLIAMS.

We, whose names are under-written, do testify, that one evening, when we were in the chamber where Margaret Rule then lay, in her late affliction, we observed her to be, by an invisible force, lifted up from the bed whereon she lay, so as to touch the garret floor, while yet neither her feet, nor any other part of her body, rested either on the bed or any other support, but were also, by the same force, lifted up from all that was under her; and all this for a considerable while, we judged it several minutes; and it was as much as several of us could do, with all our strength, to pull her down. All which happened when there was not only we two in the chamber, but we suppose ten or a dozen more, whose names we have forgotten. THOMAS THORNTON.
WILLIAM HUDSON
testifies to the substance of Thornton's testimony, to which he also hath set his hand.

Boston, January 18, 1693.
MR. COTTON MATHER,
Reverend Sir,

Yours of the 15th instant I received yesterday, and soon found I had promised myself too much by it, viz. either concurrence with, or a denial of, those fundamentals mentioned in mine, of November the 24th, finding this waived by an invitation to your library, &c. I thank God

I have the bible, and do judge that sufficient to demonstrate that cited head of Mr. Gaule to be a truth, as also those other heads mentioned as the foundations of religion. And in my apprehension, if it be asked any christian, whether God governs the world, and whether it be he only can commissionate devils, and such other fundamentals, he ought to be as ready as in the question, Who made him? (A little writing certainly might be of more use, to clear up the controverted points, than either looking over many books in a well furnished library, or than a dispute, if I were qualified for it; the inconveniencies of passion being this way best avoided.) And am not without hopes that you will yet oblige me so far, as to consider that letter, and if I err, to let me see it by scripture, &c.

Yours, almost the whole of it, is concerning the narrative I sent to you; and you seem to intimate as if I were giving characters, reflections, libels, &c. concerning yourself and relations; all which were as far from my thoughts, as ever they were in writing after either yourself, or any other minister. In the front you declare your apprehension to be, that the afflicted was under a diabolical possession; and if so, I see not how it should be occasioned by any witchcraft (unless we ascribe that power to a witch, which is only the prerogative of the Almighty, of sending or

commiffionating the devils to afflict her.) But
to your particular objections againft the narrative; and to the firft. My intelligence not
giving me any further, I could not infert that
I knew not. And it feems improbable that a
queftion fhould be put, whether fhe knew who
they were that tormented her, and at the fame
time to charge her, and that upon her life, not
to tell; and if you had done fo, I fee but little
good you could promife yourfelf or others by it,
fhe being poffeft, as alfo having it inculcated fo
much to her, of witchcraft. And as to the next
objection, about company flocking, &c. I profefs my ignorance, not knowing what you mean
by it. And, fir, that moft of the queftions did
carry with them a prefuppofing the things inquired after, is evident, if there were fuch as thofe
relating to the *blackman* and a book, and about
her hearing the prayer, &c. (related in the faid
narrative, which I find no objection againft.)
As to that which is faid of mentioning yourfelf firft difcourfing, and your hopes that your
breeding was better, (I doubt it not, nor do I
doubt your father might firft apply himfelf to
others) my intelligence is, that you firft fpake to
the afflicted or poffeffed, for which you had the
advantage of a nearer approach. The next two
objections are founded upon miftakes: I find
not in the narrative any fuch queftion, as How

many witches fit upon you? nor, that her breast was not covered, in which those material words, *with the bed-clothes*, are wholly omitted. I am not willing to retort here your own language upon you; but can tell you, that your own discourse of it publickly, at Sir W. P.'s table, has much more contributed to, &c. As to the reply, If she could she would not tell, whether either or both spake it, it matters not much. Neither does the narrative say, you felt the live thing on her belly; though I omit now to say what further demonstrations there are of it. As to that reply, That is only her fancy, I find the word *her* added. And as to your father's feeling for the live creature after you had felt it, if it were on the bed it was not so very far from her. And for the length of his prayer, possibly your witnesses might keep a more exact account of the time than those others, and I stand not for a few minutes. For the rest of the objections, I suppose them of less moment, if less can be; however, shall be ready to receive them. Those matters of greatest concern I find no objections against. These being all that yet appear, it may be thought that if the narrative be not fully exact, it was as near as memory could bear away; but should be glad to see one more perfect (which yet is not to be expected, seeing none wrote at the same time.) You mention the appendix, by which I underftand the fecond vifit; and if you be by the poffeffed belied (as being half an hour with her alone, excluding her own mother, and as telling her you had prayed for her nine times that day, and that now was her laughing time, fhe muft laugh now) I can fee no wonder in it: What can be expected lefs from the father of lies, by whom, you judge, fhe was poffeft?

And befides the above letter, you were pleafed to fend me another paper, containing feveral teftimonies of the poffeffed being lifted up, and held a fpace of feveral minutes to the garret floor, &c. but they omit giving the account, whether after fhe was down they bound her down, or kept holding her; and relate not how many were to pull her down, which hinders the knowledge what number they muft be, to be ftronger than an invifible force. Upon the whole, I fuppofe you expect I fhould believe it; and if fo, the only advantage gained is, that what has been fo long controverted between proteftants and papifts, whether miracles are ceaft, will hereby feem to be decided for the latter; it being, for ought I can fee, if fo, as true a miracle as for iron to fwim; and the devil can work fuch miracles.

But, fir, to leave thefe little difputable things, I do again pray that you would let me have the happiness of your approbation or confutation of that letter before referred to.

And now, sir, that the God of all grace may enable us zealously to own his truths, and to follow those things that tend to peace, and that yourself may be as an useful instrument in his hand, effectually to ruin the remainder of heathenish and popish superstitions, is the earnest desire and prayer of yours to command in what I may, R. C.

Postscript. — Sir, I here send you the copy of a paper that lately came to my hands; which, though it contains no wonders, yet is remarkable, and runs thus :

An account of what an Indian told Capt. Hill at Saco Fort.

The Indian told him, that the French ministers were better than the English; for before the French came among them there were a great many witches among the Indians; but now there were none; and there were witches among the English ministers, as Burroughs, who was hang'd for it.

Were I disposed to make reflections upon it, I suppose you will judge the field large enough; but I forbear.

As above, R. C.

Boston, Feb. 19, 1693.
Mr. Cotton Mather,
Reverend Sir,

I have received as yet no answer to mine of November the 24th, except an offer to peruse books, &c. relating to the doctrinals therein contained; nor to my last, of January the 18th, in which I again prayed that if I erred I might be shewed it by scripture, viz. in believing that the devil's bounds are set, which he cannot pass — that the devils are so full of malice, that it can't be added to by mankind — that where he hath power, he neither can nor will omit executing it — that it is only the Almighty that sets bounds to his rage, and who only can commission him to hurt or destroy any; and consequently to detest, as erroneous and dangerous, the belief that a witch can commission devils to afflict mortals — that he can at his or the witch's pleasure assume any shape — that the hanging or drowning of witches can lessen his power of afflicting, and restore those that were at a distance tormented by him; — and whether witchcraft ought to be understood, now in this age, to be the same that it was when the divine oracles were given forth, particularly those quoted by mr. Gaule, in that cited head, *Wonders of the Invisible World* (mr. Gaule's fourth head) to discover witches, which do so plainly shew a witch, in scripture sense, to be one that maligns, &c. and that pretends to give a sign in order to seduce, &c. For I have never understood, in my time, any such have suffered as witches, though sufficiently known; but the only witch now inquired after is one that is said to become so by making an explicit covenant with the devil,

i. e. the devil appearing to them, and making a compact, mutually promising each to other; testified by their signing his book, a material book, which he is said to keep; and that thereby they are intituled to a power, not only to afflict others, but such as is truly exorbitant, if not highly intrenching upon the prerogative of him who is the Sovereign Being: For who is he that saith, and it cometh to pass, when the Lord commandeth it not?

Such explicit covenant being, as is said, in this age, reckoned essential to complete a witch; yet I finding nothing of such covenant (or power thereby obtained) in scripture, and yet a witch therein so fully described, do pray that if there be any such scriptures I may be directed to them; for as to the many legends in this case, I make no account of them: I read indeed of a covenant with death and with hell, but suppose that to be in the heart (or *mental*) only, and see not what use such an explicit one can be of between spirits, any further than as 'tis a copy of that *mental* which is in the heart. The dire effects and consequences of such notion may be found written in indelible *Roman* characters of blood, in all countries where they have prevailed. And what less can be expected, when men are indicted for that, which it is impossible to prove, so as for any to clear himself of, viz such explicit covenant with the devil; and then, for want of better evidence, must take up with such as the nature of such secret covenant can bear, as mr. Gaule hath it, i. e. distracted stories, and strange and foreign events, &c. thereby endeavouring to find it, though by its but supposed effects. By the same rule that one is put to purge himself of such compact, by the same may all mankind.

This then being so important a case, it concerns all to know what foundations in scripture are laid for such a structure; for if they are deficient of that warrant, the more eminent the architects are, the more dangerous are they thereby rendered, &c. These are such considerations as I think will vindicate me, in the esteem of all lovers of humanity, in my endeavours to get them cleared; and, to that end, do once more pray, that you would so far oblige me as to give your approbation or confutation of the above doctrinals; but if you think silence a virtue in this case, I shall (I suppose) so far comply with it as not to lose you any more time to look over my papers. And if any others will so far oblige me, I shall not be ungrateful to them. Praying God to guide and prosper you, I am, sir, yours to my power,

R. C.

(*He that doth truth cometh to the light.*)

Boston, April the 16*th,* 1694.
Mr. Cotton Mather,
   Reverend Sir,

Having as yet received no anfwer to my laft, touching the doctrinals therein referred to, though at the delivery of it you were pleafed to promife the gentleman that prefented it that I fhould have it, and after that you acquainted the fame gentleman you were about it; the length of time fince thofe promifes makes me fuppofe you are preparing fomething for the prefs (for I would not queftion your veracity;) and I think it may not be amifs, when you do any thing of that nature for the public view, that you alfo explain fome paffages of fome late books of yours and your relations, which are hard to be underftood; to inftance in a few of many; *Wonders of the Invifible World*, page 17, " Plagues are fome of thofe woes with which the devil caufes our trouble." Page 18, " Hence come fuch plagues as that befom of deftruction which within our memory fwept away fuch a throng of people from one Englifh city, in one vifitation. Wars are fome of thofe woes with which the devil caufes our trouble." Page 16, " Hence 'tis that the devil, like a dragon keeping a guard upon fuch fruits as would refrefh a languifhing world, has hindered mankind for many ages from hitting upon thofe ufeful inventions. The benighted world muſt jog on, for thouſands of years, without the knowlege of the loadſtone, printing, and ſpectacles." Page 10, " It is not likely that every devil does know every language. 'Tis poſſible the experience, or, if I may call it ſo, the education, of all devils is not alike." *Caſes of Conſcience*, page 63, " The devil has inflicted on many the diſeaſe called the lycanthropia." *Memorable Providences relating to Witchcraft Diſc.* page 24, " I am alſo apt to think that the devils are ſeldom able to hurt us in any of our exterior concerns, without a commiſſion from ſome of our fellow worms. When foul mouth'd men ſhall wiſh harm to their neighbours, they give a commiſſion to the devil to perform what they deſire; and if God ſhould not mercifully prevent, they would go through with it. Hear this, you that in wild paſſion will give every thing to the devil; hear it, you that beſpeak a rot, a pox, or a plague, on all that ſhall provoke you; I here indict you as guilty of helliſh witchcraft in the ſight of God." *More Wonders of the Inviſible World*, p. 49, " They each of them have their ſpectres or devils commiſſioned by them, and repreſenting them." Page 14, " But ſuch a permiſſion from God for the devil to come down and break in upon mankind, muſt often times be accompanied with a commiſſion from ſome of mankind itself." *Enchantments encountered*, " These witches have driven a trade of commissioning their confederate spirits to do all sorts of mischiefs to their neighbours." Page 50, "They have bewitched some, even so far as to make them self-destroyers." Page 144, " As I am abundantly satisfied, that many of the self-murders, committed here, have been the effects of a cruel and bloody witchcraft, letting fly dæmons upon the miserable Senecas." Page 51, " We have seen some of their children dedicated to the devil, that in their infancy the imps have sucked them." *Cases of Conscience*, page 24, " They bequeath their dæmons to the children as a legacy, by whom they are often assisted to see and do things beyond the power of nature." Page 21, " There is in Spain a sort of people called Zahurs, that can see into the bowels of the earth." *On Tuesdays and Fridays, and to add that in page* 49; the words are, " For the law of God allows of no revelation from any other spirit but himself, Isa. viii. 19. It is a sin against God to make use of the devil's help, to know that which cannot be otherways known; and I testify against it as a great transgression, which may justly provoke that Holy One of Israel to let loose devils on the whole land. Although the devil's accusation may be so far regarded, as to cause an inquiry into the truth of things, (Job i. 11, 12, and ii. 5, 6) yet not so as to be an evidence or ground of conviction; for the devil's testimony ought not to be taken in whole nor in part." It is a known truth, that some unwary expressions of the primitive fathers were afterwards improved for the introducing and establishing of error, as their calling the Virgin Mary the mother of God, &c. Hence occasion and advantage were taken to propagate the idolizing of her. The like might be said of the eucharist. These assertions, above rehearsed, being apparently liable to a like mal-construction, and no less dangerous, are therefore, as I said, highly needful to be explained, and that in a most public manner. For were they to be understood literally, and as they are spoken, it must seem as if the authors were introducing among christians very dangerous doctrines, such as, were they asserted by the best of men, yet ought to be rejected by all, &c. viz. That 'tis the devil that brings the most of evils upon mankind, by way of infliction, that do befal them; and that the 'witch can commission him to the performance of these; with many other as dangerous doctrines, and such as seem in their tendency to look favourably upon the antient pagan doctrines of this country, who believed that God did hurt to none, but good to all, but that the devil must be pleased by worshiping, &c. from whom came all their miseries, as they believed. For what were all this, but to rob God of his glory in the highest manner, and give it to a devil and a witch? Is it not he that hath said, Shall there be evil in a city, and the Lord hath not done it? But if any are fond of their own notions, because some eminent men before now have asserted them, they may do well to compare them with that excellent saying (*Wonders of the Invisible World*, p. 7) "About this devil there are many things, whereof we may reasonably and profitably be inquisitive; such things I mean as are in our bibles revealed to us; according to which if we do not speak on so dark a subject, but according to our own uncertain and perhaps humoursome conjectures, there is no light in us." Or that other, p. 75, "At every other weapon the devil will be too hard for us." For 'tis most certain that other notions, weapons and practices have been taken up with, and that the event has been answerable: the devil has been too hard for such as have so done. I shall forbear to instance from the dogmatical part, and shall mention some practices that as much need explaining; *Mem. Provid. Rel. to Witchc.* pages 29, 30, 31; where account is given that it was prayed for that the afflicted might be able to declare, whom she apprehended herself afflicted by, together with the immediate answer of such prayer. To this you once replied, when it was mentioned to you, that you did not then understand the wiles of satan.

To which I have nothing to object, but it might be a good acknowledgment. But considering that the book is gone forth into all the world, I cannot but think the salve ought to be proportioned to the sore, and the notice of the devil's wiles as universal as the means recommending them. Another practice is, (pages 20, 21,) "There was one singular passion that frequently attended her; an invisible chain would be clapt about her, and she in much pain and fear cry out when they began to put it on: once I did with my own hand knock it off as it began to be fastened about her." If this were done by the power or virtue of any ordinance of divine instruction, it is well; but would have been much better if the institution had been demonstrated; or was there any physical virtue in that particular hand? But supposing that neither of these will be asserted by the author, I think it very requisite, that the world may be acquainted with the operation, and to what art or craft to refer their power of knocking off invisible chains. And thus, sir, I have faithfully discharged what in this I took to be my duty, and am so far from doing it to gain applause, or from a spirit of contradiction, that I expect to procure me many enemies thereby; but (as in cafe of a fire) where the glory of God and the good and welfare of mankind are fo nearly concerned, I thought it my duty to be no longer an idle fpectator; and can and do fay, to the glory of God, in this whole affair, I have endeavoured to keep a confcience void of offence, both towards God and towards man; and therein at the leaft have the advantage of fuch as are very jealous they have done fo much herein, as to fin in what they have done, viz. in fheltering the accufed; fuch have been the cowardice and fearfulnefs into which a regard to the diffatisfaction of other people have precipitated them; which by the way muft needs acquaint all, that for the future other meafures are refolved upon (by fuch) which, how bloody they may prove when opportunity fhall offer, is with him who orders all things according to the counfel of his own will. And now, that the fong of angels may be the emulation of men, is the earneft defire and prayer of, fir, yours to command in what I may, R. C.

Glory to God in the higheft, and on earth peace, and good will towards men.

Bofton, March the 1ft, 1694.

Mr. B——,
Worthy Sir,
After more than a year's waiting for the per-

formance of a reiterated promife from one under
fingular obligations, and a multitude of advantages to have done it fooner, the utmoft compliance I have met with is (by your hands) the
fight of four fheets of refcinded papers. But I
muft firft be obliged to return them in a fortnight, and not copied, which I have now com-
plied with: and having read them, am not at all
furprifed at the author's caution, not to admit of
fuch crude matter and impertinent abfurdities, as
are to be found in it. He feems concerned that
I take no notice of his feveral books, wherein,
as he faith, he has unanfwerably proved things.
To this I might reply, that I have fent him
letters of quotations out of thofe books, to
know how much of them he will abide by;
for I thought it hard to affix their natural confequences, till he had opportunity to explain
them. And faith, that he hath fent me mr.
Baxter's *World of Spirits*, an ungainfayable book,
&c. (though I know no ungainfayable book but
the bible;) which book, I think, no man that
has read it will give fuch a title to but the
author. He fpeaks of my reproaching his
public fermons; of which I am not confcious
to myfelf, unlefs it be about his interpretation
of a thunder ftorm (that broke into his houfe)
which favoured fo much of enthufiafm.

As to thofe papers, I have (as I read them)

noted in the margin where, in a hasty reading, I thought it needful; of which it were unreasonable for him to complain, seeing I might not take a copy, thereby to have been enabled more at leisure to digest what were needful to be said on so many heads; and as I have not flattered him, so, for telling what was so needful, with the hazard of making so many enemies by it, I have approved myself one of his best friends. And besides his own sense of the weakness of his answer, testified by the prohibition above, he has wholly declined answering to most of those things that I had his promise for; and what he pretends to speak to, after mentioning, without the needful answer or proof, drops it.

His first main work, after his definition of a witch, which he never proves (without saying any thing to mr. Gaule's scriptural description, though so often urged to it, and though himself has in his book recommended and quoted it) is to magnify the devil's power, and that as I think beyond and against the scripture; this takes him up about 11 pages; and yet in page 22d he again returns to it, and, as *I* understand it, takes part with the pharisees against our Saviour in the argument; for they charge him that he cast out devils through Beelzebub: our Saviour's answer is, (Matt. xii. 25) *Every kingdom divided against itself is brought to desolation; and every city or house divided against itself shall not stand; and if satan cast out satan, he is divided against himself; how shall then his kingdom stand?* And yet, notwithstanding this answer, together with what follows, for further illustration our author is it seems resolved to assert, that our Saviour did not in this answer deny that many did so, viz. cast out devils by Beelzebub; and, page 23, grants that the devils have a miraculous power, but yet it must not be called miraculous, and yet can be distinguished, as he intimates, only by the conscience or light within, to the no small scandal of the christian religion: though our Saviour and his apostles account this the chief or principal proof of his godhead, (*John* xx. 30, 31. *John* x. 37, 38. *John* v. 30. *Mark* xvi. 17, 18. *Acts* ii. 22. and iv. 30. with many others) and that miracles belong only to God, who also governs the world, (*Ps.* cxxxvi. 4. *Jer.* xiv. 22. *Isa.* xxxviii. 8. *Ps.* lxii. 11. *Lam.* iii. 37. *Amos* iii. 6.) But, to forbear quoting that which the scripture is most full in, do only say, that he that dares assert the devil to have such a miraculous power, had need have other scriptures than ever I have seen.

In page 12, our author proceeds, and states a question to this effect: If the devil has such powers, and cannot exert them without permission from God, what can the witch contribute thereunto? Inftead of an anfwer to this weighty objection, our author firft concedes, that the devils do ordinarily exert their powers, without the witches contributing to it; but yet, that, to the end to increafe their guilt, he may cheat a witch, by making her believe herfelf the author of them. His next is, If witchcraft be, as I fuppofe it is, the fkill of applying the plaftic fpirit of the world, &c. then the confent of the witch doth naturally contribute to that mifchief that the devil does. And his laft anfwer runs to this effect: Is it not the ordination of God, that where the devil can get the confent of a witch for the hurting of others, the hurt fhall as certainly be as if they had fet maftiff dogs upon them, or had given them poifon into their bowels? and God's providence muft be as great in delivering from one as from the other. And this it feems is not only his belief, but the moft orthodox and the moft learned anfwer that our author could pitch upon: If witchcraft be, as I fuppofe it is, &c. and is it not the ordination of God, that, &c. What is all this but precarious, and begging the queftion, and a plain dropping the argument he cannot manage? However, to amufe the ignorant, and to confound the learned, he hooks in a cramp word, if not a nonentity, viz. plaftic fpirit of the world; for who is it either knows that there is a plastic spirit, or what it is, or how this can any way serve his purpose?

He then proceeds to scripture instances of witches, &c. and where I thought it needful, I have, as I said, shewed my dissent from his judgment. He accounts it unreasonable to be held to the proof of his definition of a witch, which he makes to consist in a covenant with the devil; and chooses rather a tedious process about a pistol to defend him from it, which indeed is one particular way whereby murder has been committed, and so the doer becomes culpable. But his definition of a witch, which, as I said, still remains to be proved, is to this effect: that a witch is one that covenants with and commissions devils to do mischiefs; that she is one in covenant, or that by virtue of such covenant she can commission him to kill. The not bringing scripture to prove these two is a sufficient demonstration there is none; and so our author leaves off just where he began, viz. in a bare assertion, together with his own bigoted experiences, hinting also at multitudes of histories to confirm him in the belief of his definition. Here being all that I take notice of to be considerable.

And now, sir, if you think fit, improve your friendship with the author, for the glory of God, the sovereign being, the good and welfare of mankind, and for his real and true intereſt. As you ſee it convenient, put him in mind, that the glory of God is the end why mankind was made, and why he hath ſo many advantages to it: that the flames we have ſeen, threatening the utter extirpation of the country, muſt owe their original to theſe dangerous errors (if not hereſies) which, if they remain unextinguiſhed, may and moſt likely will be acted over again: that it is more honour to own an error in time, than tenaciouſly after full conviction to retain it. But if our author will again vindicate ſuch matters, pleaſe to acquaint him, that I ſhall not any more receive his papers, if I may not copy and uſe them; and that when he does, inſtead of ſuch abſtruſe matters, I ſtill pray his determination in thoſe things I have his promiſe for. And thus begging pardon for thus long detaining you, I am, ſir, yours to command,

R. C.

Boſton, March 18, 1694.

To the Miniſters, whether Engliſh, French or Dutch.

I, having had not only occaſion, but renewed provocation, to take a view of the myſterious doctrines which have of late been ſo much conteſted among us, could not meet with any that had ſpoken more, or more plainly, the ſenſe of those doctrines (relating to witchcraft) than the Rev. Mr. C. M.; but how clearly and consistent, either with himself or the truth, I need not now say, but cannot but suppose his strenuous and zealous asserting his opinions has been one cause of the dismal convulsions we have here lately fallen into. Supposing that his books of *Memorable Providences relating to Witchcraft*, as also his *Wonders of the Invisible World*, did contain in them things not warrantable, and very dangerous, I sent to him a letter of quotations out of those books, &c. that so, if it might have been, I might understand what tolerable sense he would put upon his own words; which I took to be a better way of proceeding, than to have affixed what I thought to be their natural consequences; and, lest I might be judged a sceptic, I gave him a full and free account of my belief relating to those doctrines, together with the grounds thereof; and prayed him, that if I erred I might be shewed it by scripture; and this I had his reiterated promise for. But after more than a year's waiting for the performance thereof, all that is done in compliance therewith is, that in February last he sent me four sheets of his writing, as his belief; but before I might receive it I must engage to deliver it back in a fortnight, and not copied. A summary account of which I shall give you, when I have first acquainted you what the doctrines were which I sent to him for his concurrence with, or confutation of, and to which I had his promise, as above.

These by way of question, viz. Whether that fourth head, cited and recommended by himself (in *Wonders of the Invisible World*) of Mr. Gaule, ought to be believed as a truth; which runs thus: "Among the most unhappy circumstances to convict a witch, one is maligning and oppugning the word, work and worship of God, and seeking by an extraordinary sign to seduce any from it. *Deut.* xiii. 1, 2. *Matt.* xxiv. 24. *Acts* xiii. 8, 10. 2 *Tim.* iii. 8. Do but mark well the places; and for this very property of thus opposing and perverting, they are all there concluded arrant and absolute witches."

And if in witchcraft the devil by means of a witch does the mischief, how is it possible to distinguish it from possession? both being said to be performed by the devil; and yet, without an infallible distinction, there can be no certainty in judgment. And whether it can be proved that the Jewish church, in any age before, or in our Saviour's time, even in the time of their greatest apostacy, did believe that a witch had power to commission devils to mischief?

So much to the questions. These were sent as my belief: That the devil's bounds are set, that he cannot pafs; that the devils are fo full of malice, that it cannot be added to by mankind; that where he hath power, he neither can nor will omit executing it; that it is only the Almighty that fets bounds to his rage, and that only can commiffion him to hurt or deftroy. And now I fhall give you the fummary account of his four fheets above mentioned, as near as memory could recollect, in ten particulars.

1. That the devils have in their natures a power to work wonders and miracles; particularly that the pharifees were not miftaken in afferting that the devils might be caft out by Beelzebub; and that our Saviour's anfwer does not oppofe that affertion; and that he hath the power of death; that he can make the moft folid things invifible, and can invifibly bring poifon, and force it down people's throats.

2. That to affert this natural, wonderful power of the devil, makes moft for the glory of God, in preferving man from its effects.

3. Yet this power is reftrained by the Almighty, as pleafeth him.

4. That a witch is one that makes a covenant with the devil.

5. That by virtue of fuch a covenant, fhe arrives at a power to commiffion him.

6. That God has ordained that when the devil is called upon by the witch, though he

were before restrained by the Almighty, the desired mischiefs ordinarily shall as certainly be performed, as if the witch had lodged poison in the bowels of her neighbour, or had set mastiff dogs on them.

7. That the witches art of applying the Plastic Spirit of the world to unlawful purposes does naturally contribute to the mischiefs done by the Devil.

8. That that God which restrained an Abimelech and a Laban from hurting, does also restrain the witch from calling upon or improving the devil, when he will not have his power so exerted.

9. That to have a familiar spirit, is to be able to cause a devil to take bodily shapes, whereby either to give responses, or to receive orders for doing mischief.

10. That this is the judgment of most of the divines in the country, whether English, Dutch, or French.

This, as I said, I took to be the most material in the four sheets sent to me as his belief, and is also all the performance he has yet made of his several promises; which ten articles being done only by memory, left through mistake or want of the original I might have committed any errors, I sent them to him, that, if there were any, they might be rectified: but instead of such an answer as might be expected from a minister and a learned gentleman, one mr. W. shewed me a letter writ by Mr. C. M. to himself, which I might read, but neither borrow nor copy, and so, if I were minded, could give but a short account of it.

And passing over his hard language, which, as I am conscious to myself I never deserved, (relating to my writing in the margin of the four sheets, and to these ten articles) so I hope I understand my duty better than to imitate him in retorting the like. Among his many words in his said letters, I meet with two small objections; one is against the word *miracle* in the first article; the word, I say, not the matter; for the works he attributes to the devil are the same, in their being above or against the course of nature and all natural causes; yet he will not admit of these to be called miracles; and hence he reckons it the greatest difficulty he meets with in this whole affair, to distinguish the works of the devil from miracles. And hence also he concedes to the devil the power to make the most solid things invisible, and invisibly to bring poison, and force it down people's throats, &c. Which I look upon to be as true miracles as that 2 *Kings*, vi. 18; and this is the sense I understand the word in; and in this sense he himself, in the four sheets, admits it; for he has an objection to this effect, viz. If the devils have such power, &c. then miracles are not ceased;

and where are we then? His anfwer is, Where! Even juft where we were before, fay I : fo that it feems the only offence here is at my ufing his words. His fecond objection (for weight) is againft the whole ninth article, and wonders how it is poffible for one man fo much to mifunderftand another; yet, as I remember, he, fpeaking of the witch of Endor, in the faid four fheets, fays, fhe had a familiar fpirit, and that a fpirit belonging to the invifible world, upon her calling, appeared to Saul, &c. and if fo, it is certain he gave refponfes. He alfo tells of Balaam, that it was known that he could fet devils on people to deftroy them; and therefore how this objection fhould bear any force I fee not. The reft of the objections are of fo fmall weight, that once reading may be fufficient to clear them up; and if this be not fo, he can, when he pleafes, by making it publick, together with the margins I writ, convince all people of the truth of what he afferts. But here it is to be noted, that the 2d, 3d, 4th and 5th articles he concedes to, as having nothing to object againft them, but that they are his belief; and that the 6th and 7th he puts for anfwer to an objection which he thus frames, viz. If the devil have fuch powers, but cannot exert them but by permiffion from God, what can the witch contribute thereto?

And thus I have faithfully performed what I undertook; and do folemnly declare, I have not intentionally in the least wronged the gentleman concerned, nor designed the least blemish to his reputation; but if it stands in competition with the glory of God, the only almighty being, his truths and his people's welfare, I suppose these too valuable to be trampled on for his sake, though in other things I am ready to my power (though with denying some part of my own interest) to serve him. Had this gentleman declined or detracted his four sheets, I see not but he might have done it, and which I think there was cause enough for him to have done; but to own the four sheets, and at the same time to disown the doctrine contained in them, and this knowing that I have no copy, renders the whole of the worse aspect.

And now I shall give you a further account of my belief, when I have first premised, that it is a prevailing belief in this country, and elsewhere, that the scriptures are not full in the description of, and in the way and means how to detect, a witch, though positive in their punishment to be by death; and that hence they have thought themselves under a necessity of taking up with the sentiments of such men or places that are thought worthy to give rules to detect them by; and have accordingly practised; viz. in searching for teats for the devil to suck; trying whether the suspected can say the Lord's prayer; and whether the afflicted falls at the fight, and rifes at the touch, of the fuppofed witch; as alfo by the afflicted or poffeffed giving account who is the witch.

Touching thefe, my belief is, that 'tis highly derogatory to the wifdom of the wife Lawgiver, to affert, that he has given a law by Mofes, the penalty whereof is death, and yet no direction to his people, whereby to know and detect the culpable, till our triumvirate, Meffrs. Perkins, Gaule and Bernard, had given us their receipts; and, that that fourth head of Mr. Gaule, being fo well proved by fcripture, is a truth, and contains a full and clear teftimony who are witches culpable of death, and that plainly and from fcripture, yet not excluding any other branch, when as well proved by that infallible rule; and, that the going to the afflicted or poffeffed, to have them divine who are witches by their fpectral fight, is a great wickednefs; even the fin of Saul (for which he alfo died) but with this difference, the one did it for augury, or to know future events; the other, in order to take away life; and, that the fearching for teats, the experiment of their faying the Lord's prayer, the falling at the fight and rifing at the touch of the fuppofed criminal, being all of them foreign from fcripture, as well as reafon, are abominations to be abhorred and repented of; and, that our Salem witchcraft, either refpecting the judges and juries, their tenderness of life, or the multitude and pertinency of witnesses, both afflicted and confessors, or the integrity of the historians, is as authentic, and made as certain, as any event of that kind in the world. And yet who is it that now sees not through it, and that these were the sentiments that have procured the sorest affliction and most lasting infamy, that ever befel this country, and most like so to do again, if the same notions be still entertained? and, finally, that these are those last times, of which the Spirit speaks expressly, *Tim.* iv. 1 ?

And now, ye that are fathers in the churches, guides to the people, and the salt of the earth, I beseech you consider these things; and if you find the glory of God diminished by ascribing such power to witches and devils; his truths opposed by these notions; and his people asperted in their doctrines and reputations, and endangered in their lives — I dare not dictate you — you know your duty as watchmen — and the Lord be with you.

But if you find my belief contrary to sound doctrine, I entreat you to shew it me by the scripture; and in the mean time blame me not if I cannot believe that there are several Almighties; for to do all sorts of wonders, beyond and above the course of nature, is certainly the work of Omnipotency. So alfo, he that fhall commiffion or empower to thefe, muft alfo be almighty; and I think it not a fufficient *falvo*, to fay they may be reftrained by the Moft High; and hope you will not put any hard conftruction on thefe my endeavours to get information (all other ways failing) in things fo needful to be known. Praying the Almighty's guidance and protection, I am

Yours to the utmoft of my power,

R. C.

Bofton, Sept. the 20*th,* 1695.

MR. SAMUEL WILLARD,

Reverend Sir,

My former, of March the 18th, directed to the Minifters (and which was lodged with yourfelf) containing feveral articles which I fent as my belief, praying them if I erred to fhew it me by fcripture, I have as yet had no anfwer to, either by word or writing, which makes me gather that they are approved of as *orthodox,* or at leaft that they have fuch foundations as that none are willing to manifeft any oppofition to them; and therefore, with fubmiffion, &c. I think that that late feafonable and well-defigned dialogue, intituled, *Some Mifcellaneous Obfervations,* &c. of which yourfelf is the fuppofed author, and which was fo ferviceable in the time of it, is yet liable to a mal-conſtruction, even to the danger of reviving what it moſt oppoſes, and of bringing thoſe practices again on foot, which in the day of them were ſo terrible to this whole country. The words, which I ſuppoſe ſo liable to miſconſtruction, are, p. 14, **B.** *Who informed them?* **S.** *The ſpectre.* **B.** *Very good, and that's the devil turned informer. How are good men like to fare, againſt whom he hath particular malice? It is but a preſumption, and wiſe men will weigh preſumptions againſt preſumptions. There is to be no examination without grounds of ſuſpicion. Some perſons credit nothing to be accounted too good to be undermined ſo far as to be ſuſpected on ſo ſlight a ground; and it is an injury done them to bring them upon examination, which renders them openly ſuſpected. I will not deny but for perſons already ſuſpected, and of ill fame, it may occaſion their being examined.* In which, theſe words, *'tis but a preſumption,* &c. and *ſome perſons credit,* &c. and *I will not deny but for perſons already ſuſpected,* &c. I take to be waiving the diſcuſſion of thoſe points, the ſpeaking to which might at that time have hindered the uſefulneſs and ſucceſs of that book, rather than any declaring the ſentiments of the author. But notwithſtanding, many perſons will be ready to underſtand this as if the author did wholly leave it with the juſtice, to judge who are ill perſons, such as the devil's accusations may fasten upon; and that the devil's accusation of a person is a presumption against them of their guilt; and that, upon such presumptions, they may be had to examination, if the justice counts them persons of ill fame; for the author I suppose knows that the bare examination will leave such a stain upon them (and it would be well if their posterity escaped it!) as the length of a holy and unblamable life will be found too short to extirpate. And if the justice may go thus far with the devil's evidence, then the addition of a story or two of some cart overset, or persons taken sick after a quarrel, might as well be thought sufficient for their commitment, in order to their trial, as 'tis called, (though this too often has been more like a stage play, or a *tragi-comic scene*) and so that otherways useful book may prove the greatest snare to revive the same practices again.

These things being so liable, as I said, to such mal-construction, it were needful that men might be undeceived, and the matter more fully demonstrated, viz. That the devil's accusation is not so much as any presumption against the life or reputation of any person; (for how are good men like to fare, if his malicious accusations may be taken as a presumption of their guilt?) and, that his accusations, as they are no presumption against persons of unspotted fame, so neither are to be heard, or any ways regarded, against persons though otherways of ill life, much less for their having long since had their names abused by his outcries, or by the malice of ill neighbours; and, that justice knows no difference of persons; that, if this evidence be sufficient to bring one person, 'tis so to bring any other, to examination, and consequently to the utmost extent of odium which such examination will certainly expose them to; for who can know any other, but that as the one may be maliciously accused by devils and a devilish report gone before it, so that another, who has not been so much as accused before, being more cunning or more seeming religious, might yet be more guilty; the whole depending upon invisible evidence, of which invisible stuff, though we have had more than sufficient, yet I find (among other reverend persons) your name to a certain printed paper, which runs thus:

Certain Proposals, made by the President and Fellows of Harvard College to the reverend Ministers of the Gospel, in the several churches of New-England.

First. To observe and record the more illustrious discoveries of the Divine Providence in the government of the world, is a design so holy, so useful, so justly approved, that the too general neglect of it in the churches of God is as justly to be lamented.

2. For the redress of that neglect, although all christians have a duty incumbent on them, yet it is in a peculiar manner to be recom-

mended unto the Minifters of the gofpel to improve the fpecial advantages which are in their hands, to obtain and preferve the knowledge of fuch notable occurrences as are fought out by all that have pleafure in the great works of the Lord.

3. The things to be efteemed memorable, are fpecially all unufual accidents in the heaven, or earth, or water; all wonderful deliverances of the diftreffed; mercies to the godly; judgments on the wicked; and more glorious fulfilments of either the promifes or threatenings in the fcriptures of truth; with apparitions, poffeffions, enchantments, and all extraordinary things, wherein the exiftence and agency of the Invifible World is more fenfibly demonftrated.

4. It is therefore propofed, that the Minifters throughout this land would manifeft their pious regards unto the works of the Lord, and the operation of his hands, by reviving their cares to take written accounts of fuch *Remarkables;* but ftill well attefted with credible and fufficient witneffes.

5. It is defired that the accounts, thus taken, of thefe remarkables, may be fent to the Prefident or Fellows of the college, by whom they fhall be carefully referved for fuch a ufe to be made of them, as may by fome fit affembly of Minifters be judged moft conducing to the glory of God, and the fervice of his people.

6. Though we doubt not that love to the name of God will be a fufficient motive to all good men to contribute what affiftance they can unto this undertaking; yet, for further encouragement, fome fingular marks of refpect fhall be ftudied for fuch good men, as will actually affift it, by taking pains to communicate any important paffages proper to be inferted in this collection.

INCREASE MATHER, Pres.

James Allen,	*John Leverette,*
Char. Morton,	*Will. Brattle,*
Sam. Willard,	*Neh. Walter,*
Cotton Mather,	

Fellows.

Cambridge, March 5, 1694.

NOTE. — It is known that Dr. Increafe Mather defigned to publifh a book concerning things rare and wonderful, occurring around him. It would feem from this circular addreffed to the clergy, that he was defirous of collecting materials for the work.

Here being an encouragement to all good men to send in such remarkables as are therein expressed, I have sent in the following; not that I think them a more sensible demonstration of the being of a future state (with rewards and punishments) or of angels good and bad, &c. than the scriptures of truth hold forth, &c.; or than any of those other demonstrations God hath given us; for this were treacherously and perfidiously to quit the post to the enemy. The sadducee, deist and atheist would hereby be put in a condition so triumphantly to deny the existence and agency thereof, as that a few stories told (which at best must be owned to be fallible and liable to misrepresentations) could not be thought infallibly sufficient to demonstrate the truth against them. I have heard that in logick a false argument is reckoned much worse than none; yet, supposing that a collection of instances may be many ways useful, not only to the present but succeeding ages, I have sent you the following remarkables, which have lately occurred, the certainty of which, if any scruple it, will be found no hard matter to get satisfaction therein. But here, not to insist on those less occurrences, as the sudden death of one of our late justices; and a like mortality that fell upon the two sons of another of them; with the fall of a man that was making provision to raise the

new northern bell, which, when it was up, the
firſt perſon, whoſe death it was to ſignify, was
ſaid to be a child of him, who, by printing and
ſpeaking, had had as great a hand in procuring
the late actions as any, if not the greateſt; and
the ſplitting the gun at Salem, where that furious
marſhal, and his father, &c. were rent to pieces,
&c. As to all theſe, it muſt be owned, that no
man knows love or hatred by all that is before
him, much leſs can they be more ſenſible demonſtrations of the exiſtence and agency of the inviſible world, than the ſcriptures of truth afford,
&c. though the rich man in the parable might
think otherwiſe, &c. who was ſeeking to ſend
ſome more ſenſible demonſtrations thereof to
his brethren, &c. In that tremendous judgment of God upon this country, by the late
amazing proſecution of the people here, under
the notion of witches; whereby twenty ſuffered
as evil doers, (beſides thoſe that died in priſon)
about ten more condemned, and a hundred im-
priſoned, and about two hundred more accuſed,
and the country generally in fears when it would
come to their turn to be accuſed; and the proſecution and manner of trial ſuch, that moſt
would have choſen to have fallen into the hands
of the barbarous enemy, rather than (under that
notion) into the hands of their brethren in
church fellowſhip; and, in ſhort, was ſuch an

affliction as far exceeded all that ever this country hath laboured under—

Yet in this mount God is seen. When it was thus bad with this distressed people, a full and a sudden stop is put, not only without, but against, the inclination of many; for out of the eater came forth meat: those very accusers, which had been improved as witnesses against so many, by the providence of the Most High, and perhaps blinded with malice, are left to accuse those in most high esteem, both magistrates and ministers, as guilty of witchcraft; which shewed our rulers, that necessity lay upon them to confound that which had so long confounded the country, as being themselves unwilling to run the same risk: this, that was in the event of it, to this country, as life from the dead, is most easy with Him, in whose hands are the hearts of all men, and was a very signal deliverance to this whole country. No less observable was it, that though at the time when the devil's testimony, by the afflicted, was first laid aside, there were great numbers of (real or pretended) afflicted; yet when this was once not judged of validity enough to be any longer brought into the court against the accused as evidence, the affliction generally ceased, and only some remainders of it in such places, where more encouragement was given to the actors, God seeming thereby plainly to decipher that sin of going to the devil, &c. as the rise and foundation of those punishments.

And thus, reverend, I have, as I understand it, performed my duty herein, for the glory of God, and the well-being of men. And for my freedom used in this and former writings, relating to the actors in this tragedy, I shall not apologize, but give you the words of one to whom some can afford the title of venerable (when he is arguing for that which they have undertaken to assert, though at other times more diminutive epithets must serve); it is the reverend mr. R. Baxter, in his book, *the Cure of Church Divisions*, pages 257, 258. " But [I pray you mark it] the way of God is to shame the sinner, how good soever in other respects, that the sin may have the greater shame, and religion may not be ashamed, as if it allowed men to sin: nor God, the author of religion, be dishonoured; nor others be without the warning: but the way of the devil is, to hide or justify the sin, as if it were for fear of disparaging the goodness of the persons that committed it; that so he may hereby dishonour religion, and godliness itself, and make men believe it is but a cover for any wickedness, and as consistent with it as a looser life is, and that he may keep the sinner from repenting, and blot out the memory of that warning which should have preserved after ages from the like falls. Scripture fhameth the profeffors (though a *David*, a *Solomon*, *Peter*, *Noah*, *or Lot*) that the religion profeft may not be afhamed, but vindicated. Satan would preferve the honour of profeffors, that the religion profeffed may bear the fhame; and fo it may fall on God himfelf."

And now that all that have had a hand in any horrid and bloody practices may be brought to give glory to God, and take the due fhame to themfelves; and that our watchmen may no longer feek to palliate, (much lefs give thanks for fuch, &c. thereby making them their own) and that the people may no longer perifh for want of knowledge in the midft of fuch means of light, nor God be any longer difhonoured by falfe fentiments in thefe matters, is the earneft defire and prayer of, fir, yours to my power,

R. C.

Mr. Cotton Mather,
    Reverend Sir,

Having long fince fent you fome doctrinals as to my belief, together with my requeft to you, that if I erred you would be pleafed to fhew it me by fcripture, viz. That the devil's bounds are fet, which he cannot pafs; that the devils are fo full of malice that it cannot be added to by mankind; that where he hath power he neither can nor will omit executing it; that 'tis only the

Almighty that sets bounds to his rage, and that only can commission him to hurt and destroy, &c. But instead of such an answer as was promised and justly expected, you were pleased to send me a book, which you since called an ungainsayable one; which book till lately I have not had opportunity so fully to consider. And to the end you may see I have now done it, I have sent to you some of the remarkables contained in the said book, intituled, "*The Certainty of the World of Spirits,*" *written by Mr.* R. B. *London, printed* 1691. It is therein conceded (preface) that to see devils and spirits ordinarily would not be enough to convince atheists. Page 88, Atheists are not to be convinced by stories; their own senses are not enough to convince them any more than sense will convince a papist from transubstantiation. (*D. Laderd.*) P. 4, No spirit can do any thing but by God's will and permission. Preface, 'Tis the free will of man that gives the devils their hurting power; and without our own consent they cannot hurt us. It is asserted, p. 222, 223, That it is a perverse opposition of popery which causes many protestants not to regard the benefits we receive by angels. And ministers are faulty, that do not pray and give thanks to God for their ministry; and that neglect to teach believers, what love and what thanks they owe to angels. P. 225,

Moft good people look fo much to God and to minifters, that they take little notice of angels, which are God's great minifters. P. 234, The author dares not, as fome have done, judge the catholick church to become antichriftian idolaters, as foon as they gave too much worfhip to faints and angels. P. 7, The bleffed fouls fhall be like the angels, therefore may appear here. P. 3, 4, 'Tis hard to know whether it be a devil or a human foul that appears, or whether the foul of a good or a bad perfon; p. 61, or the foul of fome dead friend that fuffers, and yet retains love, &c. P. 222, No doubt the fouls of the wicked carry with them their former inclinations of covetoufnefs, revenge, &c. P. 7, When revengeful things are done, as on murderers, defrauders, &c. it feems to be from the revengeful wrath of fome bad foul; if it be about money or lands, then from a worldly-minded one; fome fignifications of God's mercy to wicked fouls after this life. P. 4, 'Tis a doubt whether, befides the angels (good and bad) and the fouls of men, there is not a third fort, called fairies and goblins. It is unfearchable to us how far God leaves fpirits to free will in fmall things, fufpending his predetermining motion. P. 246, The devils have a marvellous power, if but a filly wretched witch confent. P. 10, 202, The ftories of witches and fpirits are many ways ufeful, particularly to convince atheists, and confirm believers, and to prove the operation of spirits. P. 232, To help men to understand that devils make no small number of laws, and rulers in the world, and are authors of most of the wars, and of many sermons, and of books that adorn the libraries of learned men. P. 6, 102, The devil's lying with the witch is not to be denied, and is more to exercise the lust of the witch than of the devil, who can also bring in another witch without opening the door, and so perform it by one witch with another. P. 105, Witches can raise storms, fell winds, &c. as is commonly affirmed. P. 107, In America it is a common thing to see spirits, day and night. P. 95, 96, 97, 110, Stories of a child that could not be cured of witchcraft, because the ember-weeks were past; vomited a knife a span long, cart nails, &c. and neither eat nor drank, fifteen days and nights together; a long piece of wood, four knives, and two sharp pieces of iron, every one above a span long, taken out of the stomach, &c. hair, stones, bones, vomited, &c. a thousand pounds of blood lost by one person in a year's time. P. 250, A story that makes the author think it possible that such great things, as he mentions, should be gotten down and up people's throats. P. 164, Partial credibility spoils many a good story. P. 125, The devil's substance enters into the possessed.

P. 174, Diftracted are poffeffed. P. 149, A fick woman, while fhe lay in bed, went to fee her children. P. 153, A dog appeared like a fly or a flea. P. 165, Some knowing agents direct thunder-ftorms, though the author knows not who; and that they fo often fall on churches, he knows not why. P. 2, 80, mr. I. M. and mr. C. M. recommended, together with Bodin, &c. P. 237, A crifpian, if through ignorance he believes not what he faith, may be a chriftian.

In this, fir, I fuppofe that if I have not wronged the fenfe of the author in the places quoted (which I truft you fhall not find I have done) I cannot be thought accountable for the errors or contradictions to himfelf or to the truth, if any fuch be found, particularly what he grants in the preface, of the free will of man giving the devil his hurting power; this being not only more than thofe called witch-advocates would defire to be conceded to them, but is a palpable and manifeft overturning the author's defign in all his witch ftories; (for who would confent to have the devil afflict himfelf?) as alfo his conceffion, that no fpirit can do any thing but by God's will and permiffion; I cannot perfuade myfelf but you muft be fenfible of their apparent contradictorinefs to the reft. Others there are of a very ill afpect; as p. 234, the catholicks are much encouraged in their adoration of angels and faints, if that were fo innocent as not to render them antichriftian idolaters; and that, p. 4, if admitted, will feem to lay an ungainfayable foundation for the pagan, indian and diabolift's faith, by telling us it is beyond our fearch to know how far God leaves the devils to free will, to do what they pleafe, in this world, with a fufpenfion of God's predetermination; which if it were a truth, what were more rational than to oblige him that has fuch power over us? The atheifts alfo would take encouragement if it were granted that we cannot know how far God fufpends his predetermining motion: they would thence affirm, we as little know that there is a predetermining motion, and confequently whether there be a God, and p. 165 would abundantly ftrengthen them, when fuch a learned, experienced and highly-efteemed chriftian fhall own that he knows not who it is that governs the thunder-ftorms: for it might as well difcover ignorance, who it is that difpofes of earthquakes, gun-fhot, and afflictions that befal any, with the reft of mundane events. I defign not to remark all that in the book is remarkable, fuch as the departed fouls wandering again hither to put men upon revenge, &c. favouring fo much of Pythagoras's tranfmigration of fouls, and the feparation of the foul from the body without death, as in the cafe of her that went to fee her children, while yet she did not stir out of her bed, which seems to be a new speculation; unless it determines in favour of transubstantiation, that a body may be at the same time in several places. Upon the whole, it is ungainsayable, that that book, though so highly extolled, may be justly expected to occasion the staggering of the weak, and the hardening of unbelievers in their infidelity. And it seems amazing, that you should not only give it such a recommendation, but that you should send it to me, in order (as I take it) to pervert me from the belief of those fundamental doctrinals (above recited) though I account them more firm than heaven and earth. But that which is yet more strange to me, is, that mr. B's friends did not advise him better, than in his declined age to emit such crude matter to the publick. As to the sometime reverend author, let his works praise the remembrance of him; but for such as are either erroneous and foisted upon him, or the effect of an aged imbecility, let them be detected, that they may proceed no further.

I am not ignorant that the manner of education of youth, in, I think, almost all christian schools, hath a natural tendency to propagate those doctrines of devils heretofore solely profest among ethnicks, and particularly in matters of witchcraft, &c. For, notwithstanding the council of Carthage, taking notice that the chriftian doctors did converfe much with the writings of the heathens for the gaining of eloquence, forbad the reading of the books of the gentiles; yet it feems this was only a bill without a penalty, which their fucceffors did not look upon to be binding. He that fhould in this age take a view of the fchools, might be induced to believe that the ages fince have thought, that without fuch heathen learning a man cannot be fo accomplifhed, as to have any pretence to academick literature; and that the vulgar might not be without the benefit of fuch learning, fome of their difciples have taught them to fpeak Englifh, which has given me the opportunity to fend you thefe following verfes.

Virg. Bucolicks — Ecl. 13.
Sure love is not the caufe their bones appear;
Some eyes bewitch my tender lambs, I fear.

Ecl. 8.
For me thefe herbs in Pontus, Mæris chofe;
There ev'ry powerful drug in plenty grows;
Transform'd to a wolf I often Mæris faw,
Then into fhady woods himfelf withdraw:
Oft he from deepeft fepulchres would charm
Departed fouls; and from another's farm,
Into his own ground, corn yet ftanding take.
Now from the town my charms bring Daphnis back.
Vanquifh'd with charms, from heaven the moon defcends,
Circe with charms transform'd Ulyffes' friends;
Charms in the field will burft a poifonous fnake.
Now from the town, &c.

Ovid's Metam. Lib. 7.

Her arms thrice turns about, thrice wets her crown
With gather'd dew, thrice yawns, and kneeling down,
Oh night! thou friend to secrets! you, clear fires,
That with the moon succeed when day retires;
Great Hecate thou know'st, and aid imparts,
To our design, your charms and magick arts:
And thou, oh earth, that to magicians yields
Thy powerful simples; air, winds, mountains, fields,
Soft murmuring springs, still lakes, and rivers clear,
Ye gods of woods, ye gods of night, appear;
By you, at will, I make swift streams retire
To their first fountain, while their banks admire;
Seas rough make smooth; clear skies with clouds deform;
Storms turn to calms, and make a calm a storm.
With spells and charms, I break the viper's jaw,
Cleave solid rocks, oaks from their fissures draw;
Whole woods remove, the airy mountains shake;
Earth force to groan, and ghosts from graves awake.

Lib. 14.

——————— her journey takes
To Rhegium, opposite to Zante's shore,
And treads the troubled waves, that loudly roar;
Running with unwet feet on that profound,
As if sh' had trod upon the solid ground.
This with portentous poison she pollutes,
Besprinkled with the juice of wicked roots;
In words dark and perplexed, nine times thrice,
Enchantments utters with her wicked voice, &c.

These fables of the heathens (though in themselves of no more validity than the idle tales of an indian, or the discourses of a known romancer) are become the school-learning, not to say the faith, of christians, and are the scriptures brought (instead of that most sure word) if not to prove doctrine, yet as illustrations thereof. *Cafes of Confcience concerning Witchc. page* 25: *Remarkable Providences, page* 250. This perhaps might be the caufe that in England, a people otherwife fober and religious, have for fome ages in a manner wholly refufed admitting thofe not fo educated to the work of the miniftry. Such education and practice have fo far prevailed, that it has been a means of corrupting the chriftian world, almoft to that degree as to be ungainfayable; for though there is reafon to hope that thefe diabolical principles have not fo prevailed (with multitudes of chriftians) as that they afcribe to a witch and a devil the attributes peculiar to the Almighty; yet how few are willing to be found oppofing fuch a torrent, as knowing that in fo doing they fhall be fure to meet with oppofition to the utmoft, from the many, both of magiftrates, minifters and people; and the name of fadducee, atheift, and perhaps witch too, caft upon them moft liberally, by men of the higheft profeffion in godlinefs; and if not fo learned as fome of themfelves, then accounted only fit to be trampled on, and their arguments (though both rational and fcriptural) as fit only for contempt. But though this be the deplorable dilemma, yet fome have dared from time to time (for the glory of God, and the good and fafety of men's lives, &c.) to run all thefe rifks.

And that God who has said, *My glory I will not give to another*, is able to protect those that are found doing their duty herein against all opposers; and, however otherways contemptible, can make them useful in his own hand, who has sometimes chosen the weakest instruments, that his power may be the more illustrious.

And now, reverend sir, if you are conscious to yourself, that you have, in your principles or practices, been abetting to such grand errors, I cannot see how it can consist with sincerity, to be so convinced in matters so nearly relating to the glory of God, and lives of innocents, and at the same time so much to fear disparagement among men, as to trifle with conscience, and dissemble an approving of former sentiments. You know that word, *He that honoureth me I will honour, and he that despiseth me shall be lightly esteemed.* But if you think that in these matters you have done your duty, and taught the people theirs; and that the doctrines cited from the above mentioned book are ungainsayable; I shall conclude in almost his words, He that teaches such doctrine, if through ignorance he believes not what he saith, may be a christian; but if he believes them, he is in the broad path to heathenism, devilism, popery, or atheism. It is a solemn caution, (Gal. i. 8) *But though we, or an angel from heaven, preach any other gospel unto you than that which we have preached unto you, let him be accurſed.* I hope you will not miſconſtrue my intentions herein, who am, reverend ſir, yours to command in what I may, R. C.

To the Miniſters in and near Boſton.
Jan. 12, 1696.

Chriſtianity had been but a ſhort time in the world, when there was raiſed againſt it, not only open profeſt enemies, but ſecret and inbred underminers, who ſought thereby to effect that which open force had been ſo often baffled in. And notwithſtanding that primitive purity and ſincerity, which in ſome good meaſure was ſtill retained, yet the cunning deceivers and apoſtate hereticks found opportunity to beguile the unwary, and this in fundamentals.

Among others which then ſprung up, with but too much advantage, in the third century, the maniche did ſpread his peſtiferous ſentiments, and taught the exiſtence of two beings, or cauſes of all things, viz. a good and a bad: but theſe were ſoon ſilenced by the more orthodox doctors, and anathematized by general councils. And at this day the American indians, another ſort of maniche, entertaining (thus far) the ſame belief, hold it their prudence and intereſt to pleaſe that evil being, as well by perpetrating other murders, as by their bloody ſacrifices, that ſo he may not harm them. The iron teeth of time have now almoft devoured the name of the former; and as to the latter, it is to be hoped that as chriftianity prevails among them, they will abhor fuch abominable belief.

And as thofe primitive times were not privileged againft the fpreading of dangerous herefy, fo neither can any now pretend to any fuch immunity, though profeffing the enjoyment of a primitive purity.

Might a judgment be made from the books of the modern learned divines, or from the practice of courts, or from the faith of many who call themfelves chriftians, it might be modeftly, though fadly, concluded, that the doctrine of the maniche, at leaft great part of it, is fo far from being forgotten, that it is almoft every where profeft. We in thefe ends of the earth need not feek far for inftances in each refpect to demonftrate this. The books here printed and recommended, not only by the refpective authors, but by many of their brethren, do fet forth that the devil inflicts plagues,* wars,† difeafes,‡ tempefts,§ and can render the moft folid things invifible,‖ and can do things above and againft the courfe of nature, and all natural caufes.

* Wonders of the Invifible World, p. 17, 18.—— † p. 18.——
‡ Cafes of Confcience, p. 63.—— § Remarkable Providences, p. 124.—— ‖ Wonders of the Invifible World, p. 141.

Are these the expressions of orthodox believers? or are they not rather expressions becoming a maniche, or a heathen, as agreeing far better with these than with the sacred oracles, our only rule? the whole current whereof is so diametrically opposite thereto, that it were almost endless to mention all the divine cautions against such abominable belief; he that runs may read, *Ps.* lxii. 11, and cxxxvi. 4. *Lam.* iii. 37. *Amos* iii. 6. *Jer.* iv. 22. *Ps.* lxxviii. 26, and clxviii. 6, 8. *Job* xxxviii. 22 to 34.

These places, with a multitude more, do abundantly testify, that the asserters of such power to be in the evil being, do speak in a dialect different from the scriptures, (laying a firm foundation for the indians' adorations, which agrees well with what A. Ross sets forth, in his Mistag. Poetic. p. 116, that their ancients did worship the furies and their god *Averinci*, that they might forbear to hurt them.)

And have not the courts in some parts of the world, by their practices, testified their concurrence with such belief; prosecuting to death many people upon that notion, of their improving such power of the evil one, to the raising of storms; afflicting and killing of others, though at great distance from them; doing things in their own persons above human strength; destroying cattle, flying in the air, turning them-

selves into cats, dogs, &c.? which by the way
must needs imply something of goodness to be
in that evil being, who, though he has such power, would not exert it, were it not for this people, or else that they can some way add to this
mighty power.

And are the people a whit behind in their belief? Is there any thing above mentioned, their
strong faith looks upon to be too hard for this
evil being to effect?

Here it will be answered, God permits it.
Which answer is so far an owning the doctrine,
that the devil has in his nature a power to do
all these things, and can exert this power, except
when he is restrained, that it is in effect to say
that God has made nature to fight against itself;
that he has made a creature, who has it in the
power of his nature to overthrow nature, and to
act above and against it. Which he that can
believe may as well believe the greatest contradiction. That being which can do this in the
smallest thing, can do it in the greatest. If
Moses, with a bare permission, might stretch
forth his rod, yet he was not able to bring
plagues upon the Egyptians, or to divide the
waters, without a commission from the Most
High; so neither can that evil being perform
any of this without a commission from the same
power. The scripture recites more miracles

wrought by men than by angels good and bad. Though this doctrine be so dishonourable to the only Almighty Being, as to ascribe such attributes to the evil one, as are the incommunicable prerogative of him, who is the alone Sovereign Being, yet here is not all; but, as he that steers by a false compass, the further he sails the more he is out of his way; so, though there is in some things a variation from, there is in others a further progression in, or building upon, the said doctrine of the maniche.

Men in this age are not content barely to believe such an exorbitant power to be in the nature of this evil being; but have imagined that he prevails with many to sign a book, or make a contract with him, whereby they are enabled to perform all the things above mentioned. Another account is given hereof, viz. That by virtue of such a covenant they attain power to commission him. And though the two parties are not agreed which to put it upon, whether the devil empowers the witch, or the witch commissions him; yet both parties are agreed in this, that one way or other the mischief is effected, and so the criminal becomes culpable of death. In the search after such a sort of criminals, how many countries have fallen into such convulsions, that neither the devastations made by a conquering enemy, nor the plague itself, have been so formidable. That not only good persons have thus been blemished in their reputations, but much innocent blood hath been shed, is testified even by those very books: *Cases of Conscience*, p. 33. *Remarkable Provid.* p. 179. *Memor. Provid.* p. 28.

And (to add) what less can be expected, when men, having taken up such a belief, of covenanting, afflicting and killing witches, and, comparing it with the scripture, finding no footsteps therein of such a sort of witch, have thereupon desperately concluded, that though the scripture is full in it, that a witch should not live, yet that it has not at all described the crime, nor means whereby the culpable might be detected?

And hence they are fallen so far as to reckon it necessary to make use of those diabolical and bloody ways, always heretofore practised, for their discovery; as finding that the rules, given to detect other crimes, are wholly useless for the discovery of such.

This is that which has produced that deluge of blood mentioned, and must certainly do so again, the same belief remaining.

And who can wonder, if christians that are so easily prevailed with to lay aside their swords as useless, and so have lost their ftrength, are (with Samfon) led blindfold into an idol temple, to make fport for enemies and infidels, and to do abominable actions, not only not chriftian, but againft even the light of nature and reafon? And now, reverend fathers, you who are appointed as guides to the people, and whofe lips fhould preferve knowledge; who are fet as fhepherds, and as watchmen; this matter appertains to you. I wrote to you formerly under this head, and acquainted you with my fentiments, requefting that if I erred, you would be pleafed to fhew it me by fcripture; but from your filence I gather that you approve thereof. For I may reafonably prefume, that you would have feen it your duty to have informed me better, if you had been fenfible of any error. But if in this matter you have acquitted yourfelves becoming the titles you are dignified with, you have caufe of rejoicing in the midft of calamities that afflict a finning world.

Particularly, if you have taught the people to fear God, and truft in him, and not to fear a witch or a devil — That the devil has no power to afflict any with difeafes, or lofs of cattle, &c. without a commiffion from the Moft High — That he is fo filled with malice, that whatever commiffion he may have againft any, he will not fail to execute it — That no mortal ever was, or can be, able to commission him, or to lengthen his chain in the least, and that he who only can commission him is God; and that the scriptures of truth not only assign the punishment of a witch, but give sufficient rules to detect them by; and that, according to mr. Gaule's fourth head, a witch is one that hates and opposes the word, work and worship of God, and seeks by a sign to seduce therefrom — That they who are guilty according to that head, are guilty of witchcraft, and by the law given to Moses were to be put to death: — If you have taught the people the necessity of charity, and the evil of entertaining so much as a jealousy against their neighbours for such crimes, upon the devil's suggestions to a person pretending to a spectral or diabolical sight; who utter their oracles from malice, frenzy, or a satanical delusion — That to be inquisitive of such, whose spectres they see, or who it is that afflicts, in order to put the accused's life in question, is a wickedness beyond what Saul was guilty of in going to the witch — That to consult with the dead, by the help of such as pretend to this spectral sight, and so to get information against the life of any person, is the worst sort of necromancy — That the pretending to drive away spectres, i. e. devils, with the hand, or by striking these to wound a person at a distance, cannot be without witchcraft, as pretending to a sign in order to deceive in matters of so high a nature — That 'tis ridiculous to think, by making laws against feeding, employing or rewarding of evil spirits, thereby to get rid of them — That their nature requires no sucking to support it — That it is a horrid injury and barbarity to search those parts, which even nature itself commands the concealing of, to find some excrescence to be called a teat for these to suck; which yet is said sometimes to appear as a flea-bite: — Finally, if you have taught the people what to believe and practise, as to the probation of the accused, by their saying or not saying the Lord's prayer, and as to praying that the afflicted may be able to accuse, and have not shunned in these matters to declare the whole mind of God; you have then well acquitted yourselves (in time of general defection) as faithful watchmen. But if, instead of this, you have, some by word and writing propagated, and others recommended, such doctrines, and abetted the false notions, which are so prevalent in this apostate age, it is high time to consider it. If when authority found themselves almost nonplust in such prosecutions, and sent to you for your advice what they ought to do,* and you have then thanked them for what they had already done (and

* Cases of Conscience, vlt.

thereby encouraged them to proceed in those very by-paths already fallen into) it so much the more nearly concerns you. Ezek. xxiii. 2 to 8.

To conclude: This whole people are invited and commanded to humble their souls before God, as for other causes, for the errors that may have been fallen into in these prosecutions on either hand, and to pray that God would teach us what we know not, and help us wherein we have done amiss, that we may do so no more.*

This more immediately concerns yourselves; for 'tis not supposed to be intended, that God would shew us these things by inspiration; but that such who are called to it should shew the mind of God in these things on both hands, i. e. whether there has been any error in excess or deficiency, or neither in the one nor the other. And if you do not thus far serve the publick, you need not complain of great sufferings and unrighteous discouragements, if people do not applaud your conduct, as you might other-ways have expected.† But if you altogether hold your peace at such a time as this is, your silence, at least seemingly, will speak this language; that you are not concerned, though

---

* Vide the proclamation for a fast, to be the 14th inst. as set forth by authority.

† The declaration, as drawn by the Deputies with the assistance of the Ministers; but received a nonconcurrence.

men ascribe the power and providence of the Almighty to the worst of his creatures — that if other ages or countries improve the doctrine and examples given them, either to the taking away of the life or reputations of innocents, you are well satisfied. Which, that there may be no shadow of a reason to believe but that your conduct herein may remove all such jealousies, and that God would be with you in declaring his whole mind to the people, is the earnest desire and prayer of, reverend sirs, yours to my utmost, R. C.

Mr. Benjamin Wadsworth,
Reverend Sir,

After that dreadful and severe persecution of such a multitude of people, under the notion of witches, which, in the day thereof, was the sorest trial and affliction that ever befel this country; and after many of the principal actors had declared their fears and jealousies, that they had greatly erred in those prosecutions; and after a solemn day of fasting had been kept, with prayers that God would shew us what we knew not, viz. what errors might therein have been fallen into, &c.; and after most people were convinced of the evil of some, if not of most, of those actions; at such a time as this, it might have been justly expected that the ministers would make it their work to explain the scriptures to the people; and from thence to have shown them the evil and danger of those false notions, which not only gave some occasion, but in a blind zeal hurried them into those unwarrantable practices, so to prevent a falling into the like for the future.

But instead of this, for a minister of the gospel (pastor of the old meeting) to abet such notions, and to stir up the magistrates to such prosecutions, and this without any cautions given, is what is truly amazing, and of most dangerous consequence.

It is a truth, witchcraft is, in the text then insisted on, reckoned up as a manifest work of the flesh, viz. *Gal.* v. 19. But it is as true, that in recounting those other works (which are indeed manifest fleshly works) the magistrate was not stirred up against those others; as if the rest were either not to be taken notice of by him, or as if all zeal against murder, adulteries, &c. was swallowed up and overshadowed by this against witchcraft.

The description that was then given, was, that they were such as made a covenant with the devil, and sold themselves to the evil angels. It seems faulty, when such minister is inquired of, and requested to give the reasons, or grounds in scripture, of such description, for such minister to assert that it is the inquirer's work to disprove it. And his saying further, in answer, that there are many things true, that are not asserted in scripture, seems to speak this language, viz. that the law of God is imperfect, in not describing this crime of witchcraft, though it be therein made capital.

These perfect oracles inform us, concerning Ahab, that he sold himself to work wickedness; which may signify to us, that great height of wickedness he had arrived at; which yet might be, without his being properly, or justly, accounted a witch; any more than those that are said to have made a covenant with death, and with hell, &c. Can it be thought that all those, or such as are there spoken of, are witches, and ought to suffer as witches?

As the servants and people of God have made a solemn, explicit covenant with him, (*Josh.* xxiv. 25. *Nehem.* ix. 38, &c.) so no doubt a covenant has been made by heathen indian nations, to serve and adore the devil; yet even for this, it were very hard to affix the character of a witch upon each of those heathen that so do, and accordingly to execute them as such. It is also possible, that some that have been called christians have sealed a writing, signed with their own blood, or otherways, thereby covenanting to be the devil's servants, &c.

but from far other grounds, or inducements, than what fways with the indians; thefe heathen hoping to pleafe him, that fo he may not harm them. But thefe having been educated and confirmed in the belief, that by virtue of fuch covenant they fhall have a knowledge and power more than human affifting them; this may have prevailed with fome to fo horrible a wickednefs; for none can feek evil for evil's fake; but as the ferpent, in his firft tempting man, made ufe of the knowledge of good and evil, fo to teach men that fuch effects do ufually follow fuch covenant is properly the work of the ferpent; for, without this, what inducement, or temptation, could they have to make fuch a covenant?

Thefe, having thus chofen a falfe god, may well be accounted the worft fort of idolaters. Yet it does not hence follow, that, in a fcripture fenfe, they are thereby become witches, till they have, or rather till they pretend to have, affiftances anfwerable: and do thereby endeavour to deceive others; which endeavours to deceive, by a fign, may be without any previous covenant.

But fuppofing none of all thofe feveral forts of covenants was intended, it remains that the covenant, that was underftood to be intended, in that difcourfe at the old meeting, is agreeable to the late dangerous notion that has so much prevailed, viz. That the devil appears to the persons; that they and the devil make mutual engagements each to other, confirmed by signing to the devil's book; and are from hence enabled, not only to know futurities, and things done at a distance, but are also thereby empowered to do harm to their neighbours, to raise storms, and do things above and against the course of nature. This being the notion that has occasioned the shedding so much blood in the world, it may be thought to need explaining.

For as reason knows nothing of an afflicting, covenanting witch, so it seems as foreign from scripture in general, as it is from the text then insisted on; which speaks of such wickednesses as are manifestly the works of the flesh: but such communication with spirits, the flesh doth manifestly dread even as death itself. Therefore the usual salutation of the holy angels to the best of men was, fear not; and experience shews, that the most wicked are most affrighted at the apprehensions of the appearances of devils; therefore such an explicit covenanting cannot be a manifest work of the flesh.

Yet this is manifest, that the belief of the witches power to do the things above mentioned, is an ancient belief of the heathen; and that from them it was received by the papists, as a part of their faith, who have since improved upon it and brought in the notion of a covenant. But it seems yet a further improvement, lately made by protestants, that such witches can commission devils to do those mischiefs, thereby setting the witch in the place of God; for though few of the papists are known to be thus absurd, yet when such doctrines have been preached and printed in New-England, they have met with none to oppose, but many to encourage them. Other considerable additions, or new improvements, have been made here; as the art to knock off invisible chains with the hand, to drive away spectres (i. e. devils) by brushing, and spelling words to the afflicted, &c. What has followed upon these notions, and upon such improvements, is needless here to repeat; it were unaccountable to recount that effusion of blood that has been hereby occasioned; such remaining scars, and such yet bleeding wounds, as are to be found; which none can wholly pretend ignorance of.

And if blood shall be required of that watchman that seeth the sword coming, and gives not the needful warning, how much more of such as join with the enemy, to bring in the sword to destroy them, over whom he was placed a watchman!

And if the law of God be perfect, and exceeding broad, as being given forth by the Omnifcient Lawgiver, it is exceeding high prefumption and arrogance, and highly deftructive to the lives of innocents, for any to pretend to give another, and a pretended better, defcription of a crime made thereby capital, with new rules to try fuch offenders by.

Reverend fir, the matter, being of fuch high concern, requires (and it is again prayed) that you would be pleafed to confider, and give the grounds from fcripture, or reafon, of fuch definition; or elfe that you would explode it, as inconfiftent with both. From, reverend fir, yours to my utmoft, R. C.

PART III.

ACCOUNT OF THE DIFFERENCES

IN

SALEM VILLAGE.

*Grounds of Complaint againſt Mr. Parris, &c.**

HE reaſons why we withdraw from communion with the church of Salem Village, both as to hearing the word preached, and from partaking with them at the Lord's table, are as follows:

Why we attend not on publick prayer, and preaching the word, theſe are,

1. The diſtracting and diſturbing tumults, and noiſes, made by the perſons under diabolical power and deluſions; preventing ſometimes our

---

* Some alterations have been made in the reading of the "Grounds of Complaint," in order that it may conform to the original court documents.

hearing, underſtanding, and profiting by, the word preached. We, having after many trials and experiences found no redreſs in this caſe, accounted ourſelves under a neceſſity to go where we might hear the word in quiet.

2. The apprehenſion of danger of ourſelves being accuſed as the devil's inſtruments to afflict the perſons complaining, we ſeeing thoſe, whom we have reaſon to eſteem better than ourſelves, thus accuſed, blemiſhed, and of their lives bereaved: for we ſeeing this evil, thought it our prudence to withdraw.

3. We found ſo frequent and poſitive preaching up ſome principles and practices by mr. Parris, referring to the dark and diſmal miſeries of iniquity working amongſt us, was not profitable, but offenſive.

4. Neither could we in conſcience join with mr. Parris, in the requeſts which he made in prayer, referring to the trouble then among us and upon us: therefore thought it our moſt ſafe and peaceable way to withdraw.

The reaſons why we hold not communion with them at the Lord's table, are, becauſe we eſteem ourſelves juſtly aggrieved and offended with the officer who does adminiſter, for the reaſons following:

1. From his declared and publiſhed principles, referring to our moleſtations from the in-

visible world: differing from the opinion of the generality of the orthodox ministers of this whole country.

2. His easy and strong faith and belief of the affirmations and accusations, made by those they call the afflicted.

3. His laying aside that grace (which above all we are required to put on) viz. charity towards his neighbours, and especially towards those of his church, when there is no apparent reason for the contrary.

4. His approving and practising unwarrantable and ungrounded methods, for discovering what he was desirous to know referring to the bewitched or possessed persons, as in bringing some to others, and by and from them pretending to inform himself and others, who were the devil's instruments to afflict the sick and pained.

5. His unsafe and unaccountable oath, given by him against sundry of the accused.

6. His not sending to the world so fair (if so true) account of what he wrote on examination of the afflicted.

7. Sundry unsafe, if sound, points of doctrine, delivered in his preaching, which we esteem not warrantable (if christian.)

8. His persisting in these principles, and justifying his practices; not rendering any satisfaction

to us, when regularly defired, but rather for the offending and diffatisfying ourfelves.

We, whofe names are under written, heard this paper read to our paftor, Mr. Samuel Parris, the 21ft of April, 1693.

Nathaniel *Jigarfon*,	Peter *Cloyce*, fenior,
Edward *Putman*,	Samuel *Nurfe*,
Aaron *Way*,	John *Tarboll*,
William *Way*,	Thomas *Wilkins*.

Mr. Parris's Acknowledgment.

For as much as it is the undoubted duty of all chriftians to purfue peace, *Pfal.* xxxiv. 14, even to a reaching of it, if it be poffible; (*Amos* xii. 18, 19) and whereas, through the righteous, fovereign and awful providence of God, the grand enemy to all chriftian peace has been of late tremendoufly let loofe in divers places hereabout, and more efpecially among our finful felves, not only to interrupt that partial peace which we fometimes enjoyed, but alfo, through his wiles and temptations, and our weaknefs and corruptions, to make wider breaches, and raife more bitter animofities between too many of us; in which dark and difficult difpenfations, we have been all or moft of us of one mind for a time, and afterwards of differing apprehenfions; and at laft we are but in the dark, upon ferious thoughts of all; and after many prayers, I have been moved to prefent to you (my beloved flock) the following particulars, in way of contribution towards a regaining of chriftian concord, if fo be we be not altogether unappeafeable, irreconcileable, and fo deftitute of that good fpirit, which is firft pure, then peaceable, gentle, and eafy to be entreated, *James* iii. 17. viz.

1. In that the Lord ordered the late horrid calamity (which afterward plague-like fpread in many other places) to break out firft in my family, I cannot but look upon as a very fore rebuke, and humbling providence, both to myfelf and mine, and defire fo we may improve it.

2. In that alfo in my family were fome of both parties, viz. accufers and accufed, I look alfo upon as an aggravation of that rebuke, as an addition of wormwood to the gall.

3. In the means which were ufed in my family, though totally unknown to me or mine (except fervants) till afterwards, to raife fpirits and apparitions in no better than a diabolical way, I do alfo look upon as a further rebuke of Divine Providence. And by all, I do humbly own this day, before the Lord and his people that God has been righteoufly fpitting in my face, *Numb*. xii. 14. And I defire to lie low under all this reproach, and to lay my hand on my mouth.

4. As to the management of thefe myfteries,

as far as concerns myself, I am very desirous upon further light to own any errors I have therein fallen into, and can come to a discerning of; in the mean while I do acknowledge, upon after-considerations, that were the same troubles again, (which the Lord of his rich mercy forever prevent) I should not agree with my former apprehensions in all points. As for instance,

1. I question not but God sometimes suffers the devil, as of late, to afflict in shape of not only innocent, but pious persons; or so to delude the senses of the afflicted, that they strongly conceit their hurt is from such persons, when indeed it is not.

2. The improving of one afflicted, to inquire by who afflicts the other, I fear may be, and has been, unlawfully used to satan's great advantage.

3. As to my writing, it was put upon me by authority, and therein I have been very careful to avoid the wronging of any.

4. As to my oath, I never meant it, nor do I know how it can be otherwise construed, than as vulgarly, and every one understood, yea, and upon inquiry it may be found so worded also.

5. As to any passage in preaching, or praying, in the sore hour of distress and darkness, I always intended but due justice on each hand, and that not according to men, but God, who

knows all things most perfectly; however, through weakness or sore exercise, I might sometimes, yea, and possibly sundry times, unadvisedly express myself.

6. As to several that have confessed against themselves, they being wholly strangers to me, but yet of good account with better men than myself, to whom also they are well known, I do not pass so much as a secret condemnation upon them; but rather, seeing God hath so amazingly lengthened out satan's chain, in this most formidable outrage, I much more incline to side with the opinion of those that have grounds to hope better of them.

7. As to all that have unduly suffered in these matters, either in their persons or relations, through the clouds of human weakness, and satan's wiles and sophistry, I do truly sympathize with them; taking it for granted, that such as know themselves clear of this great transgression, or that have sufficient grounds so to look upon their dear friends, have hereby been under those sore trials and temptations, that not an ordinary measure of true grace would be sufficient to prevent a bewraying of remaining corruption.

8. I am very much in the mind, and abundantly persuaded, that God, for holy ends, though for what in particular is best known to himself,

has suffered the evil angels to delude us on both hands; but how far on the one side, or the other, is much above me to say; and if we cannot reconcile till we come to a full discerning of these things, I fear we shall never come to an agreement, or at soonest not in this world.

9. Therefore, in fine, the matter being so dark and perplexed, as that there is no present appearance that all God's servants should be altogether of one mind in all circumstances, touching the same, I do most heartily, fervently and humbly beseech pardon of the merciful God, through the blood of Christ, for all my mistakes and trespasses in so weighty a matter; and also all your forgiveness of every offence, in this or other affairs, wherein you see or conceive that I have erred and offended; professing, in the presence of the Almighty God, that what I have done has been, as for substance, as I apprehended was duty, however through weakness, ignorance, &c. I may have been mistaken. I also through grace promising each of you the like of me, so again I beg, entreat and beseech you, that satan, the devil, the roaring lion, the old dragon, the enemy of all righteousness, may no longer be served by us, by our envy and strifes, where every evil work prevails whilst these bear sway, (*James* iii. 14, 15, 16) but that all from this day forward may be covered with the mantle of love, and we may on

all hands forgive each other heartily, fincerely
and thoroughly, as we do hope and pray that
God for Chrift's fake would forgive each of
ourfelves, (*Matt.* xviii. 21, to the end.) *Colofs.*
iii. 12, 13, *Put on therefore (as the elect of God,
holy and beloved) bowels of mercies, kindnefs, hum-
blenefs of mind, meeknefs, long-fuffering: forbear-
ing one another, and forgiving one another, if any
man have a quarrel againft any; even as Chrift
forgave you, fo alfo do ye.* Eph. iv. 31, 32, *Let
all bitternefs, and anger, and clamour, and evil-
fpeaking, be put away from you, with all malice.
And be ye kind one to another, tender-hearted, forgiving one another even as God for Chrift's fake
hath forgiven you.* Amen. Amen.

SAMUEL PARRIS.

Given to the diffenting brethren, for their confideration, at their requeft. *November* 26, 1694.

*The Elders and Meffengers of the churches met at
Salem Village, April* 3, 1695, *to confider and
determine what is to be done, for the compofure
of the prefent unhappy differences in that place;
after folemn invocation of God in Chrift for
his direction, do unanimoufly declare, as followeth, viz.*

1. We judge that although in the late and dark time of the confufions, wherein fatan had obtained a more than ordinary liberty, to fift this

plantation, there were fundry unwarrantable and uncomfortable fteps taken by mr. Samuel Parris, the paftor of the church in Salem Village, then under the hurrying diftractions of amazing afflictions: yet the faid mr. Parris, by the good hand of God brought unto a better fenfe of things, hath fo fully expreft it, that a chriftian charity may and fhould receive fatisfaction therewith.

2. Inafmuch as divers chriftian brethren, in the church of Salem Village, have been offended at mr. Parris, for his conduct in the time of their difficulties, which have diftreffed them; we now advife them charitably to accept the fatisfaction which he hath tendered in his chriftian acknowledgment of the errors therein committed; yea, to endeavour, as far as it is poffible, the fulleft reconciliation of their minds unto communion with him, in the whole exercife of his miniftry, and with the reft of the church. *Matt.* vi. 12, 14. *Luke* xviii. 3. *James* v. 16.

3. Confidering the extreme trials and troubles, which the difaffected brethren in the church of Salem Village have undergone, in the day of fore temptation which hath been upon them; we cannot but advife the church to treat them with bowels of much compaffion, inftead of more critical or rigorous proceedings againft them for the infirmities difcovered by them, in fuch an heart-breaking day; and if, after a patient wait-

ing for it, the said brethren cannot so far overcome the uneasiness of their spirits, in the remembrance of the disasters that have happened, as to sit under his ministry, we advise the church with all tenderness to grant them admission to any other society of the faithful, whereunto they may be desirous to be dismissed. *Gal.* vi. 1, 2. *Psal.* ciii. 13, 14. *Job* xix. 21.

4. Mr. Parris having, as we understand, with much fidelity and integrity acquitted himself, in the main course of his ministry, since he hath been pastor of the church of Salem Village; about his first call whereunto, we look upon all contests now to be both unreasonable and unseasonable; and our Lord having made him a blessing to the souls of not a few, both old and young, in this place, we advise that he be accordingly respected, honoured and supported, with all the regards that are due to a painful minister of the gospel. 1 *Thess.* v. 12, 13. 1 *Tim.* v. 17.

5. Having observed that there is in Salem Village a spirit full of contention and animosity, too sadly verifying the blemish which hath heretofore lain upon them; and that some complaints against mr. Parris have been either causeless or groundless, or unduly aggravated; we do, in the name and fear of the Lord, solemnly warn them to consider whether, if they continue to devour one another, it will not be bitterness in the latter

end; and beware left the Lord be provoked thereby utterly to deprive them of thofe which they fhould count their precious and pleafant things, and abandon them to all the defolations of a people that fin away the mercies of the gofpel. *James* iii. 16. *Gal.* v. 15. 2 *Sam.* ii. 26. *Ifa.* v. 45. *Matt.* xxi. 43.

6. If the diftempers in Salem Village fhould be (which God forbid) fo incurable, that mr. Parris, after all, find that he cannot with any comfort and fervice continue in his prefent ftation, his removal from thence will not expofe him to any hard character with us; nor, we hope, with the reft of the people of God, among whom we live. *Matt.* x. 14. *Acts* xxii. 18. All which advice we follow with our prayers, that the God of peace would bruife Satan under our feet. Now the Lord of peace himfelf give you peace always by all means.

Jos. Bridgham,	*Jer. Dummer*,	*James Allen*,
Samuel Chickley,	*Neh. Jewitt*,	*Samuel Tory*,
William Tory,	*Ephr. Hunt*,	*S. Willard*,
Jos. Boynton,	*N. Williams*,	*E. Payfon*,
R. Middlecutt,	*Incr. Mather*,	*C. Mather*.
John Walley,	*S. Phillips*,	

To the Reverend Elders of the three churches of Chrift at Bofton, with others the Elders and Brethren of other churches, late of a Council at Salem Village.

We whofe names are hereunto fubfcribed, are

bold once more to trouble you with our humble propofals: — That whereas there have been long and uncomfortable differences among us, chiefly relating to mr. Parris; and we having, as we apprehend, attended all probable means for a compofure of our troubles: and whereas we had hopes of an happy iffue, by your endeavours among us, but now are utterly fruftrated in our expectations, and that inftead of uniting, our rent is made worfe, and our breach made wider:

We humbly query, whether yourfelves, being ftraightened of time, might not omit fuch fatisfactory liberty of debating the whole of our controverfy; whereby yourfelves had not fo large an opportunity of underftanding the cafe, nor the offended fo much reafon to be fatisfied in your advice: We therefore humbly propofe, and give full liberty of proving and defending of what may be charged on either hand, leaving it to yourfelves to appoint both time and place,

1. That if yourfelves pleafe to take the trouble, with patience once more to hear the whole cafe.

2. Or that you will more plainly advife mr. Parris (the cafe being fo circumftanced that he cannot, with comfort or profit to himfelf or others, abide in the work of the miniftry among us) to ceafe his labours, and feek to

dispose himself elsewhere, as God in his providence may direct; and that yourselves would please to help us in advising to such a choice, wherein we may be more unanimous; which we hope would tend much to a composure of our differences.

3. Or that we may without any offence take the liberty of calling some other proved minister of the gospel, to preach the word of God to us and ours; and that we may not be denied our proportionable privilege, in our public disbursements in the place.

So leaving the whole case with the Lord and yourselves, we subscribe our names.

<small>Signed by 16 young men, from 16 upwards; and 52 householders, and 18 church members. This was delivered to the ministers, May 3, 1695.</small>

The copy of a paper that was handed about, touching those differences.

As to the contest between mr. Parris and his hearers, &c. it may be composed by a satisfactory answer to *Levit.* xx. 6, "And the soul that turneth after such as have familiar spirits, and after wizards, to go a whoring after them, I will set my face against that soul, and will cut him off from among his people." 1 *Chron.* x. 13, 14, "So Saul died for his transgression, which he committed against the Lord, even against the word of the Lord, which he kept not: and alſo for aſking counſel of one that had a familiar ſpirit, to inquire of it; and inquired not of the Lord; therefore he flew him," &c.

Some part of the determination of the Elders and Meſſengers of the churches, met at Salem Village, April 3, 1695, *relating to the differences there.*

If the diſtemper in Salem Village ſhould be (which God forbid) ſo incurable that mr. Parris, after all, find that he cannot with any comfort and ſervice continue in his preſent ſtation, his removal from thence will not expoſe him to any hard character with us, nor, we hope, with the reſt of the people of God, among whom we live. Matt. x. 14, *And whoſoever ſhall not receive you, nor hear your words; when you depart out of that houſe, or city, ſhake off the duſt of your feet, &c.* Acts xxii. 18. All which advice we follow with our prayers, that the God of peace would bruiſe ſatan under our feet. Now the Lord of peace give you peace always, by all means, &c.

Queſt. Whether Mr. Parris's going to Abigail Williams and others, whom he ſuppoſed to have a ſpectral ſight, to be informed who were witches and who afflicted thoſe pretended ſufferers by witchcraft, in order to their being queftioned upon their lives upon it, were not a turning after fuch as had familiar fpirits; and a greater wickednefs than Saul was guilty of, in that he did not intend thereby bodily hurt to any others?

And whether, in a crime of fuch a high nature, the making a flender and general confeffion, without any propofals of reparations, or due time for probation, ought fo far to be accounted fufficient, from fuch a paftor to his people?

And whether fuch as were accufed, or the furviving friends and relations of thofe that were any ways fufferers by accufations fo by him proved, are in duty and confcience bound to continue their refpect, honour and fupport to him, in the miniftry, after fuch known departures from the rule of God's word, and after fuch dire effects as followed thereupon, under the penalty *of the duft fhaken from his feet*, teftifying againft them, even fo as to render them in a worfe cafe than thofe of Sodom and Gomorrah?

To the Honourable Wait Winthrop, Elifha Cook and Samuel Sewall, Efquires, arbitrators, indifferently chofen, between Mr. Samuel Parris and the inhabitants of Salem Village.

The remonftrances of feveral aggrieved perfons in the faid village, with further reafons why they conceive they ought not to hear mr. Parris, nor to own him as a minister of the gospel, nor to contribute any support to him as such, for several years past; humbly offered as fit for consideration.

We humbly conceive that having, in April, 1693, given our reasons why we could not join with mr. Parris in prayer, preaching, or sacraments; if these reasons are found sufficient for our withdrawing, (and we cannot yet find but they are) then we conceive ourselves virtually discharged, not only in conscience, but also in law; which requires maintenance to be given to such as are orthodox, and blameless; the said mr. Parris having been teaching such dangerous errors, and preached such scandalous immoralities, as ought to discharge any (though ever so gifted otherways) from the work of the ministry.

Particularly in his oath against the lives of several, wherein he swears that the prisoners with their looks knock down those pretended sufferers. We humbly conceive, that he that swears to more than he is certain of, is equally guilty of perjury with him that swears to what is false. And though they did fall at such a time, yet it could not be known that they did it, much less could they be certain of it; yet did swear positively against the lives of such, as he could not have any knowledge but they might be innocent.

His believing the devil's accusations, and readily departing from all charity to persons, though of blameless and godly lives, upon such suggestions; his promoting such accusations; as also his partiality therein, in stifling the accusations of some, and at the same time vigilantly promoting others, as we conceive, are just causes for our refusal, &c.

That mr. Parris's going to Mary Walcut, or Abigail Williams, and directing others to them, to know who afflicted the people in their illnesses — we understand this to be a dealing with them that have a familiar spirit, and an implicit denying the providence of God, who alone, as we believe, can send afflictions, or cause devils to afflict any; this we also conceive sufficient to justify such refusal.

That mr. Parris, by these practices and principles, has been the beginner and procurer of the sorest afflictions, not to this Village only, but to this whole country, that did ever befal them.

We, the subscribers, in behalf of ourselves, and of several others of the same mind with us, (touching these things) having some of us had our relations by these practices taken off by an untimely death; others have been imprisoned, and suffered in our persons, reputations and estates; submit the whole to your honours decision, to determine whether we are or ought to be any ways obliged to honour, refpect and fupport fuch an inftrument of our miferies; praying God to guide your honours to act herein as may be for his glory, and the future fettlement of our village in amity and unity.

                 John Tarboll,
                 Samuel Nurfe, Attorneys for the people
                 Jos. Putman,   of the village.
                 Dan. Andrew,
Bofton, July 21, 1697.

According to the order of the aforefaid arbitrators, the faid mr. Parris had fome of his arrears paid him, as alfo a fum of money for his repairs of the minifterial houfe of the faid village, and is difmiffed therefrom.

NOTE. — Writers have generally fuppofed that Mr. Parris, after his difmiffion from Salem Village, removed to Concord, Maffachufetts. But it is now certain that he received a call to preach in Stowe, by the inhabitants of that town, Nov. 29, 1697, and on the 4th of January, 1698, the Selectmen were ordered " to make a rate of ten pounds for Mr. Parris, our prefent minifter." He is faid to have preached in Concord, Mafs., in 1705. It is certain that he commenced preaching in Dunftable in October, 1708, and continued to preach in that town three years. He died in Sudbury, Feb. 27, 1720, aged 67 years.

PART IV.

LETTERS
OF A GENTLEMAN UNINTERESTED,
ENDEAVOURING TO PROVE THE RECEIVED OPINIONS ABOUT WITCHCRAFT TO BE ORTHODOX.

Sir,

TOLD you I had fome thoughts concerning witchcraft, and an intention of conferring with the gentleman who has publifhed feveral treatifes about witchcraft, and perfons afflicted by them, lately here in New-England; but fince you have put thofe three books into my hands, I find myfelf engaged in a very hard province, to give you my opinion of them. I plainly forefee, that fhould this fcribbling of mine come to public view, it would difpleafe all parties, but that is the leaft. Moreover it is fo far out of my road to fet my thoughts to confider a matter on every fide, which in itfelf is fo abftrufe, and every ftep I advance therein, if I mifs truth

(which is a narrow and undivided line) I must tumble down headlong into the gulph of dangerous error. Yet, notwithstanding, I have forced myself to send these few lines, if so be I may clear to you a truth you now seem to be offended at, because of the ill consequences which (you think) lately have and again may be drawn from it, by the ill conduct of some men. I am not ignorant that the pious frauds of the ancient, and the inbred fire (I do not call it pride) of many of our modern, divines, have precipitated them to propagate and maintain truth as well as falsehoods, in such an unfair manner, as has given advantage to the enemy to suspect the whole doctrine, these men have profest, to be nothing but a mere trick. But it is certain, that as no lover of truth will justify an illegitimate corollary, though drawn from a true proposition; so neither will he reject a truth, because some or many men take unfair means to prove it, or draw false consequences from it. The many heresies among christians must not give a mortal wound to the essence of the christian religion; neither must any one christian doctrine be exterminated, because evil men make use of it as a cloak to cover their own self-ends; particularly, because some men, perhaps among all sorts of christians, have, under pretence of witchcraft, coloured their own malice, pride and popularity, we must not therefore conclude (1.) that there are no witches; (2.) or that witches cannot be convicted by fuch clear and undeniable proof, as the law of God requires in the cafe of death; (3.) or that a witch fo convicted ought not to be put to death.

1. That there are witches, is manifeft from the precept of Mofes, *Thou fhalt not fuffer a witch to live.* Exod. xxii. 18. For it is certain God would not have given a vain and unintelligible law, as this muft be, of putting witches to death, if there are no witches. But you object, that this doth not anfwer our cafe, for we have formed another idea of witches than what can be gathered from the fcriptures; you quote four places, viz. *Deut.* xiii. *Matt.* xxiv. *Acts* xiii. 2 *Tim.* iii. from all which you infer, that witchcraft is a maligning and oppugning the word, works and worfhip of God, and by an extraordinary fign feeking to feduce any from it; and this you readily grant. But then you fay, What is this to witches now a days, who are faid to have made an explicit covenant with the devil, and to be empowered by him to the doing of things ftrange in themfelves, and befides their natural courfe? This you fay does not follow; and herein indeed confifts the whole controverfy; therefore it is neceffary, that firft of all we clear this point, laying afide thofe prejudices we may

have from the fatal application of this doctrine to some who were (in your judgment) really, at least in law, and before men, innocent. In a word, we are seeking after truth, and truth shall and will be truth, in spite of men and devils. I do not repeat this caution to forestall you to believe the doctrine of witchcraft, as it is above defined, without inquiring into the reason and truth of it; only I desire you to inquire into it, as a thing doubtful. For no man can be certain of a negative, unless either the affirmative imply a contradiction, or he can prove it by certain testimony; to neither of which you pretend; only you alledge it cannot be proved by scripture, i. e. you cannot prove it, nor have seen it proved by any other you have read on that subject. I am not so vain as to think I can do better than the learned authors you have consulted with (though I know not what they have done, for I had no other book but the bible, to make use of on this occasion;) but because I am satisfied myself, and am willing to communicate my reasons, which I divide into three heads. 1. The appearance of angels. 2. The nature of possession; and, 3d, The scripture notion of witchcraft.

1. Good angels did appear to Abraham, and did eat, *Gen.* xv. It seems he washed their feet; it is certain he saw and heard them; therefore there is no impossibility in angels being conver-

fant with men. God is true, and whatever is contained in facred writ is true; if we poor fhallow mortals do not comprehend the manner how, that argues only our weaknefs and ignorance in this dark prifon of flefh, wherein we are enclofed during our abode in this vale of mifery, but doth not in the leaft infringe the verity of fcripture; it is fufficient that we undoubtedly know they have appeared unto men in bodily fhape, and done their errand they were fent on from God. Now if good angels have appeared, why may not bad? Surely the devils, becaufe fallen and evil, have not therefore loft the nature of angels; neither is there any contradiction in their appearing in a bodily fhape, now after, any more than before, their fall. But you will fay you muft allow of the appearances of good angels, becaufe of the fcripture teftimony; but not of bad, feeing there is no place of fcripture that clearly proves it. *Matt.* iv, The words in the gofpel do as plainly fignify the devil's outward appearance to our Saviour, when he was tempted, as can be exprefs'd; *And when the tempter came to him he faid — but he anfwered.* The fame form St. Luke ufeth to fignify the appearance of Mofes and Elias, in the transfiguration: *And behold there talked with him two men;* for what follows, ver. 31, *who appeared,* is ufed to fignify (not their appearance, but) the manner of their appearance *in great glory*. But you will urge, that it is very eafy to be underftood, that Mofes and Elias did appear, becaufe they had human bodies; but that it is unintelligible to you, how the devil, being a fpirit, can appear, a fpirit being a fubftance void of all dimenfions; therefore the words in the hiftory muft not be taken in a literal fenfe. Do not miftake: though fome philofophers are of opinion (which whether true or falfe is all one to our prefent argument) that a fpirit's fubftance is extended, and hath, befides length, breadth and depth, a fourth dimenfion, viz. effential fpiffitude; yet the fame do not fay, that pure fubftance is perceptible by our bodily fenfes; on the contrary, they tell us, that fpirits are clothed with vehicles, *i. e.* they are united to certain portions of matter, which they inform, move and actuate. Now this we muft not reject as impoffible, becaufe we cannot comprehend the formal reafon, how a fpirit acts upon matter: for who can give the reafon, that, upon the volition of the human foul, the hand fhould be lifted up, or any ways moved? for to fay the contraction of the mufcles is the mechanic caufe of voluntary motion, is not to folve the queftion, which recurs, Why, upon volition, fhould that contraction enfue which caufes that motion? All that I know the wifeft man ever faid upon this head is, that it is the will of the

Creator, who has ordered such a species of thinking creatures, by a catholic law, to be united to such portions of matter, so and so disposed; or, if you will, in the vulgar phrase, to organized bodies; and that there should be between them and the several bodies they are united to a mutual reaction and passion. Now you see how little we know of the reason of that which is most near to us, and most certain, viz. the soul's informing the body; yet you would think it a bad argument, if one should, as some have done, conclude, from this our ignorance, that there was nothing in us but matter; it is no otherways than to deny a spirit's acting a vehicle. The plainest and most certain things when denied are hardest to be proved; therefore the axiom saith well, *contra principia*, &c. There are some certain truths, which are rather to be explained to young beginners than proved, upon which all science is built; as every whole is more than its part; and of this sort I take these two following: 1. That there are two substances, *corpus* and *mens*, body and spirit, altogether different, for the ideas we have of them are quite distinct. 2. That a spirit can actuate, animate or inform a certain portion of matter, and be united to it; from whence it is very evident, that the devil, united to a portion of matter (which hereafter I'll call a vehicle) may fall under the cognizance of our senses, and be conversant with us in a bodily shape. Where then is the reason or need to run to a metaphorical and forced interpretation, when the words are so plain, and the literal sense implieth no contradiction, nor any greater difficulty than (as has been said) what ariseth from the union of the soul and body, which is most certain? Now after all to say, God *will not* permit the devil so to appear, is to beg the question, without saying any thing to the preceding argument; and it is against the sense of almost all mankind; for in all ages, and all places, there have been many witnesses of the appearances of dæmons, all of whom, that taught any thing contrary to the right worship of the true God, were certainly evil ones: and it were most presumptuous, barely to assert that all these witnesses were always deceived, and it is impossible they could all agree to deceive.

2. We come to consider the nature of possession. The man possest (*Luke* viii. 27) had a power more than natural, for he brake the bands, which he could not have done with his own strength. Now from whom had he this power? The scripture saith, he had devils a long time, and oftentimes it had caught him, &c. he was kept bound with chains and in fetters, and he brake the bands, and was driven of the devil into the wilderness. This power then was im-

mediately from the devil, and whatsoever a possessed person does, or suffers, beyond his natural power, he is enabled by the dæmon so to do; or, to speak more properly, it is the dæmon who acteth the same, as is plain from St. Mark's relation of this passage, v. 2 v. *A man with an unclean spirit.* 3 v. *And no man could bind him, no, not with chains.* 6 v. *But when he saw Jesus afar off, he came and worshiped him;* and the same he, 7 v. said *I adjure thee by God that thou torment me not;* and 9 v. *My name is Legion, for we are many.* 10 v. *And he besought him much, that he would not send them away out of the country.* It is manifest from hence, that it was not the poor man who was possest, but the devils who possessed him, by whom the chains had been plucked asunder, and the fetters broken in pieces. Now here is divine testimony, that the devils have actuated a human body to the doing of things beyond the natural strength of that body, as it was simply united to its human soul: how much more then can the devil actuate any other portion of simple matter, earth, air, fire or water, and make it a fit organ for himself to act in!

But enough of this already: let us rather inquire how the devil enters into the body of the possest, to move it at his pleasure. This I think he cannot do as a mere spirit, or by any never so strict union with the human soul; for in that case he is only a tempter or seducer, and nothing above human strength can be done: but here there being something performed (the bonds broken) by a force which could not proceed from human strength, it necessarily follows that the devils entered into the possest, otherways qualified them as a mere spirit; he did not enter without some portion of matter, to which he was united, by the intermedium whereof he acted upon and actuated the human body. Again, if it is said that the devil entered as a mere spirit, and immediately acted upon and moved that body, it follows, the devil hath a vehicle, a certain portion of matter (that body) to actuate and dispose of at will; which is absurd: 1, Because it asserts what it seems to deny, viz. the devil's having a vehicle to act immediately upon; and to be united to a portion of matter (as has been said before) is the same thing. 2, It fights against the catholic law of the union of soul and body, by which the Omnipotent hath ordained the voluntary motion of a human body to depend upon the will of its human soul, and those that are not voluntary to proceed either from its own mechanism or material force; hence we may certainly conclude, that it is by the intervening of the devil's vehicle, that he enters into the body of the possest. But what if you and I cannot agree about this notion of poffeffion, muft we therefore reject the truth itfelf, and run to a far-fetched and intolerable fenfe of the words? No, our opinions do not alter the nature of things; it is certain there were perfons poffeft, and it is as certain that the devil entered into them, either with or without a vehicle; it is all one which part of the contradiction you take, the confequence is the fame, viz. That the devil doth act immediately upon matter.

There is another acceptation of the word poffeffion in fcripture, (*Acts* xvi. 17) where one is faid to be poffeft with a fpirit of divination, the word commonly ufed to the prieftefs of Apollo, who gave refponfes; and it feems this damfel was fuch an one, for fhe brought her mafters much money, or gain, by foothfaying, till they were full of the god. Now if the hiftory of them be true, that they were demented, and knew not themfelves what they uttered, (as they word it,) their cafe is not different, but the fame with the foregoing; but if they underftood what they fpoke, then had they familiar fpirits, whereof there is frequent mention made in the old teftament, and one good king is commended for having cut off them that had fuch; therefore I think the meaning of the word was very obvious in his time; neither was it ever controverted being joined with any other name than spirit, familiar, one of our own family: that is, oft, every day conversant with us, and almost ever ready upon call to attend us. But the consideration of them, who have familiar spirits, falleth under the head of witchcraft, which we are to consider in the third place.

3. Witchcraft, to inquire into the scripture notion of it, and compare whether it be the same with that above defined. The cabalistick learning would be of great use in this search, and afford us much light; there is little doubt but that there are many great truths not commonly known. And our Saviour expressly cautions his disciples that they do not throw their pearls before swine; therefore it is no wonder that some doctrines, though unquestionably true, are not so fully described, because the authors who treat of them are afraid, lest evil men should be the more depraved by being informed: but I am in no such fear; nor can I give you any other thoughts but what are obvious to any man, from the plain sense of the scripture. Our definition we'll divide into two propositions, and handle them severally. 1 Proposition. The witch is empowered by the devil to do things strange in themselves, and beside their natural course. 2 Prop. The manner how the witch is empowered to do those strange things, is by

explicit compact, or covenant, with the devil. For clearing of the first, we will consider the four places above cited, wherein a witch is called a false prophet, a false Christ, a sorcerer, a resister of the truth, and is said to shew signs to seduce the people to seek after other gods: whence let us note three things. 1. That those terms, witch, false Christ, false prophet and sorcerer, are all synonimous, i. e. signify the same thing. 2. That a witch doth do things strange in themselves, and beyond their natural course: for it were most ridiculous to alledge that our blessed Saviour, when he said, *there shall arise false Christs, and shall shew great signs and wonders, in so much that (if it were possible) they should deceive the very elect*, meant that cunning cheats should arise, and shew legerdemain tricks; the words will in no wise bear it, and I believe you are far from thus interpreting them; so it is manifest they signify not a feigned, but a real, doing of things beyond their natural course; therefore the sorceries of Elymas and Simon were not simple delusions, but real effects, that could not have been produced by physical causes in the ordinary course of nature. 3. That the end of the witches' shewing these signs, is to seduce the people to seek after other gods; from which premises I infer, that the witches have the power of doing those wonders, or strange things, immediately from the devil: they are without the reach of nature, and therefore above human power, and no mere man can effect them; the witch then who does them must have the power of doing them from another; but who is the other? God will not give his testimony to a lie; and to say God did at any time empower a witch to work wonders, to gain belief to the doctrine of devils, were with one breath to destroy root and branch of all revealed religion; no, it cannot be, it is only God's permission, who proveth his people, whether they love him with all their heart and with all their soul. Therefore the witch has a power of doing wonders, or strange things, immediately from the devil. 2 Proposition, we will subdivide into these two. 1. That there is an express covenant between the witch and the devil. 2. That it is not reasonable to suppose this covenant to be transacted mentally. 1. The devil cannot communicate this power, by never so strict a union with the soul of the witch; for in that case he is only a tempter, and nothing above human power can be done, as has been already proved; therefore the devil, who improves the witch to do things above human power, must either appear in an external shape, and instruct him how, and upon what terms, he will enable him to do those wonders; or else he must enter into the body of the witch, and poſſeſs it. The demoniacs in the goſpel are ſuch whom the devils invade by main force, their ſoul having no further command of their bodies, which are ſubjected to the will of the devils; whoſe end is to wound and torment thoſe miſerable creatures, to throw them into the fire, and into the water: but the witch, who likewiſe is poſſeſſed, is not treated in ſuch an outrageous manner; his dæmon is tame and familiar unto him, and ſuffers him for a time to live quietly, without any further moleſtation, than prompting him to do his utmoſt endeavour to withdraw men from God; he is not bereaved of his ſenſes as the poor lunatic, but is conſcious of all he does, and willeth all his crimes: he receiveth power from the devil to do wonders, and doth them to ſerve the devil's turn. Therefore there muſt be a covenant, an expreſs covenant, between the devil and him, viz. that he ſhall obey the devil and ſerve him, and that the devil ſhall both enable him ſo to do, and alſo reward him for ſo doing; for if there is no contract between them, how comes the witch to know he has a ſupernatural power? or how can he ſo peremptorily pretend to do that which is ſo much above his natural power, not knowing he has a ſupernatural one enabling him to do the ſame? There can be no doubt but there was a very intimate commerce between ſatan and him who is called by St. Paul thou child of the devil, not as other unholy men, but in an especial manner, as being the enemy of all righteousness, who would not cease to pervert the right ways of the Lord. It is not to be supposed that he entered into this so near a relation with satan, with which he is stigmatized, that others may beware of him, without his own knowledge and consent. And is not this a covenant, an express covenant, on his part, to serve the devil incessantly; and on the devil's, to empower him to act his forceries wherewith he bewitched the people? Now I think I have from scripture fully satisfied you of the truth of what I offered in a discourse at ———. But, since, you have told me an explicit covenant with the devil signifies the devil's appearing in a bodily shape to the witch, and their signifying an express covenant, which you say cannot be proved from scripture. It were most unreasonable to imagine that the ceremonies of this hellish mystery are particularly set down in the word of God; therefore we must gather by analogy and reason the matter how this express covenant is transacted; and to that end I will set down these following considerations.

1. Under the law God did ordain his people in all their matters to have recourse immediately to himself, and depend upon him for counsel, which they were ready to obey, with full

assurance of aid and protection from him against their enemies. This the devil imitateth by setting up of oracles among the heathen, to which all the kings, nations and mighty conquerors upon earth, did come, and paid their humblest adoration to the god (as the devil blasphemously called himself) of the temple, in which they were imploring his direction and assistance in their doubtful and prosperous affairs. Again, God instituted sacrifices to put men in mind of their duty to the Creator, to whom they owe all things, even themselves; but the devil is not contented with the bare imitation hereof; the acknowledgment and worship he receiveth from the deluded world is not enough, though they offer up unto him innumerable hecatombs, unless they cause their children to pass through the fire unto him, to whom no sacrifice is so well pleasing as that of human blood. And there is no reason to think, that now, under the economy of the gospel, the devil hath left off to vie with God, and thereby to ensnare men. No, it is rather to be feared that his kingdom doth now more prevail; for by how much the light is greater, so much greater is their condemnation who do not receive it: it is reasonable to suppose that (seeing the Son of God, when he came to transact with men the wonderful covenant of their redemption, took upon him their nature, and was perfect man) the devil likewife doth counterfeit the fame, in appearing in an human fhape to them who receive him, and confederate themfelves with him, and become his vaffals.

2. Confider, it is not probable that thofe falfe apoftles mentioned, 2 *Cor.* xi. 13, erred only in ceremonies or circumftances, or that their errors, though great, did proceed rather from their ignorance than from the perverfenefs of their minds. 1 *Cor.* iii. 15. For, for fuch we may have charity and hope, that God will be merciful unto them, if they fincerely do the beft they know, though they diffent in fome, nay many things, from the practices and belief of the chriftian church; but thofe St. Paul threatens with a heavy curfe, that their end fhall be according to their works; therefore it feems they immediately ftruck at the very root and being of the chriftian religion, and were the fame with them fpoken of, 2 *Tim.* iii. 6, but with this difference, that they did not refift, but, beholding the miracles and figns which were done by the true apoftle of our Lord, wondered, and believed alfo, and were baptized; yet, being forcerers, they were unwilling to lofe that great efteem they had obtained; as it is related of Simon, who had bewitched the people of Samaria, giving out that he himfelf was fome great one, to whom they all gave heed, from the leaft to the

greateſt, ſaying, this man is the great power of God; therefore he could not brook that Peter or John ſhould have a greater power than himſelf; but offered them money, that on whomſoever he laid hands, he (that perſon) ſhould receive the Holy Ghoſt; which ſhews him, who thus deſigned to make merchandiſe of the Spirit, though baptized, to have been no true believer, but ſtill a ſorcerer, in the gall of bitterneſs, and in the bond of iniquity. Such were thoſe deceitful workers, who, not being able barefaced to reſiſt, did put on chriſtianity as a maſk, that they might undermine the truth, and introduce the doctrines of devils. Samaria and Paphos were not the only two places where the devil had ſuch agents; there was no part of the earth where his kingdom was not eſtabliſhed, and where he had not his emiſſaries before the preaching of the goſpel; and ſince the text telleth us he hath his miniſters, who imitate their maſter, by being transformed into the apoſtles of Chriſt, as he himſelf is transformed into an angel of light: whoſe deſign, in being thus transformed, cannot be to impoſe upon the Almighty; for whatever ſhape he appears in, he cannot hide his uglineſs from the eyes of him who is omniſcient; therefore he appeareth thus in the ſhape of an angel of light, either to tempt and ſeduce the bleſſed ſpirits to rebel againſt God, or to ensnare wicked men, who by their heinous crimes (being lovers of themselves, covetous, boasters, proud, blasphemers) were before disposed to be fit instruments to serve him, and to enter into league with him. Surely I, who am ignorant of the laws by which the intellectual world is governed, dare not affirm that it is impossible for satan so to appear, as to hide his deformities from the good angels, and under that vail to tempt them: but certain I am that it is more consonant to reason, to think that the apostle's intention here was to teach that the devil appeared as a glorified angel unto men, to gain ministers, whom he might imbue with the poison of his black art, and (when he had gotten full possession of them) instruct them by his own example to transform themselves into the apostles of Christ, that under that vizard they might with the greater advantage promote his ends, and join with him in doing the utmost despite to the spirit of grace.

3d Consideration: It is against the nature of this covenant, that it should be consummated by a mental colloquy between the devil and the witch. I know not how many articles it consists of; but it is certain, from what has been already proved, that the renouncing of Christ to be the Son of God, and owning the devil to be, and worshiping him as God, are the two chiefs, to which our Saviour, who was accused of casting out devils by Beelzebub, i. e. of being confederated with Beelzebub, was tempted to consent: *If thou be the Son of God, command that these stones be made bread:* and again, *throw thyself down from hence; for it is written, he will give his angels charge over thee;* and again, *all these things will I give thee, if thou wilt fall down and worship me.* Whence it is evident that here the devil laboured to insinuate into our Lord, either to do things rash and unwarrantable, or to suspect his sonship, revolt from God his father, and worship satan, that he might obtain the glory of the world. Now it has been already said, that when Jesus was tempted, the devil appeared unto him in a bodily shape; therefore it is agreeable to reason, that he doth appear in the same manner to all them, whom he also tempteth to worship him: moreover, the form of renouncing a covenant ought to bear resemblance to the form of entering into the same covenant; therefore men who are received into the mystical body of Christ by God's minister, who in God's stead expressly covenanteth with and then administereth the sacrament of baptism unto them, must in the like manner go out of, or renounce, the said covenant; and of them there are two sorts, one who, through the perverseness of their own hearts, the lucre of the world, the fear of men more than of God, abjure their Saviour, turn apoftates, turks, or pagans. The other fort is of them who contract with the devil to be his fubjects, in the initiation of whom it is not to be fuppofed that the devil will omit any material circumftance which tends both to bring them into and confirm them in his fervice. To effect which, his outward appearance, when he receives his catechumens, is of greater force than any mental contract; for many wicked men, who have denied God and Chrift, not only in their practice, but alfo blafphemoufly in profeffion, yet have repented, and at laft obtained fome hope of mercy. I dare not fay it is impoffible for a witch to repent, and find mercy; the fecrets of the Almighty are too high for me; but it is certain that thefe wretches are ftrangely hardened, by what paffes between them and the devil, in a bodily fhape, particularly their worfhiping him, which neceffarily implies his outward appearance unto them; for no man can love evil as evil, becaufe the law of felf-prefervation, deeply rooted in all men, determineth their will to purfue that which feems good, and fly from that which feems evil to them; but the inbred notion that every man has of the devil, is, that he is an enemy and deftroyer of mankind, therefore every man hath a natural averfion from him, and confequently cannot formally worſhip him as ſuch, becauſe the object of worſhip muſt be eſteemed to be propitious and placable by the worſhipers; otherwiſe, if fear alone be the adequate cauſe of adoration, it follows that the devils and damned in hell do worſhip God, which is contrary to ſcripture, which ſaith they blaſphemed, becauſe of their pains; whence it follows, that they who worſhip the devil muſt have changed the innate idea that they had of him, viz. that he is an implacable worrier of men, and take him to be benign at leaſt to his own; but this change cannot be wrought by any ſuggeſtion of ſatan into the minds of men, whom indeed he mentally tempteth to luſt, pride and malice; but it is his greateſt artifice to cauſe his inſinuations to ariſe in the hearts of men, as their own natural thoughts; and if conſcience diſcovers their author, and oppoſes them, then he varniſhes them over with the ſpecious colours of pleaſure, honour and glory; and ſo repreſents them as really good, to be willed and deſired by the ſoul, which judgeth of all things without agreeing to the ideas ſhe hath of them; but becauſe moſt objects have two, and ſome many, faces, and ſhe not always attends, therefore ſhe often errs in her choice; neverthelefs it is impoſſible for her to love an object, whoſe ſimple idea is evil; but the idea we have of the devil is such, for we cannot represent him in our minds any otherwise than the great destroyer of men, therefore no mental temptation can make us believe this our grand enemy to be ever exorable by, or in any measure favourable to us; whence it evidently follows, that the devil, to work this change of opinion his worshipers have of him, must appear unto them in a bodily shape, and impose upon them, whom, because of their great corruption and sinfulness, God hath wholly left, and given up to strong delusions, that they should believe a lie, and the father of lies; who, now appearing in a human shape, telleth them that he is not such a monster as he has been represented to them by his enemy, who calls himself God, which title of right belongs to him; and that he (if they contract to be his servants) will both amply reward them, by giving them power to do many things very suitable to their abominable depraved nature, that the christians, whatever opinion they may pretend to have of their God, cannot so much as pretend to, and also that he will protect and defend them against him, whom heretofore they have mistaken for the Almighty, and his pretended Son Christ, whom they must abjure before they can be received by or expect any benefit from him. Upon no other consideration is it possible for any man to worship the devil; for the atheists, who deny the being of a God, do likewise deny the existence of any spirit good or bad; therefore their drinking the devil's health, even upon their knees (though a most horrid crime) cannot be construed any part of worship paid to him, whom they assert to be a chimera, a mere figment of statesmen to keep the vulgar in awe. Now I have evinced to you that there are witches; that the witch receiveth power from the devil to do strange things; that there is an express covenant between the devil and the witch; that this covenant cannot be transacted mentally, but that the devil must appear in a bodily shape to the witch; therefore I conclude, that a witch in the scripture is such, who has made an explicit covenant with the devil, and is empowered by him to do things strange in themselves, and beside their natural course.

II. I persuade myself you do not expect from me any essay concerning the methods how witches may or ought to be convicted; I wish those gentlemen, whose eminent station both enables them to perform it, and likewise makes it their duty so to do, may take this province upon them, and handle it so fully as to satisfy you herein. I once intended to have provided some materials for this work, by defining four principal things relating to witchcraft, viz. 1. Witch-fits. 2. The imps that are said to attend on the witch.

3. The tranſportation of the witch through the air. 4. Laſtly, the inviſibility of the witch. But upon ſecond thought, that it was foreign from my purpoſe, who am not concerned to compoſe a juſt treatiſe of witchcraft, which would require more vacant time than my preſent circumſtances will allow; only I propoſed to give you my opinion privately; therefore I will venture to make uſe of an argument, which ſheweth neither art nor learning in the author; and it is this, That ſeeing there are witches, and that the law of God doth command them to be put to death, therefore there muſt be means to convict them, by clear and certain proof, otherwiſe the law were in vain; for no man can be juſtly condemned, who is not fairly convicted by full and certain evidence.

III. In the laſt place we are to inquire, whether a witch ought to be put to death or no? You anſwer in the negative; becauſe you ſay that that law, Thou ſhalt not ſuffer a witch to live, is *judicial*, and extendeth only to the people of the Jews; but our Saviour, or his apoſtles, have not delivered any where any ſuch command, therefore they ought to be ſuffered to live. This indeed ſeems ſomewhat plauſible at firſt view, but upon thorough examination hath no weight in it at all, for theſe reaſons, 1. All penal laws receive their ſanction from him or them who have the sovereign power in any state; as, Thou shalt not commit adultery, is a moral law, and obligatory over the consciences of men in all places and ages; but that the adulterers shall be put to death, is a judicial law, and in force only in that state where it is enacted by the sovereign. 2. The government of the Jews was a theocracy, and God himself condescended to be their King, not only as he is King of kings; for in that sense he is, always was, and ever will be, supreme Lord and Governor of all his creatures; but in an especial manner to give them laws for the government of their state, and to protect them against their enemies; in one word, to be immediately their Sovereign. 3. Our Saviour's kingdom was not of this world; he was no judge to divide so much as an inheritance between two brethren; nay, he himself submitted patiently to the unjust sentence of the governor of the country in which he lived; therefore both the rewards and punishments annexed to his laws are spiritual, and then shall have their full accomplishment, when the Son of Man at the last day shall pronounce, *come unto me ye blessed, and depart ye cursed into everlasting fire.* 4. That sovereigns, who have received the gospel of our Lord, have not therefore lost their power of enacting laws for the ruling and preserving their people, and punishing malefactors even with death; so that the criminal is as justly condemned to die by our municipal, as he was heretofore by the judicial law among the Jews. How much more then ought our law to advert against the highest of all criminals, those execrable men and women, who, though yet alive, have listed themselves under satan's banner, and explicitly sworn allegiance to him, to fight against God and Christ! Indeed all unholy men afford great matter to the devils of blaspheming; but these wretches have confederated themselves with the devils, to blaspheme and destroy all they can. And do you think that these common enemies of God and mankind ought to be suffered to live in a christian commonwealth? especially considering that we have a precedent of putting them to death from God himself, when he acted as King over his own peculiar people. But methinks I hear you saying, All this doth not satisfy me, for I am sure nothing can be added to the devil's malice; and if he could, he certainly would, appear, and frighten all men out of their wits. I answer, 1. We must not reject a truth, because we cannot resolve all the questions that may be proposed about it; otherwise all our science must be turned into scepticism, for we have not a comprehensive knowledge of any one thing.— 2. When you say, that if the devil could, he would appear and frighten all men — the lawful confequence is, not that he cannot appear at all, for we have undoubtedly proved the contrary, but that we are ignorant of the bounds that the Almighty hath fet to him, whofe malice indeed, if he were not reftrained, is fo great as to deftroy all men; but the goodnefs of our God is greater, who hath given us means to efcape his fury, if we will give earneft heed to the gofpel of our Saviour, which only is able to comfort us againft the fad and miferable condition of our prefent ftate; for not only the devils, but likewife all do confpire againft us to work our ruin. The deluge came and fwept away all the race (fave eight perfons) of mankind: the fire will in time devour what the water has left; and all this cometh to pafs becaufe of fin: but we, who have received the Lord Jefus, look for new heavens and a new earth, wherein dwelleth righteoufnefs. Therefore he, if we purify ourfelves as he is pure, will fave us (for when he appears we fhall be made like unto him, to whom be glory forever, Amen) from the great deftruction that muft come upon all the world, and inhabitants thereof. Farewell.

March 8, 1693.

Worthy Sir,   *Boston, March* 20, 1693.

The great pains you have taken for my information and satisfaction in those controverted points relating to witchcraft, whether it attain the end or not, cannot require less than suitable acknowledgments and gratitude; especially considering you had no particular obligation of office to it, and when others, whose proper province it was, had declined it. It is a great truth, that the many heresies among the christians (not the lying miracles, or witchcrafts, used by some to induce to the worship of images, &c.) must not give a mortal wound to christianity or truth; but the great question in these controverted points still is, What is truth? And in this search, being agreed in the judge or rule, there is great hopes of the issue. That there are witches, is plain from that rule of truth, the scriptures, which commands their punishment by death. But what that witchcraft is, or wherein it does consist, is the whole difficulty. That head cited from mr. Gaule, and so well proved thereby (not denied by any) makes the work yet shorter; so that it is agreed to consist in a maligning, &c. and seeking by a sign to seduce, &c. not excluding any other sorts or branches, when as well proved by that infallible rule. That good angels have appeared, is certain; though that instance of those to Abraham may admit of a various conſtruction; ſome divines ſuppoſing them to be the Trinity; others, that they were men-meſſengers, as *Judges* ii. 1; and others, that they were angels. But though this, as I ſaid, might admit of a debate, yet I ſee no queſtion of the angel Gabriel's appearance, particularly to the bleſſed virgin; for though the angels are ſpirits, and ſo not perceptible by our bodily eyes without the appointment of the Moſt High, yet he, who made all things by his word in the creation, can with a word ſpeak things into being. And whether the angels did aſſume matter (or a vehicle) and by that appear to the bodily eye; or whether by the ſame word there were an idea framed in the mind, which needed no vehicle to repreſent them to the intellects, is with the All-wiſe, and not for me to diſpute. If we poor ſhallow mortals do not comprehend the manner how, that argues only our weakneſs. Two other times did this glorious angel appear. *Dan.* viii. 16. *Dan.* ix. 21. The firſt of theſe times was in viſion, as by the text and context will appear. The ſecond was the ſame as the firſt; which, being conſidered as it will, aſcertains that angels have appeared, ſo that it is at the will of the ſender how they ſhall appear, whether to the bodily eye, or intellect only. *Matt.* i. 20. The appearance of the angel to Joſeph was in a dream, and yet a real appearance; fo was there a real appearance to the apoftle, but whether in the body or out of the body he could not tell; and that they are fent, and come not of their own motion. *Luke* i. 26, *And in the fixth month the angel Gabriel was fent from God.* Dan. ix. 23, *At the beginning of thy fupplication the commandment came forth, and I am come.* v. 21, *Being caufed to fly fwiftly, &c.* But from thefe places may be fet down, as undoubted truths or conclufions,

1. That the glorious angels have their miffion and commiffion from the Moft High.

2. That without this they cannot appear to mankind. And from thefe two will neceffarily flow a third:

3. That if the glorious angels have not that power to go till commiffioned, or to appear to mortals, then not the fallen angels; who are held in chains of darknefs to the judgment of the great day. Therefore to argue, that becaufe the good angels have appeared, the evil may or can, is to me as if, becaufe the dead have been raifed to life by holy prophets, therefore men, wicked men, can raife the dead. As the fufferings, fo the temptations, of our Saviour were (in degree) beyond thofe common to man. He being the fecond Adam, or public head, the ftrongeft affaults were now improved; and we read that he was tempted, that he might be able

to fuccour them that are tempted; as alfo that he was led of the Spirit into the wildernefs, that he might be tempted, &c. But how the tempter appeared to him who was God Omnifcient; whether to the bodily eye, or to the intellect, is as far beyond my cognizance, as for a blind man to judge of colours. But from the whole fet down this fourth conclufion:

4. That when the Almighty Free Agent has a work to bring about for his own glory, or man's good, he can employ not only bleffed angels, but the evil ones, in it, as 2 *Cor.* xii. 7, *And left I fhould be exalted above meafure, there was given to me a thorn in the flefh, the meffenger of fatan to buffet me.* 1 *Sam.* xvi. 14, 15 & 23, *An evil fpirit from the Lord troubled him*, &c. It is a great truth, that we underftand little, very little, and that in common things; how much lefs then in fpirituals, fuch as are above human cognizance! But though upon the ftricteft fcrutiny in fome natural things we can only difcover our ignorance, yet we muft not hence deny what we do know, or fuffer a rape to be committed upon our reafon and fenfes in the dark. And to fay that the devil by his ordinary power can act a vehicle, i. e. fome matter diftinct from himfelf, who is wholly a fpirit, and yet this matter not to be felt nor heard, and at the fame time to be feen; or may be felt, and not heard, nor

seen, &c. seems to me to be a chimera, invented at first to puzzle the belief of reasonable creatures, and since calculated to a roman latitude, to uphold the doctrine of transubstantiation; who teach, that under the accidents of bread is contained the body of our Saviour, his human body, as long and as broad, &c. for here the power of the Almighty must not be confined to be less than the devil's, and it is he that has said, *hoc est meum corpus*. As to the consent of almost all ages, I meddle not now with it, but come to the fifth conclusion:

5. That when the Divine Being will employ the agency of evil spirits for any service, it is with him to determine how they shall exhibit themselves, whether to the bodily eye, or intellect only; and whether it shall be more or less formidable. To deny these three last, were to make the devil an independent power, and consequently a God. As to the nature of possessions by evil spirits, for the better understanding of it, it may be needful to compare it with its contraries; and to instance in Samson, of whom it was foretold, that he should begin to deliver Israel. And how was he enabled to this work? *Judges* xiii. 25, *The spirit of the Lord began to move him at times in the camp*, &c. Chap. xv. 13, 14. v. *And they bound him with two new cords, and brought him up from the rock; and when they came*

to Lehi, the Philistines shouted against him; and the spirit of the Lord came mightily upon him, and the cords that were upon his arms became as flax, that was burnt with fire, and his bands loosed from his hands, &c. I might instance further; but this may suffice to show that he had more than a natural strength, as also whence his strength was, viz. he was empowered by the spirit from God. And now will any say, that it was not Samson, but the spirit, that did these things; or, that these being things done, bonds broken, &c. by a force that could not proceed from human strength, that therefore the spirit entered into him otherwise qualified than as a mere spirit; or, that the spirit entered not without some portion of matter, and by the intermediation thereof acted Samson's body? If any say this and more too, this doth not alter the truth, which remains, viz. that the spirit of God did enable Samson to the doing of things beyond his natural strength. And now what remains but, upon parity of reason, to apply this to the case of possession? which may be summed up in this sixth conclusion:

6. That God, for wise ends, only known to himself, may and has empowered devils to possess and strangely to actuate human bodies, even to the doing of things beyond the natural strength of that body. And for any to tell of a

vehicle, or matter used in it, I must observe that general rule, *Colos*. ii. 8, " Beware lest any spoil you through philosophy, and vain deceit, after the tradition of men, after the rudiments of the world, and not after Christ." To come next to that of witchcraft, and here taking that cited head of mr. Gaule to be uncontroverted, set it as a seventh conclusion:

7. That witchcraft consists in a maligning and opposing the word, work and worship of God, and seeking by any extraordinary sign to seduce any from it. *Deut.* xiii. 12. *Matt.* xxiv. 24. *Acts* xiii. 8, 10. 2 *Tim.* iii. 8. Do but mark well the places; and for this very property of thus opposing and perverting, they are all there concluded arrant and absolute witches; and it will be easily granted, that the same that is called witch, is called a false Christ, a false prophet, and a sorcerer, and that the terms are synonimous; and that what the witches aim at is, to seduce the people to seek after other gods. But here the question will be, whether the witch really do things strange in themselves, and beyond their natural course, and all this by a power immediately from the devil. In this inquiry, as we have nothing to do with unwritten verities, so but little with cabalistic learning, which might perhaps but lead us more astray; as in the instance of their charging our Saviour with

casting out devils by Beelzebub; his answer is, if satan be divided against himself, his kingdom hath an end. But seeing all are agreed, set this eighth conclusion:

8. That God will not give his testimony to a lie. To say that God did at any time empower a witch to work wonders,* to gain belief to the doctrine of devils, were with one breath to destroy the root and branch of all revealed religion. And hence it is clear the witch has no such wonder-working power from God. And must we then conclude she has such a miraculous power from the devil? If so, then it follows, that either God gives the devil leave to empower the witch to make use of this seal, in order to deceive, or else that the devil has this power independent of himself. To assert the first of these were in effect to say, that though God will not give his testimony to a lie, yet that he may empower the devil to set to it God's own seal, in order to deceive. And what were this but to overthrow all revealed religion? The last, if asserted, must be to own the devil to be

---

*Jos. Glanvil, in his *Saducismus Triumphatus*, published in London in 1681, and which was considered good authority in the trials in 1692, says "a witch is one who can do or seem to do strange things beyond the known power of art and ordinary nature by virtue of a confederacy with evil spirits." It was the strict application of the above rule or test, in the case of George Burroughs, that cost him his life.

an unconquered enemy, and confequently a fovereign deity, and deferving much thanks, that he exerts his power no more. Therefore in this dilemma it is wifdom for fhallow mortals to have recourfe to their only guide, and impartially to inquire, whether the witches really have fuch a miraculous or wonder-working power. And it is remarkable that the apoftle, *Gal.* v. 20, reckons up witchcraft among the works of the flefh; which, were it indeed a wonder-working power, received immediately from the devil, and wholly beyond the power of nature, it were very improper to place it with drunkennefs, murthers, adulteries, &c. all manifeft flefhly works. 'Tis alfo remarkable, that witchcraft is generally in fcripture joined with fpiritual whoredom, i. e. idolatry. This thence will plainly appear to be the fame; only pretending to a fign, in order to deceive, feems to be yet a further degree: and in this fenfe Manaffeh and Jezebel, 2 *Chron.* xxxiii. 6; 2 *Kings* ix. 22, ufed witchcraft and whoredoms. *Nahum* iii. 4, the idolatrous city is called miftrefs of witchcrafts. But to inftance in one place inftead of many, 2 *Thefs.* ii. 3 to 12, particularly 9 and 10 *v*. *Even him, whofe coming is after the working of fatan, with all power and figns, and lying wonders, and with all deceivablenefs. And for this caufe God fhall fend them ftrong delufions that they fhould believe a lie, that they all might be damned, who believe not the truth, &c.* This that then was spoken in the prophecy of that man of sin, that was to appear, how abundantly does history testify the fulfilment of it, particularly to seduce to the worship of images! Have not the images been made to move, to smile, &c.? Too tedious were it to mention the hundredth part of what undoubted history doth abundantly testify. And hence do set down this ninth conclusion:

9. That the man of sin, or seducer, &c. makes use of lying wonders to the end to deceive, and that God in righteous judgment *may send strong delusions that they should believe a lie, that they might be damned, who believe not the truth,* &c.

'Tis certain that the devil is a proud being, and would be thought to have a power equal to the Almighty; and it cannot but be very grateful to him to see mortals charging one another with doing such works by the devil's power, as in truth is the proper prerogative of the Almighty, Omnipotent Being. The next head should have been about an explicit covenant between the witch and the devil, &c. But in this, the whole of it, I cannot persuade myself but you must be sensible of an apparent leaning to education (or tradition) the scriptures being wholly silent on it; and supposing this to fall in as a dependent on what went before, I shall say the less to it; for if the devil has no such power to communicate upon such compact, then the whole is a fiction; though I cannot but acknowledge you have said so much to uphold that doctrine, that I know not how any could have done more. However, as I said, I find not myself engaged (unless scripture proof were offered) to meddle with it: for as you have in such cases your reason for your guide, so I must be allowed to use that little that I have, and do only say, that as God is a spirit, so he must be worshiped in spirit and in truth; so also that the devil is a spirit, and that his rule is in the hearts of the children of disobedience, and that an explicit covenant of one nature or another can have little force, any further than as the heart is engaged in it. And so I pass to the last, viz. whether a witch ought to be put to death; and without accumulation of the offence do judge, that where the law of any country is to punish by death such as seduce and tempt to the worship of strange gods (or idols, or statues) by as good authority may they, no doubt, punish these as capital offenders, who are distinguished by that one remove, viz. to their seducing is added a sign, i. e. they pretend to a sign in order to seduce. And thus, worthy sir, I have freely given you my thoughts upon yours, which you so much obliged me with the sight of; and upon the whole, though I cannot in the general but commend your caution in not afserting many things contended for by others, yet muſt ſay, that in my eſteem there is retained ſo much as will ſecure all the reſt : (to inſtance) if a ſpirit has a vehicle, i. e. ſome portion of matter which it acts, &c. hence as neceſsarily may be inferred that doctrine of *incubus* and *succubus*, and why not that alſo of procreation by ſpirits both good and bad? Thus was Alexander the Great, the Britiſh Merlin, and Martin Luther, and many others, ſaid to be begotten. Again, if the witch had ſuch a wonder-working power, why not to afflict? Will not the devil thus far gratify her? And have none this miraculous power, but the covenanting witch? Then the offence lies in the covenant; then it is not only hard, but impoſsible, to find a witch by ſuch evidence as the law of God requires; for it will not be ſuppoſed that they call witneſs to this covenant; therefore it will here be neceſsary to admit of ſuch as the nature of ſuch covenant will bear (as mr. Gaule hath it in his fifth head, i. e.) the teſtimony of the afflicted, with their ſpectral ſight, to tell who afflicts themſelves or others; the experiment of ſaying the Lord's prayer, falling at the ſight, and riſing at the touch, ſearching for teats, (i. e. excreſcences of nature) ſtrange and foreign ſtories of the death of ſome cattle, or overſetting ſome cart. And what can juries have better to guide them to find out this covenant by?

It is matter of lamentation, and let it be for a lamentation, to confider how thefe things have opened the floodgates of malice, revenge, uncharitablenefs and bloodfhed, and what multitudes have been fwept away by this torrent.

In *Germany*, countries depopulated; in *Scotland*, no lefs than 4000 are faid to have fuffered by fire and halter at one heat.

Thus we may fay with the prophet *Ifa.* lix. 10, *We grope for the wall like the blind, and we grope as if we had no eyes: we ftumble at noonday as in the night, we are in defolate places as dead men:* and this by feeking to be wife above what is written, in framing to ourfelves fuch crimes and fuch ordeals (or ways of trial) as are wholly foreign from the direction of our only guide, which fhould be a light to our feet, and a lanthorn to our paths; but inftead of this, if we have not followed the direction, we have followed the example, of pagan and papal Rome, thereby rendering us contemptible and bafe before all people, according as we have not kept his ways, but have been partial in his law.

And now, that we may, in all our fentiments and ways, have regard to his teftimonies, and give to the Almighty the glory due to his name, is the earnest desire and prayer of, sir, yours to command, R. C.

Sir,

Since your design of giving copies of our papers, if not to the public, at least out of your hands, I find myself obliged to make a reply to your answer, lest silence should be construed an assent to the positions whereby, I think, truth would be scandalized.

I remember that some have taught that it is not certain there is any such thing really in being as matter; because the ideas which we have of our own and all other bodies may be caused to arise in us by God, without the real existence of the objects they represent. But this opinion is not only absurd and false, but likewise atheistical, destroying the veracity of the Almighty, whom it asserts to have determined us by a fatal necessity to believe things to be, which are not; and I wonder that you should allude unto it, because that angels have appeared in a dream, in a vision; for we dream also of trees, birds, &c. Are there therefore no such things in nature, because we sometimes dream to see and hear them, when we are asleep? St. Paul in his vision was so far from believing the objects that were represented to him to come by the intermedium of his senses, that he declares, he does not know whether he was in the body or out of the body; therefore the inftance is in no wife proper. For Abraham and the Bleffed Virgin did fee and hear; and if there were not fuch things really, as were reprefented to them by their fenfes, they were deluded, by being made to believe they faw and heard what was not. There is none who denieth God caufeth thoughts to arife in men's minds; but thence to infer he maketh objects which are not, by forming their ideas in our minds, to appear to us through the miniftry of our fenfes as though they were, is a piece not only of vain, but very dangerous, philofophy.

It is true, the good angels will not appear without the appointment of God; they will not do any one action, but according to the laws he has prefcribed to them. But you fay they cannot, (which does not follow from your premifes) fuppofing their not appearing to proceed from the defect of their power, and not the rectitude of their will; which fallacy has deceived you into a third conclufion: for the fallen angels are not fo held under chains of darknefs, but that they can, and do, go to and fro on the earth, feeking whom they may devour. Before their fall they could have appeared if fent, and would not then do anything without a divine command; but now they have rebelled against God, and do all they can to despite him; therefore their not appearing now (if it were true they never did, they never shall, appear) must proceed from a restraint they are under, which is accidental, not essential to their nature; so that the true conclusion is, the fallen angels, while they are under forcible restraint from God to the contrary, cannot appear. But what this (being cleared from the ambiguity you express it in) maketh to the purpose, I know not, unless God had promised for a determinate time to detain them under this restraint.

I do not understand what you intend by the dead being raised by holy men; the most natural inference is, that, in imitation of them, wicked men, by their enchantments calling on a dæmon to appear in the shape of the dead, will pretend that they also can raise the dead.

The Romanists are much obliged to you for making transubstantiation (so much contended for by them) to be of as old a date as the appearance of devils, and that the one implieth no more contradiction than the other: if so, we do well to think seriously whether we are not guilty of great sin in separating from them; for certainly whatever private men's notions in this age may be, yet it is matter of great moment, that all antiquity (the sadducees, the elder brethren of our Hobbists, excepted) hath believed the appearance of evil spirits and their delusions.

I should be too officious if I offered to explain how matter, real matter, may fall under the cognisance of one of our senses, and not the rest. It is for you to shew the impossibility thereof, if you will build any thing upon your assertion; to prove which, your first argument is (it seems to me) a chimera; which is not enough, when there are many to whom it seems to be a truth. Your second is very dangerous, and highly derogatory of the honour of God, between whom and the devil you make comparison more than once, as the power of the Almighty must not be considered to be less than the devil's. And again, to deny these three last were to make the devil an independent power, and consequently a God. These expressions (which cannot but be very pleasing to the devil, who vainly boasts himself to be a being without dependence) are altogether groundless, and very unmeet to proceed from a christian. Consider what you are doing; to establish a doctrine (the contrary whereof the greatest part of mankind does believe) you run upon such precipices, as, if you are mistaken, (and that is not impossible) must totally destroy all religion, natural and revealed; for suppose it were generally believed, according to you, that the devil cannot appear, because if he could he must be a God, independent, an unconquered enemy, and he doth appear to us as we hear he hath to multitudes, both of the paft and prefent ages; in fuch a cafe what remains for us to do, but to fall down and worfhip him?

Upon the head of poffeffion, you have recourfe to that inftance of *Samfon*, who was empowered by God to the doing of things beyond the natural ftrength of common men; and thence you fay, we may at leaft learn the nature of poffeffion by evil fpirits. This comparifon is indeed very odious, and I had rather think you have fallen into it unawares; for what greater blafphemy, than that God and the devil do act the bodies, which the one and the other do poffefs, in the fame manner? If the hypothefis I laid down had not pleafed you, yet you ought not (for fear of being deceived by vain philofophy) to have run to fo horrible an extreme, as to affimilate God's manner of working to the devil's, which neceffarily implies, that either their powers are equal, or at leaft that they do not differ in kind, but in degree only; than which nothing can be more impious or abfurd: for the moft poffible perfect creature is infinitely diftant from the Creator, and there can be no comparifon between them.

On the head of witchcraft, you acknowledge the witch has not his wonder-working power from God; but then you say, the devil has no such power to give; for if he had, he must be ———. This way of reasoning, as I noted before, is very dangerous, and I think ought not to be used; besides, there is a great fallacy in your dilemma; which, because I perceive you lay the whole weight of the matter upon it, I will evince unto you. The devil, though superlatively arrogant and proud, nevertheless depends on the First Cause for his being, and all his powers, without whose influx he or any other creature cannot subsist a moment, but must either return to their primitive nothing, or be continually preserved by the same power, by the which they were at first produced; therefore the being and powers of all creatures (because they immediately flow from God) are good, and consequently the simple actions, as they proceed from those powers, are in their own nature likewise good, the evil proceeding only from the rebellious will of the creature; wherefore it is no paradox, but a certain truth, that the same action in respect of the first cause is good, but in respect of the second is evil; for instance, the act of copulation is in itself good, instituted by God, and may be explicitly willed and desired by the soul, which sinneth not for exerting the simple act, but for exerting it contrary to the laws prescribed by God: as in wedlock and adultery there is the same special natural action, which, considered simply, as flowing from a power given to man by God, is certainly good; but considered with relation to the rebellious will of the adulterer (who lieth with his neighbour's wife, whom he is forbid to touch) is a very great evil. We may say the same of all human actions; the executioner and the murtherer do the same natural act of striking and killing: the difference consists in the rectitude of the one's, and depravation of the other's, will. These things premised, what more reason have we to conclude that the devil (because he shews signs and wonders to gain belief to lies, which is very contrary to the will of God) must be therefore an independent power, than that the adulterer, the murtherer, or any other sinner (because their actions being evil, of which God cannot be the cause) must be independent beings? The deceit of the last is very palpable, and I doubt not but you will readily acknowledge it; for it is obvious from what has been said, to the meanest capacity, to distinguish between the action itself, which is good, and flows from God, and the circumstances of the action, the choice whereof proceeds from the iniquity of the will, wherein doth solely consist the sin; the parallel is so exact, that I cannot see the least shadow of reason, why we ought not in like manner to distinguish whatever effect is produced by the devil; to whom (as to man) God, having given powers, and a will to rule those powers, is truly and properly the cause of all the actions (in a natural, but not moral sense) that flow from the powers he has given. Therefore the wonder-working power of the devil, and the effects thereof, considered as acts of one of God's creatures, are not evil but good; the using that power (which proceeds from the rebellion of satan) to bear testimony to a lie, is that one, which constitutes the evil thereof.

And now I have done with your argument, wherein you have indeed shewn great skill and dexterity in turning to your advantage what, being fairly stated, makes against you, as the appearance of angels, &c. observing nicely the rules of art, and particularly that grand one of concealing, nay dissembling, the same art; as when you quote that scripture concerning vain philosophy (of which, though altogether foreign from the matter in hand, yet) you intend to serve yourself with the unthinking, who measure the sense of words by their jingle, not knowing how to weigh the things they signify; and truly herein your end is very artificial: for you intend both to throw dirt at them that differ from you, and at the same time to cover yourself with such a subtle web, through which you may see, and not be seen. What follows is rather a rhetorical lecture, such as the patriots of sects (who commonly explain the holy scriptures according to their own dogmas, and so obtrude human invention for the pure word of God) use with their auditors, to recommend any principle they have a mind to establish, than an impartial and thorough disquisition of a controverted point; wherefore I do not think myself obliged to take any further notice of it; especially seeing truth, which for the most part is little regarded in such florid discourses, and not any prejudice of education, interest or party, did set me about this subject. I have never been used to compliment in points of controversy, therefore I hope you will not be angry because I have given you my thoughts naked and plain. I have not the least motion in my mind of accusing you of any formal design to injure religion; I only observe unto you, that your over eager contention to maintain your principle has hurried you to assert many things of much greater danger, both in themselves and their consequences, than those you would seem to avoid; which do amount to no more than that men, being (in the ordinary course of providence) the depositories of both divine and human laws, may (instead of using them to preserve) pervert them to destroy; which indeed is very lamentable. But it is the inevitable consequent of our depraved nature, and cannot be wholly remedied, till sin, and the grand author of sin, the devil, be entirely conquered, and God be all in all; to whom, with the Son, and Holy Ghost, be glory for ever, Amen.

Sir, your affectionate friend to serve you.
Boston, July 25, 1694.

Worthy Sir,   *Boston, August* 17, 1694.

Yours of July 25 being in some sort surprising to me, I could do no less than say somewhat, as well to vindicate myself from those many reflections, mistakes and hard censures therein, as also to vindicate what I conceive to be important truth; and to that end find it needful to repeat some part of mine, viz. conclusion

1. That the glorious angels have their mission and commission from the Most High.

2. That without this they cannot appear to mankind.

3. That if the glorious angels have not that power to go till commissioned, or to appear to mortals, then not the fallen angels, who are held in chains of darkness to the judgment of the great day.

4. That when the Almighty Free Agent has a work to bring about for his own glory, or man's good, he can employ not only the blessed angels, but evil ones, in it.

5. That when the Divine Being will employ the agency of evil spirits for any service, it is with him the manner how they shall exhibit themselves, whether to the bodily eye, or intellect only, or whether it shall be more or less formidable.

To deny these three last, were to make the devil an independent power, and consequently a God.

The bare recital of these is sufficient to vindicate me from that reiterated charge, of denying all appearances of angels or devils.

That the good angels cannot appear without mission and commission from the Most High, is, you say, more than follows from the premises; but if you like not such negative deduction, though so natural, it concerns you (if you will assert this power to be in their natures, and their non-appearance only to proceed from the rectitude of their wills, and that without such commission they have a power to appear to mortals, and upon this to build so prodigious a structure, &c.) very clearly to prove it by scripture; for christians have good reason to take the apostle's warning (if some philosophers have taught that man is nothing but matter, and others that 'tis not certain there is any matter at all) *to take heed lest they should be spoiled through vain philosophy*, &c. but that this should be alluded to such as never heard of either notion, or that it was asserted that those real appearances to Joseph, and to the apostle, were through the ministry of the senses, is as vain as such philosophy. As to the dead being raised, had I used art or rhetorick enough to explain my meaning to you, I needed not now to rejoin,—that 'tis as good an argument to say, that because holy prophets have raised the dead, therefore wicked men have a power to raise the dead, as 'tis to say, because good angels have appeared, therefore the evil have a power to appear; for who can doubt, but if the Almighty shall commission a wicked man to it, he also shall raise the dead? as is intimated, Matt. vii. 22, *And in thy name done many wonderful works.* As to comparisons being odious, particularly that concerning Samson, I think it needful here to add these scriptures further to confirm the fourth conclusion. 2 *Sam.* xxiv. 1, compared with 1 *Chron.* xxi. 1. In one 'tis *God moved*, &c. and in the other *Satan provoked David to number the people.* 2 Chron. xviii. 21, *And the Lord said, thou shalt entice him and thou shalt also prevail; go out and do even so;* all which, with many more that might be produced, will shew the truth of the conclusion; so that 'tis no odious comparison to say, that as the Almighty can make use of good, so also of evil spirits, for the accomplishing of his own wise ends, and can empower either without the help of a vehicle: for poffeffions muft be numbered among God's afflictive difpenfations, who alfo orders all the circumftances thereof. But if any object, God is not the author of evil, &c. you have furnifhed me with a very learned anfwer, by diftinguifhing between the act, and the evil of the act, and to which 'tis adapt, but will no wife fuit where it is placed, till it be firft proved that the devil hath of himfelf fuch power not only of appearing at pleafure, but of working miracles, and to the Almighty referved only the power of reftraining; for, till this be proved, the dilemma muft remain ftable. He that afferts, that becaufe good angels have appeared, therefore the fallen angels have a power of themfelves to appear to mortals, and that they cannot be employed by the Almighty, nor that he does not order the manner and circumftances of fuch appearance, what doth he lefs than make the devil an independent power, and confequently a God? So he that afferts that the devil hath a power of himfelf, and independent, to work wonders, and miracles, and to empower witches to do like in order to deceive, &c. what doth he lefs than own him to be an unconquered enemy, and confequently a fovereign deity? and who is he that is culpable? he that afcribes fuch attributes to the evil one, or he that afferts that the fo doing gives him (or afcribes to him) fuch power as is the prerogative of him only who is Almighty? And here, fir, it highly concerns you to confider your foundations, what proof from fcripture is to be found for your affertions, and who it is you are contending for: for hitherto nothing like a proof hath been offered from fcripture, which abounds fo with the contrary, that he that runs may read; as, *Shall there be evil in the city, and the Lord hath not done it? Who is he that faith, and it cometh to pafs, when the Lord commandeth not? Who among the gods of the heathen* (of which the devil is one) *can give rain?* &c.

But I fhall not be tedious in multiplying proofs, to that which all feem to own. For as to that ftale plea of univerfality, do fay that I have read of one, if not feveral, general councils, that have not only difapproved, but anathematifed them that have afcribed fuch powers to the devils. And feveral national proteftant churches at this day, in their exhortations before the facrament (among other enormous crimes) admonifh all that believe any fuch power in the witch, &c. to withdraw, as unmeet to partake at the Lord's table.

And I believe chriftians in general, if they were afked, would own that what powers the devil may at any time have to appear, to afflict, deftroy, or caufe tempefts, &c. muft be by power or commiffion from the Sovereign Being; and that, having fuch a commiffion, not only hail, but frogs, lice, or fleas, fhall be empowered to plague a great king and kingdom. And if fo, this fandy ftructure of the devil's appearance, and working wonders, at pleafure, and of empowering witches to afflict, &c. (for to this narrow crifis is that whole doctrine reduced) the whole difappears at the firft fhaking.

Thus, worthy fir, I have given you my fentiments, and the grounds thereof, as plainly and as concife as I was able; though 'tis indeed a fubject that calls for the ableft pens to difcufs, acknowledging myfelf to be infufficient for thefe things. However, I think I have done but my duty, for the glory of God, the fovereign being; and have purpofely avoided fuch a reply as fome parts of yours required; and pray that not only you and I, but all mankind, may give to the Almighty the glory due unto his name.

From, fir, yours to command, R. C.

Witchcraft is manifeftly a work of the flefh.

PART V.

AN IMPARTIAL ACCOUNT

OF THE MOST MEMORABLE

MATTERS OF FACT,

TOUCHING THE SUPPOSED WITCHCRAFT
IN NEW-ENGLAND.

R. PARRIS had been some years a minister in Salem Village,* when this sad calamity, as a deluge, overflowed them, spreading itself far and near. He was a gentleman of liberal education; and, not meeting with any great encouragement, or advantage, in merchandising, to which for some time he applied himself, betook himself to the work of the ministry; this Village being then vacant, he met with so much encouragement, as to settle in that capacity among them.

After he had been there about two years, he

* Mr. Parris was settled over the Village church Nov. 19th, 1689.

obtained a grant from a part of the town, that the houfe and land he occupied, and which had been allotted by the whole people to the miniftry, fhould be and remain to him, &c. as his own eftate in fee fimple. This occafioned great divifions both between the inhabitants themfelves, and between a confiderable part of them and their faid minifter; which divifions were but as a beginning, or prelude, to what immediately followed.

It was the latter end of *February*, 1691, when divers young perfons* belonging to mr. Parris's family, and one or more of the neighbourhood, began to act after a ftrange and unufual manner, viz. as by getting into holes, and creeping under chairs and ftools, and to ufe fundry odd poftures and antick geftures, uttering foolifh, ridiculous fpeeches, which neither they themfelves nor any others could make fenfe of. The phyficians that were called could affign no reafon for this; but it feems one of them, having recourfe to the old fhift, told them, he was afraid they were bewitched. Upon fuch fuggeftions, they that were concerned applied themfelves to fafting and prayer, which was attended not only in their own private families, but with calling in the help of others. *March the* 11*th*, mr. Parris

---

*Elizabeth Parris, his daughter, aged nine years, and Abigail Williams, his niece, aged eleven years.

invited feveral neighbouring minifters to join with him in keeping a folemn day of prayer at his own houfe. The time of the exercife, thofe perfons were for the moft part filent; but after any one prayer was ended, they would act and fpeak ftrangely and ridiculoufly; yet were fuch as had been well educated, and of good behaviour; the one, a girl of 11 or 12 years old, would fometimes feem to be in a convulfion fit, her limbs being twifted feveral ways, and very ftiff, but prefently her fit would be over.

A few days before this folemn day of prayer, mr. Parris's Indian man and woman made a cake of rye meal, with the children's water, and baked it in the afhes, and, as is faid, gave it to the dog; this was done as a means to difcover witchcraft; foon after which, thofe ill affected or afflicted perfons named feveral that they faid they faw, when in their fits, afflicting them.

The firft complained of was the faid Indian woman, named Tituba: fhe confeffed that the devil urged her to fign a book, which he prefented to her, and alfo to work mifchief to the children, &c. She was afterwards committed to prifon, and lay there till fold for her fees. The account fhe fince gives of it is, that her mafter did beat her, and otherways abufe her, to make her confefs and accufe (fuch as he called) her fifter-witches; and that whatfoever fhe faid by way of confessing, or accusing others, was the effect of such usage: her master refused to pay her fees, unless she would stand to what she had said.

The children complained likewise of two other women, to be the authors of their hurt, viz. Sarah Good, who had long been counted a *melancholy* or *distracted* woman; and one Osborn, an old *bed-ridden* woman; which two were persons so ill thought of, that the accusation was the more readily believed; and, after examination before two Salem magistrates, were committed. *March 9th*, mr. Lawson (who had been formerly a preacher at the said village) came thither, and hath since set forth, in print, an account of what then passed; about which time, as he saith, they complained of goodwife Cory, and goodwife Nurse, members of churches at the Village and at Salem, many others being by that time accused.

March 21. Goodwife Cory was examined before the magistrates of Salem, at the meeting house in the Village, a throng of spectators being present to see the novelty. Mr. Noyes, one of the ministers of Salem, began with prayer; after which the prisoner being called, in order to answer to what should be alledged against her, she desired that she might go to prayer; and was answered by the magistrates, that they did not come to hear her pray, but to examine her.

The number of the afflicted were at that time about ten, viz. mrs. Pope, mrs. Putman, goodwife Bibber and goodwife Goodall, Mary Wolcott, Mercy Lewes (at Thomas Putman's) and Dr. Grigg's maid, and three girls, viz. Elizabeth Parris, daughter to the minister, Abigail Williams, his niece, and Ann Putman; which last three were not only the beginners, but were also the chief, in these accusations. These ten were most of them present at the examination, and did vehemently accuse her of afflicting them, by biting, pinching, strangling, &c. and they said they did in their fits see her likeness coming to them, and bringing a book for them to sign. Mr. Hathorn, a magistrate of Salem, asked her why she afflicted those children. She said, she did not afflict them. He asked her who did then. She said, I do not know, how should I know? She said, they were poor disstracted creatures, and no heed ought to be given to what they said. Mr. Hathorn and mr. Noyes replied that it was the judgment of all that were there present, that they were bewitched, and only she (the accused) said they were distracted. She was accused by them, that the *black man* whispered to her in her ear now (while she was upon examination) and that she had a yellow bird, that did use to suck between her fingers, and that the said bird did suck now in the assembly. Order being given to look in that place to fee if there were any fign, the girl that pretended to fee it faid, that it was too late now, for fhe had removed a pin, and put it on her head; it was upon fearch found, that a pin was there fticking upright. When the accufed had any motion of their body, hands or mouth, the accufers would cry out; as when fhe bit a lip, they would cry out of being bitten; if fhe grafped one hand with the other, they would cry out of being pinched by her, and would produce marks; fo of the other motions of her body, as complaining of being preft, when fhe leaned to the feat next her; if fhe ftirred her feet, they would ftamp, and cry out of pain there. After the hearing, the faid Cory was committed to Salem prifon, and then their crying out of her abated.

March 24, goodwife Nurfe * was brought before mr. Hathorn and mr. Curwin (magiftrates)

* The folly and madnefs of the witchcraft delufion was ftrikingly manifefted at the examination of goodwife Nurfe. Parris, who was taking notes at the time, informs us that the noife of the accufing girls and fpeakers was fo great, that he could not proceed with his minutes. He has, however, given us enough of her examination to fhow the great diftrefs fhe was thrown into by her falfe accufers. Looking around the crowded meeting houfe, and not difcovering one fympathizing countenance, fhe faid, " I have got nobody to look to but God;" and in her agony fhe lifted her arms and fpread out her hands, and exclaimed, " O Lord, help me!" Mr. Hathorn met this appeal to Heaven with this remark,—" It is very awful to fee thefe agonies in an old profeffor, charged with contracting with the devil."

in the meeting-house. Mr. Hale,* minister of Beverly, began with prayer; after which she, being accused of much the same crimes, made the like answers, asserting her own innocence with earnestness. The accusers were mostly the same, Thomas Putman's wife, &c.† complaining much. The dreadful shrieking from her and others was very amazing, which was heard at a great distance. She was also committed to prison.

A child of Sarah Good's was likewise apprehended, being between 4 and 5 years old. The accusers said this child bit them, and would shew such like marks, as those of a small set of teeth, upon their arms: as many of the afflicted as the child cast its eye upon, would complain they were in torment: which child they also committed.

Concerning those that had been hitherto examined and committed, it is among other things observed, by Mr. Lawson (in print) that they were by the accusers charged to belong to a company that did muster in arms, and were reported by them to keep days of fast, thankf-

---

* Rev. John Hale, who was more connected with Salem witchcraft than has been generally supposed.

† Thomas Putman's wife, and her daughter, Ann Junr., as she was called, were most severely afflicted by witches. Thomas was for many years Parish Clerk, and near neighbour to Mr. Parris. Sergt. Thomas Putman, as he was styled, did more to carry forward the witchcraft delusion, than any other person.

giving and facraments; and that thofe afflicted (or accufers) did in the affembly cure each other, even with a touch of their hand, when ftrangled and other ways tortured, and would endeavour to get to the afflicted to relieve them thereby (for hitherto they had not ufed the experiment of bringing the accufed to touch the afflicted, in order to their cure) and could foretel one another's fit to be coming, and would fay, look to fuch a one, fhe will have a fit prefently, and fo it happened; and that at the fame time when the accufed perfon was prefent, the afflicted faid they faw her fpectre or likenefs in other places of the meeting-houfe fucking their familiars.

The faid mr. Lawfon being to preach at the Village, after the pfalm was fung, Abigail Williams faid, *Now ftand up and name your text;* after it was read, fhe faid, *it was a long text.* Mrs. Pope in the beginning of fermon faid to him, *now there is enough of that.* In fermon, he referring to his doctrine, Abigail Williams faid to him, *I know no doctrine you had; if you did name one, I have forgot it.* Ann Putman, an afflicted girl, faid, *there was a yellow bird fat on his hat as it hung on the pin in the pulpit.*

March 31, 1692, was fet apart as a day of folemn humiliation at Salem, upon the account of this bufinefs; on which day Abigail Williams faid, *that fhe faw a great number of perfons in the*

Village at the administration of a mock sacrament, where they had bread as red as raw flesh, and red drink.

April 1. Mercy Lewis affirmed, *that she saw a man in white, with whom she went into a glorious place,* viz. in her fits, *where was no light of the sun, much less of candles, yet was full of light and brightness, with a great multitude in white glittering robes, who sang the song in Rev.* v. 9. *and the* cxlix Psalm; *and was given that she might tarry no longer in this place.* This white man is said to have appeared several times to others of them, and to have given them notice how long it should be before they should have another fit.

April 3. Being sacrament day at the Village, Sarah Cloyce, sister to goodwife Nurse, a member of one of the churches, was (though it seems with difficulty prevailed with to be) present; but being entered the place, and mr. Parris naming his text, *John,* vi. 70, *Have not I chosen you twelve? and one of you is a devil;* (for what cause may rest as a doubt, whether upon the account of her sister's being committed, or because of the choice of that text) she rose up and went out; the wind shutting the door forcibly, gave occasion to some to suppose she went out in anger, and might occasion a suspicion of her; however, she was soon after complained of, examined and committed.

April 11. By this time the number of the accused and accusers being much increased, there was a publick examination at Salem, six of the magistrates with several ministers being present. There appeared several who complained against others with hideous clamours and screechings. Goodwife Proctor was brought thither, being accused or cried out against: her husband coming to attend and assist her, as there might be need, the accusers cried out of him also, and that with so much earnestness, that he was committed with his wife. About this time, besides the experiment of the afflicted falling at the sight, &c. they put the accused upon saying the Lord's prayer, which one among them performed, except in that petition, *deliver us from evil*, she exprest it thus, *deliver us from* all *evil:* this was looked upon as if she prayed against what she was now justly under, and being put upon it again, and repeating those words, *hallowed be thy name* she exprest it, *hollowed be thy name:* this was counted a depraving the words, as signifying to make void, and so a curse rather than a prayer: upon the whole it was concluded that she also could not say it, &c. Proceeding in this work of examination and commitment, many were sent to prison. As an instance, see the following mittimus.

To their Majesties' Gaol-keeper in Salem.

You are in their majesties' names hereby required to take into your care, and safe custody, the bodies of William Hobs and Deborah his wife, Mary Easty, the wife of Isaac Easty, and Sarah Wild, the wife of John Wild, all of Topsfield; and Edward Bishop of Salem Village, husbandman, and Sarah his wife, and Mary Black, a negro of lieutenant Nathaniel Putman, of Salem Village; also Mary English, the wife of Philip English, merchant, in Salem; who stand charged with high suspicion of sundry acts of witchcraft, done or committed by them lately upon the bodies of Ann Putman, Mary Lewis and Abigail Williams, of Salem Village; whereby great hurt and damage hath been done to the bodies of the said persons, according to the complaint of Thomas Putman and John Buxton, of Salem Village, exhibited; whom you are to secure in order to their further examination. — Fail not.

John Hathorn,
Jona. Curwin, } assistants.

Dated Salem, April 22, 1692.

To marshal George Herrick,
of Salem, Essex.

You are in their majesties' names hereby required to convey the above named to the gaol at Salem. — Fail not.

John Hathorn,
Jona. Curwin, } assistants.

Dated Salem, April 22, 1692.

The occasion of Bishop's being cried out of, was, he being at an examination in Salem, when at the inn an afflicted Indian was very unruly, whom he undertook, and so managed him, that he was very orderly; after which, in riding home, in company of him and other accusers, the Indian fell into a fit, and clapping hold with his teeth on the back of the man that rode before him, thereby held himself upon the horse; but said Bishop striking him with his stick, the Indian soon recovered, and promised he would do so no more; to which Bishop replied, that he doubted not but he could cure them all, with more to the same effect. Immediately after he was parted from them, he was cried out of, &c.

May 14, 1692. Sir William Phips arrived with commission from their majesties to be governor, pursuant to the new charter, which he now brought with him, the ancient charter having been vacated by king Charles and king James, (by which they had a power not only to make their own laws, but also to choose their own governor and officers) and the country for some years was put under an absolute commission-government, till the Revolution, at which time, though more than two thirds of the people were for reassuming their ancient government, (to which they had encouragement by his then royal highness's proclamation) yet some that might have been better employed (in another station) made it their business (by printing, as well as speaking) to their utmost to divert them from such a settlement; and so far prevailed, that for about seven weeks after the Revolution, here was not so much as a face of any government; but some few men upon their own nomination would be called a committee of safety; but at length the assembly prevailed with those that had been of the government, to promise that they would reassume; and accordingly a proclamation was drawn, but before publishing it, it was underwritten, that they would not have it understood that they did reassume charter-government; so that between government and no government, this country remained till sir William arrived: agents being in this time empowered in England, which no doubt did not all of them act according to the minds or interests of those that empowered them, which is manifest by their not acting jointly in what was done; so that this place is perhaps a single instance (even in the best of reigns) of a charter not restored after so happy a revolution. This settlement by sir William Phips's having come governor put an end to all disputes of these things; and being arrived, and having read his commission, the first thing he exerted his power in, was said to be his giving orders that irons should be put upon those in prison; for though for some time after these were committed, the accusers ceased to cry out of them, yet now the cry against them was renewed, which occasioned such order; and though there was partiality in the executing it (some having them taken off almost as soon as put on) yet the cry of these accusers against such, ceased after this order.

May 24. Mrs. Cary, of Charlestown, was examined and committed. Her husband, mr. Jonathan Cary, has given account thereof, as also of her escape, to this effect:

"I having heard, some days, that my wife was accused of witchcraft, being much disturbed at it, by advice we went to Salem Village, to see if the afflicted knew her; we arrived there 24th May; it happened to be a day appointed for examination; accordingly, soon after our arrival, mr. Hathorn and mr. Curwin, &c. went to the meeting-house, which was the place appointed for that work; the minister began with prayer; and having taken care to get a convenient place, I observed that the afflicted were two girls of about ten years old, and about two or three others, of about eighteen; one of the girls talked most, and could discern more than the rest. The prisoners were called in one by one, and as they came in were cried out of, &c. The prisoners were placed about seven or eight feet from the juſtices, and the accuſers between the juſtices and them; the priſoners were ordered to ſtand right before the juſtices, with an officer appointed to hold each hand, left they ſhould therewith afflict them; and the priſoners' eyes muſt be conſtantly on the juſtices; for if they looked on the afflicted, they would either fall into their fits, or cry out of being hurt by them. After an examination of the priſoners, who it was afflicted theſe girls, &c. they were put upon ſaying the Lord's prayer, as a trial of their guilt. After the afflicted ſeemed to be out of their fits, they would look ſteadfaſtly on ſome one perſon, and frequently not ſpeak; and then the juſtices ſaid they were ſtruck dumb, and after a little time would ſpeak again; then the juſtices ſaid to the accuſers, Which of you will go and touch the priſoner at the bar? Then the moſt courageous would adventure, but before they had made three ſteps would ordinarily fall down as in a fit. The juſtices ordered that they ſhould be taken up and carried to the priſoner, that ſhe might touch them; and as ſoon as they were touched by the accuſed, the juſtices would ſay, they are well, before I could diſcern any alteration; by which I obſerved that the juſtices underſtood the manner of it. Thus far I was only as a ſpectator; my wife alſo was there part of the time, but no notice taken of her by the afflicted, except once or twice they came to her and asked her name.

"But I having an opportunity to discourse mr. Hale (with whom I had formerly acquaintance) I took his advice what I had best to do, and desired of him that I might have an opportunity to speak with her that accused my wife; which he promised should be, I acquainting him that I reposed my trust in him. Accordingly he came to me after the examination was over, and told me I had now an opportunity to speak with the said accuser, viz. Abigail Williams, a girl of 11 or 12 years old; but that we could not be in private at mr. Parris's house, as he had promised me; we went therefore into the alehouse, where an Indian man attended us, who it seems was one of the afflicted: to him we gave some cider: he shewed several scars, that seemed as if they had been long there, and shewed them as done by witchcraft, and acquainted us that his wife, who also was a slave, was imprisoned for witchcraft. And now, instead of one accuser, they all came in, and began to tumble down like swine; and then three women were called in to attend them. We in the room were all at a stand, to see who they would cry out of; but in a short time they cried out, Cary; and immediately after a warrant was sent from the justices to bring my wife before them, who were sitting in a chamber near by, waiting for this.

"Being brought before the justices, her chief accusers were two girls. My wife declared to the justices, that she never had any knowledge of them before that day. She was forced to stand with her arms stretched out. I requested that I might hold one of her hands, but it was denied me; then she desired me to wipe the tears from her eyes, and the sweat from her face, which I did; then she desired she might lean herself on me, saying she should faint.

"Justice Hathorn replied, she had strength enough to torment those persons, and she should have strength enough to stand. I speaking something against their cruel proceedings, they commanded me to be silent, or else I should be turned out of the room. The Indian before mentioned was also brought in, to be one of her accusers: being come in, he now (when before the justices) fell down and tumbled about like a hog, but said nothing. The justices asked the girls who afflicted the Indian; they answered, she, (meaning my wife) and that she now lay upon him; the justices ordered her to touch him, in order to his cure, but her head must be turned another way, lest, instead of curing, she should make him worse, by her looking on him,

her hand being guided to take hold of his; but
the Indian took hold of her hand, and pulled her
down on the floor, in a barbarous manner; then
his hand was taken off, and her hand put on his,
and the cure was quickly wrought. I, being
extremely troubled at their inhuman dealings,
uttered a hasty speech, *That God would take
vengeance on them, and desired that God would
deliver us out of the hands of unmerciful men.*
Then her mittimus was writ. I did with difficulty and charge obtain the liberty of a room,
but no beds in it; if there had been, could have
taken but little rest that night. She was committed to Boston prison; but I obtained a ha-
beas corpus to remove her to Cambridge prison,
which is in our county of Middlesex. Having
been there one night, next morning the jailer
put irons on her legs (having received such a
command;) the weight of them was about eight
pounds: these irons and her other afflictions soon
brought her into convulsion fits, so that I thought
she would have died that night. I sent to entreat that the irons might be taken off; but all
entreaties were in vain, if it would have saved
her life, so that in this condition she must continue. The trials at Salem coming on, I went
thither, to see how things were managed; and
finding that the spectre evidence was there received, together with idle, if not malicious

stories, against people's lives, I did easily perceive which way the rest would go; for the same evidence that served for one, would serve for all the rest. I acquainted her with her danger; and that if she were carried to Salem to be tried, I feared she would never return. I did my utmost that she might have her trial in our own county, I with several others petitioning the judge for it, and were put in hopes of it; but I soon saw so much, that I understood thereby it was not intended, which put me upon consulting the means of her escape; which through the goodness of God was effected, and she got to Rhode-Island, but soon found herself not safe when there, by reason of the pursuit after her; from thence she went to New-York, along with some others that had escaped their cruel hands; where we found his excellency Benjamin Fletcher, esq. governor, who was very courteous to us. After this, some of my goods were seized in a friend's hands, with whom I had left them, and myself imprisoned by the sheriff, and kept in custody half a day, and then dismissed; but to speak of their usage of the prisoners, and the inhumanity shewn to them at the time of their execution, no sober christian could bear. They had also trials of cruel mockings; which is the more, considering what a people for religion, I mean the profession of it, we have been; thofe that fuffered being many of them church members, and moft of them unfpotted in their converfation, till their adverfary the devil took up this method for accufing them.   Per JONATHAN CARY."

May 31. Capt. John Aldin was examined in Salem, and committed to Bofton prifon. The prifon-keeper, feeing fuch a man committed, of whom he had a good efteem, was after this the more compaffionate to thofe that were in prifon on the like account; and refrained from fuch hard things to the prifoners, as before he had ufed. Mr. Aldin himfelf has given an account of his examination, in thefe words :

An account how John Aldin, fenior, was dealt with at Salem Village.

John Aldin, fenior, of Bofton, in the county of Suffolk, mariner, on the 28th day of May, 1692, was fent for by the magiftrates of Salem, in the county of Effex, upon the accufation of a company of poor diftracted or poffeffed creatures or witches; and being fent by mr. Stoughton, arrived there the 31ft of May, and appeared at Salem Village, before mr. Gidney, mr. Hathorn and mr. Curwin.

Thofe wenches being prefent, who played their juggling tricks, falling down, crying out, and staring in people's faces; the magistrates demanded of them several times, who it was of all the people in the room that hurt them: one of these accusers pointed several times at one captain Hill, there present, but spake nothing; the same accuser had a man standing at her back to hold her up; he stooped down to her ear, then she cried out, Aldin, Aldin afflicted her; one of the magistrates asked her if she had ever seen Aldin, she answered no; he asked how she knew it was Aldin; she said the man told her so.

Then all were ordered to go down into the street, where a ring was made; and the same accuser cried out, There stands Aldin, a bold fellow, with his hat on before the judges; he sells powder and shot to the Indians and French, and lies with the Indian squaws, and has Indian papooses. Then was Aldin committed to the marshal's custody, and his sword taken from him; for they said he afflicted them with his sword. After some hours Aldin was sent for to the meeting-house in the Village, before the magistrates; who required Aldin to stand upon a chair, to the open view of all the people.

The accusers cried out that Aldin pinched them, then, when he stood upon the chair, in the sight of all the people, a good way distant from them. One of the magistrates bid the marshal to hold open Aldin's hands, that he might not pinch thofe creatures. Aldin afked them why they fhould think that he fhould come to that Village to afflict thofe perfons that he never knew or faw before. Mr. Gidney bid Aldin confefs, and give glory to God. Aldin faid, he hoped he fhould give glory to God, and hoped he fhould never gratify the devil; but appealed to all that ever knew him, if they ever fufpected him to be fuch a perfon, and challenged any one, that could bring in any thing upon their own knowledge, that might give fufpicion of his being fuch an one. Mr. Gidney faid he had known Aldin many years, and had been at fea with him, and always looked upon him to be an honeft man, but now he faw caufe to alter his judgment. Aldin anfwered, he was forry for that, but he hoped God would clear up his innocency, that he would recal that judgment again; and added, that he hoped that he fhould with Job maintain his integrity till he died. They bid Aldin look upon the accufers, which he did, and then they fell down. Aldin afked mr. Gidney what reafon there could be given, why Aldin's looking upon *him* did not ftrike *him* down as well; but no reafon was given that I heard. But the accufers were brought to Aldin to touch them, and this touch they faid made them well. Aldin began to fpeak of the providence of God, in fuffering thefe creatures to accufe innocent perfons. Mr. Noyes afked Aldin why he would offer to fpeak of the providence of God: God by his providence (faid mr. Noyes) governs the world, and keeps it in peace; and fo went on with difcourfe, and ftopt Aldin's mouth as to that. Aldin told mr. Gidney, that he could affure him that there was a lying fpirit in them, for I can affure you that there is not a word of truth in all thefe fay of me. But Aldin was again committed to the marfhal, and his mittimus written, which was as follows:

To mr. John Arnold, keeper of the prifon in Bofton, in the county of Suffolk.

Whereas captain John Aldin, of Bofton, mariner, and Sarah Rice, wife of Nicholas Rice, of Reading, hufbandman, have been this day brought before us, John Hathorn and Jonathan Curwin, efquires; being accufed and fufpected of perpetrating divers acts of witchcraft, contrary to the form of the ftatute, in that cafe made and provided: thefe are therefore, in their majefties king William and queen Mary's names, to will and require you to take into your cuftody the bodies of the faid John Aldin and Sarah Rice, and them fafely keep, until they fhall be delivered by due courfe of law, as you will anfwer the contrary at your peril; and this fhall be your sufficient warrant. Given under our hands at Salem Village, the 31ſt of May, in the fourth year of the reign of our ſovereign lord and lady, William and Mary, now king and queen over England, &c. Anno Domini 1692.

John Hathorn,
Jona. Curwin, } aſſiſtants.

To Boſton, Aldin was carried by a conſtable; no bail would be taken for him; but was delivered to the priſon-keeper, where he remained fifteen weeks; and then, obſerving the manner of trials, and evidence then taken, was at length prevailed with to make his eſcape, and being returned, was bound over to anſwer at the ſuperior court at Boſton, the laſt Tueſday in April, anno 1693; and was there cleared by proclamation, none appearing againſt him.

Per JOHN ALDEN.

At the examination, and at other times, it was uſual for the accuſers to tell of the black man, or of a ſpectre, as being then on the table, &c. The people about would ſtrike with ſwords, or ſticks, at thoſe places. One juſtice broke his cane at this exerciſe; and ſometimes the accuſers would ſay, they ſtruck the ſpectre, and it is reported ſeveral of the accuſed were hurt and wounded thereby, though at home at the ſame time.

The juftices proceeding in thefe works of examination and commitment to the end of May, there were by that time about a hundred perfons imprifoned upon that account.

June 2. A fpecial commiffion of oyer and terminer having been iffued out, to mr. Stoughton, the new lieutenant governor, major Saltonftall, major Richards, major Gidney, mr. Wait Winthrop, captain Sewall, and mr. Sergeant, a quorum of whom fat at Salem this day, where the moft that was done this week was the trial of one Bifhop,* alias Oliver, of Salem; who had long undergone the repute of a witch, occafioned by the accufations of one Samuel Gray; he, about twenty years fince, having charged her with fuch crimes; and though upon his deathbed he teftified his forrow and repentance for fuch accufations, as being wholly groundlefs, yet the report, taken up by his means, continued, and fhe being accufed by thofe afflicted, and upon fearch a teat, as they call it, being found, fhe was brought in guilty by the jury; fhe received her fentence of death, and was executed June 10, but made not the

* Bridget Bifhop kept a fmall beer-fhop on the old Ipfwich road, at Danvers Plains, where Meffrs. Perley & Currier's ftore now ftands. Rev. John Hale, of Beverly, in his depofition, given on the 20th of May, 1692, fays that he was informed by the wife of John Trafk, that Bridget entertained people in her houfe at night, in drinking and playing fhovel-board.

least confession of anything relating to witch-craft.

June 15. Several ministers in and near Boston, having been to that end consulted by his excellency, exprest their minds to this effect, viz.

That they were affected with the deplorable state of the afflicted; that they were thankful for the diligent care of the rulers to detect the abominable witchcrafts which have been committed in the country, praying for a perfect discovery thereof; but advised to a cautious proceeding, lest many evils ensue, &c. and that tenderness be used towards those accused, relating to matters presumptive and convictive, and also to privacy in examinations; and to consult mr. Perkins and mr. Bernard what tests to make use of in the scrutiny: that presumptions and convictions ought to have better grounds than the accusers affirming that they see such persons' spectres afflicting them; and that the devil may afflict in the shape of good men; and that falling at the sight, and rising at the touch, of the accused, is no infallible proof of guilt; that seeing the devil's strength consists in such accusations, our disbelieving them may be a means to put a period to the dreadful calamities. Nevertheless they humbly recommend to the government, the speedy and vigorous prosecution of such as have rendered themselves obnoxious, according to the direction given in the laws of God, and the wholesome statutes of the English nation, for the detection of witchcraft.

This is briefly the substance of what may be seen more at large in *Cases of Conscience.* (*ult.*) And one of them since taking occasion to repeat some part of this advice, (*Wonders of the Invisible World*, p. 83) declares (notwithstanding the dissatisfaction of others) that if his said book may conduce to promote thankfulness to God for such executions, he shall rejoice, &c.

The 30th of June, the court according to adjournment again sat; five more were tried, viz Sarah Good and Rebecca Nurse, of Salem Village; Susanna Martin, of Amsbury; Elizabeth How of Ipswich; and Sarah Wildes of Topsfield: these were all condemned that session, and were all executed on the 19th of July.

At the trial of Sarah Good, one of the afflicted fell in a fit; and after coming out of it she cried out of the prisoner, for stabbing her in the breast with a knife, and that she had broken the knife in stabbing of her; accordingly a piece of the blade of a knife was found about her. Immediately information being given to the court, a young man was called, who produced a haft and part of the blade, which the court having viewed and compared, saw it to be the same; and upon inquiry the young man affirmed, that yesterday he happened to break that knife, and that he cast away the upper part. This afflicted person being then present, the young man was dismissed, and she was bidden by the court not to tell lies; and was improved after (as she had been before) to give evidence against the prisoners.

At the execution, mr. Noyes urged Sarah Good to confess, and told her she was a witch, and she knew she was a witch; to which she replied, you are a liar; I am no more a witch than you are a wizard; and if you take away my life, God will give you blood to drink.

At the trial of Rebecca Nurse, it was remarkable that the jury brought in their verdict not guilty; immediately all the accusers in the court, and suddenly after all the afflicted out of court, made an hideous outcry, to the amazement not only of the spectators, but the court also seemed strangely surprised: one of the judges exprest himself not satisfied; another of them, as he was going off the bench, said they would have her indicted anew. The chief judge said he would not impose upon the jury; but intimated as if they had not well considered one expression of the prisoner when she was upon trial, viz. that when one Hobbs, who had confessed herself to be a witch, was brought into the court to witness against her, the prisoner, turning her head to her, said, *What, do you bring her? she is one of us*, or to that effect; this, together with the clamours of the accusers, induced the jury to go out again, after their verdict, not guilty. But not agreeing, they came into the court; and she being then at the bar, her words were repeated to her, in order to have her explanation of them; and she making no reply to them, they found the bill, and brought her in guilty; these words being the inducement to it, as the foreman has signified in writing, as follows:

July 4, 1692. I, Thomas Fisk, the subscriber hereof, being one of them that were of the jury last week at Salem court, upon the trial of Rebecca Nurse, &c.* being desired by some of the relations to give a reason why the jury brought her in guilty, after her verdict not guilty; I do hereby give my reasons to be as follows, viz.

When the verdict was, not guilty, the honoured court was pleased to object against it, saying to them, that they think they let slip the words which the prisoner at the bar spake against herself, which were spoken in reply to goodwife Hobbs and her daughter, who had been faulty in setting their hands to the devil's book, as they

---

* A most estimable and intelligent woman, who, with her amiable and excellent sister, Mary Esty, of Topsfield, were executed. — Their sister, Mary Cloyce, escaped with imprisonment.

had confessed formerly; the words were, *What, do these persons give in evidence again me now? they used to come among us.* After the honoured court had manifested their dissatisfaction of the verdict, several of the jury declared themselves desirous to go out again, and thereupon the court gave leave; but when we came to consider of the case, I could not tell how to take her words as an evidence against her, till she had a further opportunity to put her sense upon them, if she would take it; and then, going into court, I mentioned the words aforesaid, which by one of the court were affirmed to have been spoken by her, she being then at the bar, but made no reply, nor interpretation of them; whereupon these words were to me a principal evidence against her. THOMAS FISK.

When goodwife Nurse was informed what use was made of these words, she put in this following declaration into the court:

These presents do humbly shew to the honoured court and jury, that I being informed that the jury brought me in guilty, upon my saying that goodwife Hobbs and her daughter were of our company; but I intended no otherways, than as they were prisoners with us, and therefore did then, and yet do, judge them not legal evidence againſt their fellow priſoners. And I being ſomething hard of hearing, and full of grief, none informing me how the court took up my words, and therefore had no opportunity to declare what I intended, when I ſaid they were of our company. Rebecca Nurse.

After her condemnation ſhe was by one of the miniſters of Salem excommunicated; yet the governor ſaw cauſe to grant a reprieve; which when known (and ſome ſay immediately upon granting) the accuſers renewed their diſmal outcries againſt her, inſomuch that the governor was by ſome Salem gentlemen prevailed with to recall the reprieve, and ſhe was executed with the reſt.

The teſtimonials of her chriſtian behaviour, both in the courſe of her life and at her death, and her extraordinary care in educating her children, and ſetting them good examples, &c. under the hands of ſo many, are ſo numerous, that for brevity they are here omitted.

It was at the trial of theſe that one of the accuſers cried out publicly of mr. Willard, miniſter in Boſton, as afflicting of her: ſhe was ſent out of the court, and it was told about ſhe was miſtaken in the perſon.

Auguſt 5, the court again ſitting, ſix more were tried on the ſame account, viz. mr. George Burroughs, fometime minifter of Wells, John Proctor, and Elizabeth Proctor his wife, with John Willard, of Salem Village, George Jacobs fenior, of Salem, and Martha Carrier, of Andover; thefe were all brought in guilty, and condemned; and were all executed, *Auguft* 19, except Proctor's wife, who pleaded pregnancy.

Mr. Burroughs was carried in a cart with the others, through the ftreets of Salem to execution. When he was upon the ladder, he made a fpeech for the clearing of his innocency, with fuch folemn and ferious expreffions, as were to the admiration of all prefent: his prayer (which he concluded by repeating the Lord's prayer) was fo well worded, and uttered with fuch compofednefs, and fuch (at leaft feeming) fervency of fpirit, as was very affecting, and drew tears from many, fo that it feemed to fome that the fpectators would hinder the execution. The accufers faid the black man ftood and dictated to him. As foon as he was turned off, mr. Cotton Mather, being mounted upon a horfe, addreffed himfelf to the people, partly to declare that he [Burroughs] was no ordained minifter, and partly to poffefs the people of his guilt, faying that the devil has often been transformed into an angel of light; and this fomewhat appeafed the people, and the executions went on. When he was cut down, he was dragged by the halter to a hole, or grave, between the rocks, about two feet deep, his shirt and breeches being pulled off, and an old pair of trowsers of one executed put on his lower parts; he was so put in, together with Willard and Carrier, that one of his hands and his chin, and a foot of one of them, were left uncovered.

John Willard had been employed to fetch in several that were accused; but taking dissatisfaction from his being sent to fetch up some that he had better thoughts of, he declined the service; and presently after he himself was accused of the same crime, and that with such vehemency, that they sent after him to apprehend him. He had made his escape as far as Nashawag, about forty miles from Salem; yet it is said those accusers did then presently tell the exact time, saying, Now Willard is taken.

John Proctor * and his wife being in prison, the sheriff came to his house and seized all the goods, provisions and cattle that he could come at, and sold some of the cattle at half price, and killed others, and put them up for the West-Indies; threw out the beer out of a barrel, and carried away the barrel; emptied a pot of broth,

* John Proctor was a respectable farmer; and great efforts were made by his friends, not only at Salem Village, but also at Ipswich, his native town, to save his life; but they were unsuccessful. A copy of his will, made during his imprisonment and while under sentence of death, is in the Probate-Court Records at Salem.

and took away the pot, and left nothing in the houſe for the ſupport of the children. No part of the ſaid goods are known to be returned. Proctor earneſtly requeſted mr. Noyes to pray with and for him; but it was wholly denied, becauſe he would not own himſelf to be a witch.

During his impriſonment he ſent the following letter, in behalf of himſelf and others.

Salem Priſon, July 23, 1692.
Mr. Mather, Mr. Allen, Mr. Moody, Mr. Willard, and Mr. Baily.

Reverend Gentlemen,

The innocency of our caſe, with the enmity of our accuſers and our judges and jury, whom nothing but our innocent blood will ſerve, having condemned us already before our trials, being ſo much incenſed and enraged againſt us by the devil, makes us bold to beg and implore your favourable aſſiſtance of this our humble petition to his excellency, that if it be poſſible our innocent blood may be ſpared, which undoubtedly otherwiſe will be ſhed, if the Lord doth not mercifully ſtep in; the magiſtrates, miniſters, juries, and all the people in general, being ſo much enraged and incenſed againſt us by the deluſion of the devil, which we can term no other, by reaſon we know in our own conſciences we are all innocent persons. Here are five persons who have lately confessed themselves to be witches, and do accuse some of us of being along with them at a sacrament, since we were committed into close prison, which we know to be lies. Two of the five are (Carrier's sons) young men, who would not confess any thing till they tied them neck and heels, till the blood was ready to come out of their noses; and it is credibly believed and reported this was the occasion of making them confess what they never did, by reason they said one had been a witch a month, and another five weeks, and that their mother had made them so, who has been confined here this nine weeks. My son William Proctor, when he was examined, because he would not confess that he was guilty, when he was innocent, they tied him neck and heels till the blood gushed out at his nose, and would have kept him so twenty-four hours, if one, more merciful than the rest, had not taken pity on him, and caused him to be unbound. These actions are very like the popish cruelties. They have already undone us in our estates, and that will not serve their turns without our innocent blood. If it cannot be granted that we can have our trials at Boston, we humbly beg that you would endeavour to have these magistrates changed, and others in their rooms; begging alfo and befeeching you would be pleafed to be here, if not all, fome of you, at our trials, hoping thereby you may be the means of faving the fhedding of our innocent blood. Defiring your prayers to the Lord in our behalf, we reft your poor afflicted fervants.   JOHN PROCTOR, &c.

He pleaded very hard at execution for a little refpite of time, faying that he was not fit to die; but it was not granted.

Old Jacobs* being condemned, the fheriff and officers came and feized all he had; his wife had her wedding ring taken from her, but with great difficulty obtained it again. She was forced to buy provifions of the fheriff, fuch as he had taken, towards her own fupport, which not being fufficient, the neighbours in charity relieved her.

Margaret Jacobs being one that had confeffed her own guilt, and teftified againft her grandfather Jacobs, mr. Burroughs and John Willard, fhe the day before execution came to mr. Burroughs, acknowledging that fhe had belied them, and begged mr. Burroughs's forgivenefs; who not only forgave her, but alfo prayed with and for her. She wrote the following letter to her father:

* George Jacobs, Sen., after his execution, was buried on his farm, at Danvers Port, where his grave is to be feen at this day.

From the dungeon in Salem prison, Aug. 20, 1692.
Honoured Father,

After my humble duty remembered to you, hoping in the Lord of your good health, as blessed be God I enjoy, though in abundance of affliction, being close confined here in a loathsome dungeon; the Lord look down in mercy upon me, not knowing how soon I shall be put to death, by means of the afflicted persons; my grandfather having suffered already, and all his estate seized for the king. The reason of my confinement is this: I having, through the magistrates' threatenings, and my own vile and wretched heart, confessed several things contrary to my conscience and knowledge, though to the wounding of my own soul, (the Lord pardon me for it); but oh! the terrors of a wounded conscience who can bear? But blessed be the Lord, he would not let me go on in my sins, but in mercy, I hope to my soul, would not suffer me to keep it in any longer, but I was forced to confess the truth of all before the magistrates, who would not believe me; but 'tis their pleasure to put me in here, and God knows how soon I shall be put to death. Dear father, let me beg your prayers to the Lord on my behalf, and send us a joyful and happy meeting in heaven. My mother, poor woman, is very crazy, and remembers her kind love to you, and to uncle, viz. D. A. So leaving you to the protection of the Lord, I rest your dutiful daughter,

MARGARET JACOBS.

At the time appointed for her trial, she had an imposthume in her head, which was her escape.

September 9, six more were tried, and received sentence of death, viz. Martha Cory, of Salem Village; Mary Easty, of Topsfield; Alice Parker and Ann Pudeater, of Salem; Dorcas Hoar, of Beverly, and Mary Bradberry, of Salisbury. Sept. 16, Giles Cory was prest to death.

September 17, nine more received sentence of death, viz. Margaret Scot, of Rowley; goodwife Reed, of Marblehead; Samuel Wardwell and Mary Parker, of Andover; also Abigail Falkner, of Andover, who pleaded pregnancy; Rebecca Eames, of Boxford, Mary Lacy and Ann Foster, of Andover, and Abigail Hobbs, of Topsfield. Of these, eight were executed, Sept. 22, viz. Martha Cory, Mary Easty, Alice Parker, Ann Pudeater, Margaret Scot, William Reed, Samuel Wardwell and Mary Parker.

Giles Cory * pleaded not guilty to his indict-

---

* Giles Cory was executed Sept. 19th, 1692, about noon. The day following, Sergt. Thomas Putman, of Salem Village, sent a letter to Judge Sewall, informing him of a revelation from his daughter Ann, wherein a spectre revealed to her the fact that Giles

ment, but would not put himself on trial by the jury (they having cleared none upon trial) and knowing there would be the same witnesses against him, rather chose to undergo what death they would put him to. In pressing, his tongue being prest out of his mouth, the sheriff with his cane forced it in again when he was dying.

Cory, some seventeen years before, was suspected of causing the death of a man in his employ. The coroner's jury, which sat upon the body, rendered a verdict of murder, by bruising,—he having, as they expressed it, "clodders of blood about the heart." We may suppose that the remembrance of this occurrence may have prejudiced the minds of many against Cory, although there was not a particle of evidence that he caused, or was knowing to, the death of the man in his employ, and living in his house. The courts took no notice of the affair, and it was generally forgotten, until recalled by his prosecution for witchcraft. The story of the murder seems to have been used at the time to palliate the dreadful deed of pressing him to death, by inducing the public to believe that he suffered a just punishment, in consequence of his having, seventeen years before, pressed a man to death with his feet.

It is generally supposed, and we think correctly, that Giles Cory, seeing that no one escaped, and that a trial was but a farce, refused to plead. But Ann Putman informs us, that the ghost of the man, whom it was said Cory murdered, appeared to her the night before his execution, and told her that when goodman Cory made his witch-covenant, the devil stipulated with him, and gave him assurance, that he should never be hanged, let what would come; but was careful not to tell him he should be pressed to death. The ghost in the winding sheet further informed Ann, that Cory's heart was hardened that he should not hearken to the importunity of the court to plead either guilty or not guilty, so that he might at least die a more easy death than by pressing — Because, continued the spectre, it must be done to *him* as he has done to *me*, the ghost of the murdered man!

He was the first in New-England that was ever prest to death.

The cart, going to the hill with these eight to execution, was for some time at a set; the afflicted and others said that the devil hindered it, &c.

Martha Cory, wife to Giles Cory, protesting her innocency, concluded her life with an eminent prayer upon the ladder.

Wardwell, having formerly confessed himself guilty, and after denied it, was soon brought upon his trial; his former confession and spectre testimony was all that appeared against him. At execution, while he was speaking to the people, protesting his innocency, the executioner being at the same time smoking tobacco, the smoke coming in his face interrupted his discourse; those accusers said that the devil did hinder him with smoke.

Mary Easty, sister also to Rebecca Nurse, when she took her last farewell of her husband, children and friends, was, as is reported by them present, as serious, religious, distinct and affectionate as could well be exprest, drawing tears from the eyes of almost all present. It seems, besides the testimony of the accusers and confessors, another proof, as it was counted, appeared against her: it having been usual to search the accused for teats, upon some parts of her body, not here to be named, was found an excrescence, which they called a teat. Before her death she presented the following petition:

"To the honourable judge and bench now sitting in judicature in Salem, and the reverend ministers, humbly sheweth, That whereas your humble poor petitioner, being condemned to die, doth humbly beg of you to take it into your judicious and pious consideration, that your poor and humble petitioner, knowing my own innocency (blessed be the Lord for it) and seeing plainly the wiles and subtilty of my accusers, by myself, cannot but judge charitably of others, that are going the same way with myself, if the Lord step not mightily in. I was confined a whole month on the same account that I am now condemned, and then cleared by the afflicted persons, as some of your honours know; and in two days time I was cried out upon by them again, and have been confined, and now am condemned to die. The Lord above knows my innocence then, and likewise doth now, as at the great day will be known by men and angels. I petition to your honours not for my own life, for I know I must die, and my appointed time is set; but the Lord he knows if it be possible that no more innocent blood be shed, which undoubtedly cannot be avoided in the way and course you go in. I queſtion not but your honours do to the utmoſt of your powers, in the diſcovery and detecting of witchcraft and witches, and would not be guilty of innocent blood for the world; but by my own innocency I know you are in the wrong way. The Lord in his infinite mercy direct you in this great work, if it be his bleſſed will, that innocent blood be not ſhed. I would humbly beg of you that your honours would be pleaſed to examine ſome of thoſe confeſſing witches, I being confident there are ſeveral of them have belied themſelves and others, as will appear, if not in this world, I am ſure in the world to come, whither I am going; and I queſtion not but yourſelves will ſee an alteration in theſe things. They ſay, myſelf and others have made a league with the devil; we cannot confeſs; I know and the Lord knows (as will ſhortly appear) they belie me, and ſo I queſtion not but they do others; the Lord alone, who is the ſearcher of all hearts, knows, as I ſhall anſwer it at the tribunal ſeat, that I know not the leaſt thing of witchcraft, therefore I cannot, I durſt not, belie my own ſoul. I beg your honours not to deny this my humble petition, from a poor, dying, innocent perſon, and I queſtion not but the Lord will give a bleſſing to your endeavours.

Mary Easty."

After execution, mr. Noyes, turning him to the bodies, faid, What a fad thing it is to fee eight firebrands of hell hanging there!

In October, 1692, one of Wenham complained of mrs. Hale, whofe hufband, the minifter of Beverly, had been very forward in thefe profecutions; but being fully fatisfied of his wife's fincere chriftianity caufed him to alter his judgment; for it was come to a ftated controverfy, among the New-England divines, whether the devil could afflict in a good man's fhape; it feems nothing elfe could convince him, yet when it came fo near to himfelf he was foon convinced, that the devil might fo afflict. Which fame reafon did afterwards prevail with many others, and much influenced to the fucceeding change at trials.

October 7. Edward Bifhop and his wife having made their efcape out of prifon, this day mr. Corwin, the fheriff, came and feized his goods and chattels, and had it not been for his fecond fon (who borrowed ten pound and gave it him) they had been wholly loft. The receipt follows; but it feems they muft be content with fuch a receipt as he would give them:

Received, this 7th day of October, 1692, of Samuel Bifhop, of the town of Salem, of the county of Effex, in New-England, cordwainer, in full fatisfaction, a valuable fum of money, for the goods and chattels of Edward Bifhop, fenior, of the town and county aforesaid, husbandman; which goods and chattels being seized, for that the said Edward Bishop, and Sarah his wife, having been committed for witchcraft and felony, have made their escape; and their goods and chattels were forfeited unto their majesties, and now being in possession of the said Samuel Bishop; and in behalf of their majesties, I do hereby discharge the said goods and chattels, the day and year above written, as witness my hand,

GEORGE CORWIN, *Sheriff.*

But before this, the said Bishop's eldest son having married into that family of the Putmans, who were chief prosecutors in this business, he holding a cow to be branded lest it should be seized, and having a push or boil upon his thigh, with his straining it broke; this is that that was pretended to be burnt with the said brand, and is one of the bones thrown to the dogmatical to pick, in *Wonders of the Invisible World,* p. 143. The other, of a corner of a sheet, pretended to be taken from a spectre; it is known that it was provided the day before by that afflicted person; and the third bone of a spindle is almost as easily provided, as the piece of the knife; so that Apollo needs not herein be consulted, &c.

Mr. Philip English, and his wife, having made their escape out of prison, mr. Corwin, the sheriff, seized his estate, to the value of about fifteen hundred pound, which was wholly lost to him, except about three hundred pound value (which was afterward restored.)

After goodwife Hoar was condemned, her

eftate was feized, and was alfo bought again for eight pound.

George Jacobs, fon to old Jacobs, being accufed, he fled; then the officers came to his houfe; his wife was a woman crazy in her fenfes, and had been fo feveral years. She it feems had been alfo accufed. There were in the houfe with her only four fmall children, and one of them fucked her eldeft daughter, being in prifon: the officer perfuaded her out of the houfe, to go along with him, telling her fhe fhould fpeedily return; the children ran a great way after her, crying.

When fhe came where the afflicted were, being afked, they faid they did not know her; at length one faid, Don't you know *Jacobs*, the old witch? and then they cried out of her, and fell down in their fits. She was fent to prifon, and lay there ten months; the neighbours of pity took care of the children to preferve them from perifhing.

About this time a new fcene was begun; one Jofeph Ballard, of Andover, whofe wife was ill, (and after died of a fever) fent to Salem for fome of thofe accufers, to tell him who afflicted his wife; others did the like: horfe and man were fent from feveral places to fetch thofe accufers who had the fpectral fight, that they might thereby tell who afflicted thofe that were any ways ill.

When thefe came into any place where fuch were, ufually they fell into a fit: after which, being afked who it was that afflicted the perfon, they would, for the moft part, name one who they faid fat on the head, and another that fat on the lower parts, of the afflicted. Soon after Ballard's fending (as above) more than fifty of the people of Andover were complained of, for afflicting their neighbours. Here it was that many accufed themfelves of riding upon poles through the air; many parents believing their children to be witches, and many hufbands their wives, &c. When thefe accufers came to the houfe of any upon fuch account, it was ordinary for other young people to be taken in fits, and to have the fame fpectral fight.

Mr. Dudley Bradftreet, a juftice of peace in Andover, having granted out warrants againft and committed, thirty or forty to prifon, for the fuppofed witchcrafts, at length faw caufe to forbear granting out any more warrants. Soon after which, he and his wife were cried out of; himfelf was (by them) faid to have killed nine perfons by witchcraft, and he found it his fafeft courfe to make his efcape.

A dog being afflicted at Salem Village, thofe that had the fpectral fight being fent for, they accufed mr. John Bradftreet, (brother to the juftice,) that he afflicted the faid dog, and now rid upon him. He made his escape into Piscatuqua government, and the dog was put to death, and was all of the afflicted that suffered death.

At Andover, the afflicted complained of a dog, as afflicting them, and would fall into their fits at the dog's looking upon them; the dog was put to death.

A worthy gentleman of Boston being about this time accused by those at Andover, he sent by some particular friends a writ to arrest those accusers in a thousand pound action for defamation, with instructions to them to inform themselves of the certainty of the proof, in doing which their business was perceived, and from thenceforward the accusations at Andover generally ceased.

In October some of these accusers were sent for to Gloucester, and occasioned four women to be sent to prison; but Salem prison being so full it could receive no more, two were sent to Ipswich prison. In November they were sent for again by lieutenant Stephens, who was told that a sister of his was bewitched; in their way, passing over Ipswich-bridge, they met with an old woman, and instantly fell into their fits. But by this time the validity of such accusations being much questioned, they found not that encouragement they had done elsewhere, and soon withdrew.

These accusers swore that they saw three persons sitting upon lieutenant Stephens's sister till she died; yet bond was accepted for those three.

And now nineteen persons having been hanged, and one prest to death, and eight more condemned, in all twenty-eight, of which above a third part were members of some of the churches in New-England, and more than half of them of a good conversation in general, and not one cleared; about fifty having confest themselves to be witches, of which not one executed; above an hundred and fifty in prison, and above two hundred more accused; the special commission of oyer and terminer comes to a period, which has no other foundation than the governor's commission; and had proceeded in the manner of swearing witnesses, viz. by holding up the hand, (and by receiving evidences in writing) according to the ancient usage of this country; as also having their indictments in English. In the trials, when any were indicted for afflicting, pining and wasting the bodies of particular persons by witchcraft, it was usual to hear evidence of matter foreign, and of perhaps twenty or thirty years standing, about oversetting carts, the death of cattle, unkindness to relations, or unexpected accidents befalling after some quarrel. Whether this was admitted by the law of England, or by what other law, wants to be determined; the executions feemed mixt, in preffing to death for not pleading, which moft agrees with the laws of England; and fentencing women to be hanged for witchcraft, according to the former practice of this country, and not by burning, as is faid to have been the law of England. And though the confeffing witches were many, yet not one of them that confeffed their own guilt, and abode by their confeffion, was put to death.

Here followeth what account fome of thofe miferable creatures give of their confeffion under their own hands:

"We, whofe names are under written, inhabitants of Andover, when as that horrible and tremendous judgment beginning at Salem Village, in the year 1692, (by fome called witchcraft) firft breaking forth at mr. Parris's houfe, feveral young perfons being feemingly afflicted, did accufe feveral perfons for afflicting them, and many there believing it fo to be; we being informed that if a perfon were fick, the afflicted perfon could tell what or who was the caufe of that ficknefs: Jofeph Ballard, of Andover (his wife being fick at the fame time) he either from himfelf, or by the advice of others, fetched two of the perfons, called the afflicted perfons, from Salem Village to Andover: which was the beginning of that dreadful calamity that befel us in Andover. And the authority in Andover, believing the said accusations to be true, sent for the said persons to come together to the meeting-house in Andover (the afflicted persons being there.) After mr. Barnard had been at prayer, we were blindfolded, and our hands were laid upon the afflicted persons, they being in their fits, and falling into their fits at our coming into their presence (as they said) and some led us and laid our hands upon them, and then they said they were well, and that we were guilty of afflicting of them; whereupon we were all seized as prisoners, by a warrant from a justice of the peace, and forthwith carried to Salem. And by reason of that sudden surprisal, we knowing ourselves altogether innocent of that crime, we were all exceedingly astonished and amazed, and affrighted even out of our reason; and our nearest and dearest relations, seeing us in that dreadful condition, and knowing our great danger, apprehending that there was no other way to save our lives, as the case was then circumstanced, but by our confessing ourselves to be such and such persons, as the afflicted represented us to be, they out of tender love and pity persuaded us to confess what we did confess. And indeed that confession, that it is said we made, was no other than what was suggested to us by some gentlemen; they telling us, that we were witches, and they knew it, and we knew it, and they knew that we knew it, which made us think that it was fo; and our underftanding, our reafon and our faculties almoft gone, we were not capable of judging our condition; as alfo the hard meafures they ufed with us rendered us uncapable of making our defence; but faid any thing and every thing which they defired; and moft of what we faid was but in effect a confenting to what they faid. Sometime after, when we were better compofed, they telling of us what we had confeffed, we did profefs that we were innocent, and ignorant of fuch things. And we hearing that Samuel Wardwell had renounced his confeffion, and quickly after was condemned and executed, fome of us were told that we were going after Wardwell.

Mary Ofgood,	Abigail Barker,
Mary Tiler,	Sarah Wilfon,
Deliv. Dane,	Hannah Tiler."

It may here be further added, concerning thofe that did confefs, that befides that powerful argument, of life (and freedom from hardfhips, not only promifed, but alfo performed to all that owned their guilt) there are numerous inftances, too many to be here inferted, of the tedious examinations before private perfons, many hours together; they all that time urging them to confess (and taking turns to persuade them) till the accused were wearied out by being forced to stand so long, or for want of sleep, &c. and so brought to give an assent to what they said; they then asking them, Were you at such a witch-meeting? or, Have you signed the devil's book? &c. Upon their replying, Yes, the whole was drawn into form, as their confession.

But that which did mightily further such confessions was, their nearest relations urging them to it. These, seeing no other way of escape for them, thought it the best advice that could be given; hence it was that the husbands of some, by counsel often urging, and utmost earnestness, and children upon their knees intreating, have at length prevailed with them to say they were guilty.

As to the manner of trials, and the evidence taken for convictions at Salem, it is already set forth in print, by the rev. mr. Cotton Mather, in his *Wonders of the Invisible World*, at the command of his excellency sir William Phips; with not only the recommendation, but thanks of the lieutenant governor; and with the approbation of the rev. mr. I. M. in his postscript to his *Cases of Conscience;* which last book was set forth by the consent of the ministers in and near Boston. Two of the judges have alfo given their fentiments in thefe words, p. 147.

> The reverend and worthy author having, at the direction of his excellency the governor, fo far obliged the publick, as to give fome account of the fufferings brought upon the country by witch-crafts, and of the trials which have paffed upon feveral executed for the same:
> Upon perufal thereof, we find the matters of fact and evidence truly reported, and a profpect given of the methods of conviction, ufed in the proceedings of the court at Salem.
> WILLIAM STOUGHTON,
SAMUEL SEWALL.
>
> *Boston, Oct.* 11, 1692.

And confidering that this may fall into the hands of fuch as never faw thofe *Wonders*, it may be needful to tranfcribe the whole account he has given thereof, without any variation (but with one of the indictments annexed to the trial of each) which is thus prefaced, pp. 81, 82, 83.

"But I fhall no longer detain my reader from his expected entertainment, in a brief account of the trials which have paffed upon some of the malefactors lately executed at Salem for the witchcrafts whereof they ftood convicted. For my own part I was not prefent at any of them; nor ever had I any perfonal prejudice againft the perfons thus brought upon the ftage; much lefs, at the furviving relations of thofe perfons, with and for whom I would be as hearty a mourner, as any man living in the world: *The*

Lord comfort them! But having received a command so to do, I can do no other than shortly relate the chief matters of fact, which occurred in the trials of some that were executed, in an abridgment collected out of the court-papers, on this occasion put into my hands. You are to take the truth, just as it was; and the truth will hurt no good man. There might have been more of these; and if some other worthy hands did not perhaps intend something further in these collections; for which cause I have only singled out four or five, which may serve to illustrate the way of dealing, wherein witchcrafts used to be concerned; and I report matters, not as an advocate, but as an historian.

"These were some of the gracious words inserted in the advice, which many of the neighbouring ministers did this summer humbly lay before our honourable judges: 'We cannot but with all thankfulness acknowledge the success, which the merciful God has given unto the sedulous and assiduous endeavours of our honourable rulers, to detect the abominable witchcrafts which have been committed in the country; humbly praying that the discovery of those mysterious and mischievous wickednesses may be perfected.' If, in the midst of the many dissatisfactions among us, the publication of these trials may promote such a pious thankfulnefs unto God, for juftice being fo far executed among us, I fhall rejoice that God is glorified; and pray that no wrong fteps of ours may ever fully any of his glorious works."

The Indictment of George Burroughs.

Effex fs.   *Anno Regni Regis & Reginæ Willielmi & Mariæ, nunc Angliæ, &c. quarto.*——

The jurors for our fovereign lord and lady the king and queen prefent, that George Burroughs, late of Falmouth, in the province of the Maffachufetts Bay, in New England, clerk, the 9th day of May, in the fourth year of the reign of our fovereign lord and lady William and Mary, by the grace of God, of England, Scotland, France and Ireland, king and queen, defenders of the faith, &c., and divers other days and times, as well before as after, certain deteftable arts, called witchcrafts and forceries, wickedly and felonioufly hath ufed, practifed and exercifed, at and within the townfhip of Salem, in the county of Effex, aforefaid, in, upon and againft one Mary Wolcott, of Salem Village, in the county of Effex, fingle woman; by which faid wicked arts the faid Mary Wolcott, the 9th day of May, in the fourth year abovefaid, and divers other days and times, as well before as after, was and is tortured, afflicted, pined, confumed, wafted, and tormented, againft the peace of our fovereign lord and lady, the king and queen, and againft the form of the ftatute in that cafe made and provided.

Witneffes, *Mary Wolcott, Sarah Vibber, Mercy Lewis,* Ann Putman, *Eliz. Hubbard.*

Endorfed by the grand jury, *Billa Vera.*

There was alfo a fecond indictment, for afflicting Elizabeth Hubbard. The witneffes to the faid indictment were *Elizabeth Hubbard, Mary Wolcott* and *Ann Putman.*

The third indictment was for afflicting Mercy Lewis: the witneffes, the faid *Mercy Lewis,*

Mary Wolcott, Elizabeth Hubbard and *Ann Putman*.

The fourth, for acts of witchcraft on Ann Putman: the witnesses, the said *Ann Putman, Mary Wolcott, Elizabeth Hubbard*, and Mary Warren.

The Trial of G. B.* as printed in Wonders of the Invisible World, from p. 94 to 104.

Glad should I have been, if I had never known the name of this man, or never had this

---

* The trial of Rev. George Burroughs appears to have attracted general notice, from the circumstance of his being a former clergyman in Salem village, and supposed to be a leader amongst the witches. — Dr. Cotton Mather says he was not present at any of the trials for witchcraft; how he could keep away from that of Burroughs, we cannot imagine. — His father, Dr. Increase Mather, informs us that he attended this single trial, and says, " had I been one of George Burrough's judges, I could not have acquitted him; for several persons did upon oath testify, that they saw him do such things as no man that had not a devil to be his familiar, could perform." Burroughs was apprehended in Wells, in Maine; so say his children. They also inform us, that he was buried by his friends after the inhuman treatment of his body from the hands of his executioners, at Gallows Hill, in Salem. He is represented as being a small, black haired, dark complexioned man, of quick passions, and possessing great strength. His power of muscle, which discovered itself early when Burroughs was a member of Cambridge College, and which we notice in the slight rebutting evidence offered by his friends at his trial, convinces us that he lifted the gun, and the barrel of molasses by the power of his own well-strung muscles, and not by any help from the devil, as was supposed by the Mathers, both father and son. Alas! that a man's own strong arm should thus prove his ruin.

occasion to mention so much as the first letters of his name; but the government requiring some account of his trial to be inserted in this book, it becomes me with all obedience to submit unto the order.

1. This G. B. was indicted for witchcrafts; and, in the prosecution of the charge against him, he was accused by five or six of the bewitched, as the author of their miseries; he was accused by eight of the confessing witches, as being a head actor at some of their hellish rendezvous, and who had the promise of being a king in satan's kingdom, now going to be erected; he was accused by nine persons, for extraordinary lifting, and such feats of strength as could not be done without a diabolical assistance; and for other such things he was accused, until about thirty testimonies were brought in against him; nor were these judged the half of what might have been considered, for his conviction: however, they were enough to fix the character of a witch upon him, accord-

---

In regard to the reputation of Rev. George Burroughs, Judge Sullivan, in his history of Maine, says: — " He was a man of bad character, and of a cruel disposition." — Our researches lead us to form a very different opinion. And all the weight of character enlisted against him, fails to counteract the favourable impression made by his christian conduct, during his imprisonment, and at the time of his execution. We find Georgius Burroughs in the Harvard catalogue list of graduates for the year 1670.

ing to the rules of reasoning, by the judicious *Gaule* in that case directed.

2. The court being sensible that the testimonies of the parties bewitched used to have a room among the suspicions, or presumptions, brought in against one indicted for witchcraft, there were now heard the testimonies of several persons who were most notoriously bewitched, and every day tortured by invisible hands, and these now all charged the spectres of G. B. to have a share in their torments. At the examination of this G. B. the bewitched people were grievously harassed with preternatural mischiefs, which could not possibly be dissembled; and they still ascribed it unto the endeavours of G. B. to kill them. And now, upon his trial, one of the bewitched persons testified, that in her agonies a little black-haired man came to her, saying his name was B. and bidding her set her hand unto a book, which he shewed unto her; and bragging that he was a conjurer above the ordinary rank of witches; that he often persecuted her with the offer of that book, saying, she should be well, and need fear nobody, if she would but sign it: but he inflicted cruel pains and hurts upon her, because of her denying so to do. The testimonies of the other sufferers concurred with these; and it was remarkable, that whereas biting was one of the ways which

the witches ufed for the vexing of the fufferers, when they cried out of **G. B.** biting them, the print of his teeth would be feen on the flefh of the complainers; and juft fuch a fet of teeth as **G. B.**'s would then appear upon them, which could be diftinguifhed from thofe of fome other men's.

Others of them teftified, that in their torments **G. B.** tempted them to go unto a facrament, unto which they perceived him with a found of trumpet fummoning other witches; who quickly after the found would come from all quarters unto the rendezvous. One of them, falling into a kind of a trance, afterwards affirmed, that **G. B.** had carried her into a very high mountain, where he fhowed her mighty and glorious kingdoms, and faid he would give them all to her, if fhe would write in his book; but fhe told him, they were none of his to give, and refufed the motion, enduring much mifery for that refufal.

It coft the court a wonderful deal of trouble to hear the teftimonies of the fufferers; for when they were going to give in their depofitions, they would for a long while be taken with fits, that made them uncapable of faying anything. The chief judge afked the prifoner, who he thought hindered thefe witneffes from giving their teftimonies; and he anfwered, he fuppofed it was the devil. That honourable perſon then replied, How comes the devil ſo loth to have any teſtimony borne againſt you? which caſt him into very great confuſion.

3. It hath been a frequent thing for the bewitched people to be entertained with apparitions of ghoſts of murdered people, at the ſame time that the ſpectres of the witches trouble them. Theſe ghoſts do always affright the beholders, more than all the other ſpectral repreſentations; and when they exhibit themſelves, they cry out of being murdered by the witchcrafts or other violences of the perſons who are then in ſpectre preſent. It is further conſiderable, that once or twice theſe apparitions have been ſeen by others, at the very ſame time they have ſhown themſelves to the bewitched; and ſeldom have there been theſe apparitions, but when ſomething unuſual and ſuſpected hath attended the death of the party thus appearing. Some, that have been accuſed by theſe apparitions, accoſting the bewitched people, who had never heard a word of any ſuch perſons ever being in the world, have, upon a fair examination, freely and fully confeſſed the murders of thoſe very perſons, although theſe alſo did not know how the apparitions had complained of them. Accordingly ſeveral of the bewitched had given in their teſtimony, that they had been troubled with the apparitions of

two women, who faid they were **G. B.**'s two wives; and that he had been the death of them; and that the magiftrates muft be told of it, before whom, if **B.** upon his trial denied it, they did not know but that they fhould appear again in the court. Now **G. B.** had been infamous, for the barbarous ufage of his two fucceffive wives, all the country over. Moreover, it was teftified, the fpectre of **G. B.** threatening the fufferers, told them he had killed (befides others) mrs. Lawfon and her daughter Ann. And it was noted, that thefe were the virtuous wife and daughter of one, at whom this **G. B.** might have a prejudice, for being ferviceable at Salem Village, from whence himfelf had in ill terms removed fome years before; and that when they died, which was long fince, there were fome odd circumftances about them, which made fome of the attendants there fufpect fomething of witchcraft, though none imagined from what quarter it fhould come.

Well, **G. B.** being now upon his trial, one of the bewitched perfons was caft into horror at the ghofts of **B.**'s two deceafed wives, then appearing before him, and crying for vengeance againft him. Hereupon feveral of the bewitched perfons were fucceffively called in, who all, not knowing what the former had feen and faid, concurred in their horror of the apparition, which they affirmed that he had before him. But he, though much appalled, utterly denied that he discerned anything of it, nor was it any part of his conviction.

4. Judicious writers have assigned it a great place in the conviction of witches, when persons are impeached by other notorious witches to be as ill as themselves, especially if the persons have been much noted for neglecting the worship of God. Now, as there might have been testimonies enough of G. B's antipathy to prayer, and the other ordinances of God, though by his profession singularly obliged thereunto; so there now came in against the prisoner, the testimonies of several persons, who confessed their own having been horrible witches, and, ever since their confessions, had been themselves terribly tortured by the devils and other witches, even like the other sufferers, and therein undergone the pains of many deaths for their confessions,

These now testified, that G. B. had been at witch-meetings with them; and that he was the person who had seduced and compelled them into the snares of witchcraft; that he promised them fine clothes for doing it; that he brought poppets to them, and thorns to stick into those poppets, for the afflicting of other people: and that he exhorted them, with the rest of the crew, to bewitch all Salem Village; but be sure to do it gradually, if they would prevail in what they did.

When the Lancashire witches were condemned, I do not remember that there was any confiderable further evidence, than that of the bewitched, and than that of fome that had confeffed. We fee fo much already againft **G. B.** But this being indeed not enough, there were other things to render what had already been produced credible.

5. A famous divine recites this among the convictions of a witch; the teftimony of the party bewitched, whether pining or dying; together with the joint oaths of fufficient perfons, that have feen certain prodigious pranks, or feats, wrought by the party accufed. Now God had been pleafed fo to leave **G. B.** that he had enfnared himfelf, by feveral inftances, which he had formerly given, of a preternatural ftrength; and which were now produced againft him. He was a very puny man, yet he had often done things beyond the ftrength of a giant. A gun of about feven feet barrel, and fo heavy that ftrong men could not fteadily hold it out, with both hands, there were feveral teftimonies given in by perfons of credit and honour, that he made nothing of taking up fuch a gun behind the lock with but one hand, and holding it out, like a piftol, at arm's end. **G. B.** in his vindication was fo foolifh as to fay, that an Indian was there, and held it out, at the fame time: whereas, none

of the spectators ever saw any such Indian; but
they supposed the black man (as the witches call
the devil, and they generally say he resembles
an Indian) might give him that assistance.
There was evidence likewise brought in, that he
made nothing of taking up whole barrels filled
with molasses, or cider, in very disadvantageous
postures, and carrying them off, through the most
difficult places, out of a canoe to the shore.

Yea, there were two testimonies, that **G. B.**
with only putting the fore-finger of his right
hand into the muzzle of an heavy gun, a fowl-
ing piece of about six or seven feet barrel, lifted
up the gun, and held it out at arm's end; a gun
which the deponents, though strong men, could
not with both hands lift up, and hold out at the
but-end, as is usual. Indeed one of these witnesses was over-persuaded by some persons to be
out of the way upon **G. B.**'s trial; but he came
afterwards, with sorrow for his withdrawing, and
gave in his testimony. Nor were either of these
witnesses made use of as evidence in the trial.

6. There came in several testimonies, relating
to the domestic affairs of **G. B.** which had a very
hard aspect upon him; and not only proved him
a very ill man, but also confirmed the belief of
the character which had been already fastened on
him. 'Twas testified, that, keeping his two successive wives in a strange kind of slavery, he

would, when he came home from abroad, pretend to tell the talk which any had with them: that he has brought them to the point of death, by his harſh dealings with his wives, and then made the people about him to promiſe that in caſe death ſhould happen they would ſay nothing of it: that he uſed all means to make his wives write, ſign, ſeal and ſwear a covenant never to reveal any of his ſecrets: that his wives had privately complained unto the neighbours about frightly apparitions of evil ſpirits, with which their houſe was ſometimes infeſted; and that many ſuch things had been whiſpered among the neighbourhood. There were alſo ſome other teſtimonies, relating to the death of people, whereby the conſciences of an impartial jury were convinced that **G. B.** had bewitched the perſons mentioned in the complaints. But I am forced to omit ſeveral ſuch paſſages in this as well as in all the ſucceeding trials, becauſe the ſcribes who took notice of them have not ſupplied me.

7. One mr. Ruck, brother-in-law to this **G. B.** teſtified, that **G. B.** and he himſelf, and his ſiſter, who was **G. B.**'s wife, going out for two or three miles, to gather ſtrawberries, Ruck, with his ſiſter, the wife of **G. B.** rode home very ſoftly, with **G. B.** on foot, in their company; **G. B.** ſtept aſide a little into the buſhes, whereupon

they halted and hollowed for him: he not answering, they went away homewards, with a quickened pace, without any expectation of seeing him in a considerable while; and yet, when they were got near home, to their astonishment they found him on foot, with them, having a basket of strawberries. G. B. immediately then fell to chiding his wife, on the account of what she had been speaking to her brother of him on the road; which when they wondered at, he said, he knew their thoughts. Ruck, being startled at that, made some reply, intimating that the devil himself did not know so far; but G. B. answered, my God makes known your thoughts unto me. The prisoner now at the bar had nothing to answer unto what was thus witnessed against him, that was worth considering; only he said, Ruck and his wife left a man with him, when they left him; which Ruck now affirmed to be false; and when the court asked G. B. what the man's name was, his countenance was much altered, nor could he say who it was. But the court began to think that he then stept aside, only that by the assistance of the black man he might put on his invisibility, and in that fascinating mist gratify his own jealous humour, to hear what they said of him: which trick of rendering themselves invisible, our witches do in their confessions pretend that they sometimes are masters of; and it is the more credible, because there is demonstration that they often render many other things utterly invisible.

8. Faultering, faulty, unconstant and contrary answers, upon judicial and deliberate examination, are counted some unlucky symptoms of guilt in all crimes, especially in witchcrafts. Now there never was a prisoner more eminent for them than G. B. both at his examination and on his trial. His tergiversations, contradictions, and falsehoods were very sensible; he had little to say, but that he had heard some things, that he could not prove, reflecting upon the reputation of some of the witnesses: only he gave in a paper to the jury, wherein, although he had many times before granted not only that there are witches, but also that the present sufferings of the country are the effects of horrible witchcrafts, yet he now goes to evince it, that there neither are, nor ever were, witches, that having made a compact with the devil, can send a devil to torment other people at a distance. This paper was transcribed out of Ady; which the court presently knew, as soon as they heard it. But he said, he had taken none of it out of any book; for which his evasion afterwards was, that a gentleman gave him the discourse in a manuscript, from whence he transcribed it.

9. The jury brought him in guilty; but when

he came to die, he utterly denied the fact, whereof he had been thus convicted.

The Indictment of Bridget Bishop.

Essex ss.   *Anno Regni Regis & Reginæ Willielmi & Mariæ, nunc Angliæ, &c. quarto.——*

The jurors for our sovereign lord and lady the king and queen present, that Bridget Bishop, alias Oliver, the wife of Edward Bishop, in Salem, in the county of Essex, sawyer, the nineteenth day of April, in the fourth year of the reign of our sovereign lord and lady William and Mary, by the grace of God, of England, Scotland, France and Ireland, king and queen, defenders of the faith, &c. and divers other days and times, as well before as after, certain detestable arts, called witchcrafts and sorceries, wickedly and feloniously hath used, practised and exercised, at and within the township of Salem, in the county of Essex, aforesaid, in, upon and against one Mercy Lewis, of Salem Village, in the county aforesaid, single woman; by which said wicked arts the said Mercy Lewis, the said 19th day of April, in the fourth year abovesaid, and divers other days and times, as well before as after, was and is hurt, tortured, afflicted, pined, consumed, wasted and tormented, against the peace of our sovereign lord and lady, the king and queen, and against the form of the statute in that case made and provided.

Endorsed, *Billa Vera.*

Witnesses, *Mercy Lewis, Nathaniel Ingersoll,* mr. *Samuel Parris, Thomas Putman,* junior, *Mary Wolcott,* junior, *Ann Putman,* junior, *Eliz. Hubbard,* and *Abigail Williams.*

There was also a second indictment, on the said Bishop, for afflicting and practising witchcraft on *Abigail Williams.* Witnesses to the said indictment were, the said Abigail Williams, mr. Parris, Nathaniel Ingersoll, Thomas Putman, Ann Putman, Mary Wolcott, Elizabeth Hubbard.

The third indictment was for afflicting *Mary Wolcott;* witnesses to which said indictment were, Mary Wolcott, Mary Lewis, mr. Samuel Parris, Nathaniel Ingersoll, Thomas Putman, Ann Putman, Elizabeth Hubbard, Abigail Williams.

The fourth indictment was for afflicting *Elizabeth Hubbard;* witnesses to which said indictment were, the said Elizabeth Hubbard, Mercy Lewis, mr. Parris, Nathaniel Ingersoll, Thomas Putman, Ann Putman, Mary Wolcott, Abigail Williams.

The fifth indictment was for afflicting *Ann Putman;* witnesses to which said indictment were the said Ann Putman, mr. Samuel Parris, Nathaniel Ingersoll, Thomas Putman, Mercy Lewis, Mary Wolcott, Abigail Williams, Elizabeth Hubbard.

The Trial of Bridget Bishop, *as printed in Wonders of the Invisible World, June* 2, 1692, *from p.* 104 *to p.* 114.

1. She was indicted for bewitching several persons in the neighbourhood. The indictment being drawn up, according to the form in such cases usual, and pleading not guilty, there were brought in several persons, who had long undergone many kinds of miseries, which were preternaturally inflicted, and generally ascribed unto an horrible witchcraft. There was little occasion to prove the witchcraft, it being evident and no-

torious to all beholders. Now to fix the witchcraft on the prisoner at the bar, the first thing used was the testimony of the bewitched; whereof several testified, that the shape of the prisoner did oftentimes very grievously pinch them, choke them, bite them, and afflict them; urging them to write their names in a book, which the said spectre called *ours*. One of them did further testify, that it was the shape of this prisoner, with another, which one day took her from her wheel, and carrying her to the river side, threatened there to drown her, if she did not sign the book mentioned; which yet she refused. Others of them did also testify, that the said shape did, in her threats, brag to them, that she had been the death of sundry persons, then by her named. Another testified, the apparition of ghosts unto the spectre of Bishop, crying out, *You murdered us*. About the truth whereof, there was in the matter of fact but too much suspicion.

2. It was testified, that at the examination of the prisoner, before the magistrates, the bewitched were extremely tortured. If she did but cast her eyes on them, they were presently struck down; and this in such a manner as there could be no collusion in the business. But upon the touch of her hand upon them, when they lay in their swoons, they would immediately revive; and not upon the touch of any one's else. More-

over, upon some special actions of her body, as the shaking of her head, or the turning of her eyes, they presently and painfully fell into the like postures. And many of the like accidents now fell out, while she was at the bar; one at the same time testifying, that she said, she could not be troubled to see the afflicted thus tormented.

3. There was testimony likewise brought in, that a man striking once at a place where a bewitched person said the shape of this Bishop stood, the bewitched cried out that he had torn her coat, in the place then particularly specified; and the woman's coat was found to be torn in the very place.

4. One Deliverance Hobbs, who had confessed her being a witch, was now tormented by the spectres for her confession. And she now testified, that this Bishop tempted her to sign the book again, and to deny what she had confessed. She affirmed, that it was the shape of this prisoner which whipped her with iron rods, to compel her thereunto. And she affirmed, that this Bishop was at a general meeting of the witches in a field, at Salem Village, and there partook of a diabolical sacrament, in bread and wine, then administered.

5. To render it further unquestionable, that the prisoner at the bar was the person truly charged in this witchcraft, there were produced

many evidences of other witchcrafts, by her perpetrated. For instance, John Cook testified, that about five or six years ago, one morning about sunrise, he was, in his chamber, assaulted by the shape of this prisoner; which looked on him, grinned at him, and very much hurt him with a blow on the side of the head; and that on the same day, about noon, the same shape walked in the room where he was, and an apple strangely flew out of his hand into the lap of his mother, six or eight feet from him.

6. Samuel Gray testified, that about fourteen years ago, he waked on a night, and saw the room where he lay full of light; and that he then saw plainly a woman between the cradle and the bedside, which looked upon him. He rose, and it vanished, though he found the doors all fast. Looking out at the entry door, he saw the same woman in the same garb again; and said, *In God's name, what do you come for?* He went to bed, and had the same woman again assaulting him. The child in the cradle gave a great screech, and the woman disappeared. It was long before the child could be quieted; and though it were a very likely, thriving child, yet from this time it pined away, and after divers months died in a sad condition. He knew not Bishop, nor her name; but when he saw her after this, he knew by her countenance, and

apparel, and all circumstances, that it was the apparition of this Bishop, which had thus troubled him.

7. John Bly and his wife testified, that he bought a sow of Edward Bishop, the husband of the prisoner, and was to pay the price agreed unto another person. This prisoner, being angry that she was thus hindered from fingering the money, quarrelled with Bly; soon after which the sow was taken with strange fits, jumping, leaping, and knocking her head against the fence; she seemed blind and deaf, and would neither eat nor be sucked. Whereupon a neighbour said, she believed the creature was *overlooked*; and sundry other circumstances concurred, which made the deponents believe that Bishop had bewitched it.

8. Richard Coman testified, that eight years ago, as he lay awake in his bed, with a light burning in the room, he was annoyed with the apparition of this Bishop, and of two more that were strangers to him, who came and oppressed him, so that he could neither stir himself, nor wake any one else; and that he was the night after molested again in the like manner, the said Bishop taking him by the throat, and pulling him almost out of the bed. His kinsman offered for this cause to lodge with him; and that night, as they were awake, discoursing together, this

Coman was once more visited by the guests which had formerly been so troublesome, his kinsman being at the same time struck speechless, and unable to move hand or foot. He had laid his sword by him; which those unhappy spectres did strive much to wrest from him, but he held too fast for them. He then grew able to call the people of his house; but although they heard him, yet they had not power to speak or stir, until at last one of the people crying out, What's the matter? the spectres all vanished.

9. Samuel Shattock testified, that in the year 1680, this Bridget Bishop often came to his house upon such frivolous and foolish errands, that they suspected she came indeed with a purpose of mischief; presently whereupon, his eldest child, which was of as promising health and sense as any child of its age, began to droop exceedingly; and the oftener that Bishop came to his house, the worse grew the child. As the child would be standing at the door, he would be thrown and bruised against the stones, by an invisible hand, and in like sort knock his face against the sides of the house, and bruise it after a miserable manner. Afterwards this Bishop would bring him things to dye, whereof he could not imagine any use; and when she paid him a piece of money, the purse and money were unaccountably conveyed out of a locked

box, and never seen more. The child was immediately hereupon taken with terrible fits, whereof his friends thought he would have died: indeed he did nothing but cry and sleep, for several months together; and at length his understanding was utterly taken away. Among other symptoms of an enchantment upon him, one was, that there was a board in the garden, whereon he would walk; and all the invitations in the world would never fetch him off. About seventeen or eighteen years after, there came a stranger to Shattock's house, who, seeing the child, said, *This poor child is bewitched; and you have a neighbour living not far off who is a witch.* He added, *Your neighbour has had a falling out with your wife; and she said in her heart, your wife is a proud woman, and she would bring down her pride in this child.* He then remembered that Bishop had parted from his wife in muttering and menacing terms, a little before the child was taken ill. The abovesaid stranger would needs carry the bewitched boy with him to Bishop's house, on pretence of buying a pot of cider. The woman entertained him in a furious manner; and flew also upon the boy, scratching his face till the blood came, and saying, *Thou rogue, what! dost thou bring this fellow here to plague me?* Now it seems the man had said, before he went, that he would fetch blood of her. Ever after the boy was followed by grievous fits, which the doctors themselves generally ascribed unto witchcraft; and wherein he would be thrown still into fire or water, if he were not constantly looked after; and it was verily believed that Bishop was the cause of it.

10. John Louder testified, that upon some little controversy with Bishop about her fowls, going well to bed, he awaked in the night by moonlight, and clearly saw the likeness of this woman grievously oppressing him; in which miserable condition she held him, unable to help himself, till near day. He told Bishop of this, but she utterly denied it, and threatened him very much. Quickly after this, being at home on a Lord's day, with the doors shut about him, he saw a black pig approach him; at which he going to kick, it vanished away. Immediately after, sitting down, he saw a black thing jump in at the window, and come and stand before him: the body was like that of a monkey, the feet like a cock's, but the face much like a man's. He being so extremely frighted that he could not speak, this monster spoke to him, and said, *I am a messenger sent unto you, for I understand that you are in some trouble of mind, and if you will be ruled by me, you shall want for nothing in this world.* Whereupon he endeavoured to clap his hands upon it; but he could feel no

substance, and it jumped out of the window again; but immediately came in by the porch, though the doors were shut, and said, *You had better take my counsel.* He then struck at it with a stick, but struck only the groundsel, and broke the stick. The arm with which he struck was presently disenabled, and it vanished away. He presently went out at the back door, and spied this Bishop, in her orchard, going towards her house; but he had not power to set one foot forward unto her. Whereupon, returning into the house, he was immediately accosted by the monster he had seen before; which goblin was now going to fly at him; whereat he cried out, *The whole armour of God be between me and you!* so it sprang back, and flew over the apple-tree, shaking many apples off the tree in its flying over. At its leap, it flung dirt with its feet against the stomach of the man; whereon he was then struck dumb, and so continued for three days together. Upon the producing of this testimony, Bishop denied that she knew this deponent. Yet their two orchards joined, and they had often had their little quarrels for some years together.

11. William Stacy testified, that receiving money of this Bishop for work done by him, he was gone but about three rods from her, and, looking for his money, found it unaccountably gone from him. Some time after, Bishop asked

him whether his father would grind her grift for her. He demanded why. She replied, Becaufe folks count me a witch. He anfwered, No queftion but he will grind it for you. Being then gone about fix rods from her, with a fmall load in his cart, fuddenly the off wheel flumpt, and funk down into an hole, upon plain ground, fo that the deponent was forced to get help for the recovering of the wheel. But ftepping back to look for the hole which might give him this difafter, there was none at all to be found. Some time after he was awakened in the night; but it feemed as light as day; and he perfectly faw the fhape of this Bifhop in the room, troubling him; but upon her going out, all was dark again. He charged Bifhop afterwards with it, and fhe denied it not, but was very angry. Quickly after, this deponent having been threatened by Bifhop, as he was in a dark night going to the barn, he was very fuddenly taken or lifted up from the ground, and thrown againft a ftone wall; after that he was again hoifted up, and thrown down a bank, at the end of his houfe. After this, again paffing by this Bifhop, his horfe, with a fmall load, ftriving to draw, all his gears flew to pieces, and the cart fell down; and this deponent going then to lift a bag of corn, of about two bufhels, could not lift it with all his might.

Many other pranks of this Bifhop, this deponent was ready to teftify. He alfo teftified, that he verily believed the faid Bifhop was the inftrument of his daughter Prifcilla's death; of which fufpicion, pregnant reafons were affigned.

12. To crown all, John Bly and William Bly teftified, that, being employed by Bridget Bifhop to help take down the cellar-wall of the old houfe, wherein fhe formerly lived, they did in holes of the faid old wall find feveral poppets made up of rags and hogs' briftles, with headlefs pins in them, the points being outward: whereof fhe could now give no account unto the court, that was reafonable or tolerable.

13. One thing that made againft the prifoner was, her being evidently convicted of grofs lying in the court, feveral times, while fhe was making her plea. But befides this, a jury of women found a preternatural teat upon her body; but upon a fecond fearch, within three or four hours, there was no fuch thing to be feen. There was alfo an account of other people, whom this woman had afflicted; and there might have been many more, if they had been inquired for; but there was no need of them.

14. There was one very ftrange thing more, with which the court was newly entertained. As this woman was, under a guard, paffing by the great and fpacious meeting-houfe of Salem, fhe gave a look towards the houfe; and imme-

diately a dæmon, invifibly entering the meetinghoufe, tore down a part of it; fo that though there were no perfon to be feen there, yet the people, at the noife running in, found a board, which was ftrongly faftened with feveral nails, tranfported unto another quarter of the houfe.

The Indictment of Sufanna Martin.

Effex fs *Anno Regni Regis & Reginæ Willielmi & Mariæ nunc Angeliæ, &c. quarto.*——

The jurors for our fovereign lord and lady the king and queen prefent, that Sufanna Martin, of Amefbury, in the county of Effex, widow, the fecond day of May, in the fourth year of the reign of our fovereign lord and lady William and Mary, by the grace of God, of England, Scotland, France and Ireland, king and queen, defenders of the faith, &c. and divers other days and times, as well before as after, certain deteftable arts, called witchcrafts and forceries, wickedly and felonioufly hath ufed, practifed and exercifed, at and within the townfhip of Salem, in the county of Effex, aforefaid, in, upon and againft one Mary Wolcott, of Salem Village, in the county of Effex, fingle woman; by which faid wicked arts the faid Mary Wolcott, the fecond day of May, in the fourth year aforefaid, and at divers other days and times, as well before as after, was and is tortured, afflicted, pined, confumed, wafted and tormented; as alfo for fundry other acts of witchcraft by faid Sufanna Martin committed and done before and fince that time, againft the peace of our fovereign lord and lady, William and Mary, king and queen of England, their crown and dignity, and againft the form of the ftatute, in that cafe made and provided.

Returned by the grand jury, *Billa vera.*

Witneffes — *Sarah Vibber, Mary Wolcott, Samuel Parris, Elizabeth Hubbard and Mercy Lewis.*

The fecond indictment was for afflicting *Mercy Lewis.* Witneffes — Samuel Parris, Ann

Putman, Sarah Vibber, Elizabeth Hubbard, Mary Wolcott and Mercy Lewis.

The Trial of SUSANNA MARTIN, *June* 29, 1692; *as is printed in Wonders of the Invisible World, from p.* 114 *to p.* 116.

1. Sufanna Martin pleading not guilty to the indictment of witchcraft brought in againft her, there were produced the evidences of many perfons very fenfibly and grievoufly bewitched, who all complained of the prifoner at the bar, as the perfon whom they believed the caufe of their miferies. And now, as well as in the other trials, there was an extraordinary endeavour by witchcrafts, with cruel and frequent fits, to hinder the poor fufferers from giving in their complaints; which the court was forced with much patience to obtain, by much waiting and watching for it.

There was now alfo an account given of what had paffed at her firft examination before the magiftrates; the caft of her eye then ftriking the afflicted people to the ground, whether they faw that caft or no. There were thefe among other paffages between the magiftrates and the examinant:

Magiftrate. Pray, what ails thefe people?
Martin. I don't know.
Mag. But, what do you think ails them?

Martin. I do not defire to fpend my judgment upon it.

Mag. Don't you think they are bewitched?

Martin. No, I do not think they are.

Mag. Tell us your thoughts about them, then.

Martin. No, my thoughts are my own when they are in, but when they are out they are another's. Their mafter——

Mag. Their mafter! Who do you think is their mafter?

Martin. If they be dealing in the black art, you may know as well as I.

Mag. Well, what have you done towards this.

Martin. Nothing at all.

Mag. Why, 'tis you or your appearance.

Martin. I can't help it.

Mag. Is it not your mafter? How comes your appearance to hurt thefe?

Martin. How do I know? He that appeared in the fhape of Samuel, a glorified faint, may appear in any one's fhape.

It was then alfo noted in her, as in others like her, that if the afflicted went to approach her, they were flung down to the ground; and when fhe was afked the reafon of it, fhe faid, I cannot tell; it may be the devil bears me more malice than another.

3. The court accounted themfelves alarmed by thefe things to inquire further into the converfa-

tion of the prisoner, and see what there might occur to render these accusations further credible. Whereupon John Allen, of Salisbury, testified, that he refusing, because of the weakness of his oxen, to cart some staves at the request of this Martin, she was displeased at it, and said, it had been as good that he had, for his oxen should never do him much more service. Whereupon this deponent said, Dost thou threaten me, thou old witch? I'll throw thee into the brook; which to avoid, she flew over the bridge, and escaped. But as he was going home, one of his oxen tired, so that he was forced to unyoke him that he might get him home. He then put his oxen, with many more, upon Salisbury-beach, where cattle used to get flesh. In a few days, all the oxen upon the beach were found by their tracks to have run unto the mouth of Merrimack-river, and not returned; but the next day they were found come ashore upon Plum-island. They that sought them used all imaginable gentleness; but they would still run away with a violence that seemed wholly diabolical, till they came near the mouth of Merrimack-river, when they ran right into the sea, swimming as far as they could be seen. One of them then swam back again, with a swiftness amazing to the beholders, who stood ready to receive him, and help up his tired carcass; but the beast ran furiously up into the island, and from thence through the marshes, up into Newbury-town, and so up into the woods; and after a while was found near Amesbury. So that, of fourteen good oxen, there was only this saved: the rest were all cast up, some in one place, and some in another, drowned.

4. John Atkinson testified, that he exchanged a cow with a son of Susanna Martin, whereat she muttered, and was unwilling he should have it. Going to receive this cow, though he hamstringed her, and haltered her, she of a tame creature grew so mad, that they could scarce get her along. She broke all the ropes that were fastened unto her; and though she was tied fast unto a tree, yet she made her escape, and gave them such further trouble, as they could ascribe to no cause but witchcraft.

5. Bernard Peache testified, that, being in bed, on a Lord's-day night, he heard a scrabbling at the window, whereat he then saw Susanna Martin come in, and jump down upon the floor. She took hold of this deponent's feet, and, drawing his body up into an heap, she lay upon him near two hours; in all which time he could neither speak nor stir. At length, when he could begin to move, he laid hold on her hand, and pulling it up to his mouth, he bit three of her fingers, as he judged, to the bone; whereupon

she went from the chamber down the stairs, out at the door. This deponent thereupon called unto the people of the house to advise them of what passed; and he himself followed her. The people saw her not; but there being a bucket at the left hand of the door, there was a drop of blood on it, and several more drops of blood upon the snow, newly fallen abroad. There was likewise the print of her two feet, just without the threshold; but no more sign of any footing further off.

At another time this deponent was desired by the prisoner to come to husking of corn, at her house; and she said, *If he did not come, it were better that he did.* He went not; but the night following, Susanna Martin, as he judged, and another, came towards him. One of them said, *Here he is;* but he, having a quarterstaff, made a blow at them: the roof of the barn broke his blow; but, following them to the window, he made another blow at them, and struck them down; yet they got up, and got out, and he saw no more of them.

About this time, there was a rumour about the town, that Martin had a broken head; but the deponent could say nothing to that.

The said Peache also testified, the bewitching of cattle to death, upon Martin's discontents.

6. Robert Downer testified, that this prisoner

being some years ago prosecuted at court for a witch, he then said unto her, *he believed she was a witch.* Whereat she being dissatisfied, said, *that some she-devil would shortly fetch him away;* which words were heard by others, as well as himself. The night following, as he lay in his bed, there came in at the window, the likeness of a cat, which flew upon him, and took fast hold of his throat, lay on him a considerable while, and almost killed him; at length he remembered what Susanna Martin had threatened the day before, and with much striving he cried out, *Avoid, thou she-devil; in the name of God the Father, the Son, and the Holy Ghost, avoid:* whereupon it left him, leaped on the floor, and flew out at the window.

And there also came in several testimonies, that, before ever Downer spoke a word of this accident, Susanna Martin and her family had related how this Downer had been handled.

7. John Kembal testified, that Susanna Martin, upon a causeless disgust, had threatened him about a certain cow of his, that she should never do him any more good, and it came to pass accordingly; for soon after the cow was found stark dead on the dry ground, without any distemper to be discerned upon her; upon which he was followed with a strange death upon more of his cattle; whereof he lost in one spring, to

the value of 30 *l.* But the said John Kembal had a further testimony to give in against the prisoner, which was truly admirable. Being desirous to furnish himself with a dog, he applied himself to buy one of this Martin, who had a bitch with whelps in her house; but she not letting him have his choice, he said he would supply himself then at one Blezdel's. Having marked a puppy which he liked at Blezdel's, he met George Martin, the husband of the prisoner, going by, who asked whether he would not have one of his wife's puppies; and he answered, no. The same day one Edmund Eliot, being at Martin's house, heard George Martin relate where this Kembal had been, and what he had said; whereupon Susanna Martin replied, *If I live I'll give him puppies enough.* Within a few days after this, Kembal coming out of the woods, there arose a little black cloud in the N. W. and Kembal immediately felt a force upon him, which made him not able to avoid running upon the stumps of trees that were before him, although he had a broad, plain cart-way before him; but though he had his axe on his shoulder to endanger him in his falls, he could not forbear going out of his way to tumble over them. When he came below the meeting-house, there appeared to him a little thing like a puppy, of a darkish colour, and it shot backwards and forwards between his legs. He had the courage to use all possible endeavours to cut it with his axe, but he could not hit it; the puppy gave a jump from him, and went, as to him it seemed, into the ground. Going a little further, there appeared unto him a black puppy, somewhat bigger than the first, but as black as a coal. Its motions were quicker than those of his axe. It flew at his belly, and at his throat, so over his shoulders one way, and then over his shoulders another way. His heart now began to fail him, and he thought the dog would have tore his throat out; but he recovered himself, and called upon God in his distress, and naming the name of Jesus Christ, it vanished away at once. The deponent spoke not one word of these accidents, for fear of affrighting his wife. But the next morning, Edmund Eliot going into Martin's house, this woman asked him where Kembal was. He replied, At home, a-bed, for ought he knew. She returned, They say he was frighted last night. Eliot asked, With what? She answered, With puppies. Eliot asked where she heard of it, for he had heard nothing of it. She rejoined, About the town; although Kembal had mentioned the matter to no creature living.

8. William Brown testified, that Heaven having blessed him with a most pious and prudent wife, this wife of his one day met with Susanna

Martin; but when she approached just unto her, Martin vanished out of sight, and left her extremely affrighted. After which time the said Martin often appeared unto her, giving her no little trouble; and when she did come, she was visited with birds, that sorely pecked and pricked her; and sometimes a bunch like a pullet's egg would rise on her throat, ready to choke her, till she cried out, *Witch, you shan't choke me!* While this good woman was in this extremity, the church appointed a day of prayer on her behalf; whereupon the trouble ceased; she saw not Martin as formerly; and the church, instead of their fast, gave thanks for her deliverance. But a considerable while after, she being summoned to give in some evidence at the court against this Martin, quickly this Martin came behind her, while she was milking her cow, and said unto her, *For thy defaming me at court, I'll make thee the miserablest creature in the world.* Soon after which, she fell into a strange kind of distemper, and became horribly frantic, and uncapable of any reasonable action; the physicians declaring that her distemper was preternatural, and that some devil had certainly bewitched her; and in that condition she now remained.

9. Sarah Atkinson testified, that Susanna Martin came from Amesbury, to their house at Newbury, in an extraordinary season, when it was not

fit for any one to travel. She came (as she said to Atkinson) all that long way on foot. She bragged and showed how dry she was; nor could it be perceived that so much as the soles of her shoes were wet. Atkinson was amazed at it, and professed that she should herself have been wet up to the knees, if she had then come so far; but Martin replied, *she scorned to be drabbled*. It was noted that this testimony, upon her trial, cast her into a very singular confusion.

10. John Pressy testified, that being one evening very unaccountably bewildered near a field of Martin, and several times as one under an enchantment, returning to the place he had left, at length he saw a marvellous light, about the bigness of an half bushel, near two rods out of the way. He went and struck at it with a stick, and laid it on with all his might. He gave it near forty blows, and felt it a palpable substance. But, going from it, his heels were struck up, and he was laid with his back on the ground; sliding, as he thought, into a pit; from whence he recovered, by taking hold on a bush; although afterwards he could find no such pit in the place. Having after his recovery gone five or six rods, he saw Susanna Martin standing on his left hand, as the light had done before; but they changed no words with one another. He could scarce find his house in his return; but at length he

got home, extremely affrighted. The next day it was upon inquiry underftood, that Martin was in a miferable condition, by pains and hurts that were upon her.

It was further teftified by this deponent, that after he had given in fome evidence againft Sufanna Martin many years ago, fhe gave him foul words about it, and faid, *he fhould never profper; more particularly, that he fhould never have more than two cows: that though he were ever fo likely to have more, yet he fhould never have them;* and that, from that very day to this, namely for twenty years together, he could never exceed that number, but fome ftrange thing or other ftill prevented his having any more.

11. Jarvis Ring teftified, that about feven years ago he was oftentimes grievoufly oppreffed in the night, but faw not who troubled him, until at length he, lying perfectly awake, plainly faw Sufanna Martin approach him: fhe came to him, and forcibly bit him by the finger; fo that the print of the bite is now, fo long after, to be feen upon him.

12. But, befides all thefe evidences, there was a moft wonderful account of one Jofeph Ring produced on this occafion. This man has been ftrangely carried about, by dæmons, from one witch-meeting to another, for near two years together; and for one quarter of this time they

made him and kept him dumb, though he is now again able to speak. There was one T. H. who, having, as 'tis judged, a design of engaging this Joseph Ring in a snare of devilism, contrived a wile to bring this Ring two shillings in debt unto him. Afterwards this poor man would be visited with unknown shapes, and this T. H. sometimes among them : which would force him away with them, unto unknown places, where he saw meetings, feasting, dancings; and after his return, wherein they hurried him along through the air, he gave demonstrations to the neighbours, that he had been so transported. When he was brought unto these hellish meetings, one of the first things they still did unto him was, to give him a knock on the back, whereupon he was ever, as if bound with chains, uncapable of stirring out of the place, till they should release him. He related, that there often came to him a man, who presented him a book, whereto he would have him set his hand; promising him that he should then have even what he would; and presenting him with all the delectable things, persons and places that he could imagine; but he refusing to subscribe, the business would end with dreadful shapes, noises and screeches, which almost scared him out of his wits. Once, with a book, there was a pen offered him, and an inkhorn, with liquor in it, that seemed like blood; but he never touched it.

This man did now affirm, that he faw the prifoner at feveral of thefe hellifh rendezvous.

Note. This woman was one of the moft impudent, fcurrilous, wicked creatures, in the world: and fhe now, throughout her whole trial, difcovered herfelf to be fuch an one. Yet when fhe was afked what fhe had to fay for herfelf, her chief plea was, that fhe had led a moft virtuous and holy life.

The Indictment of Elizabeth How.

Effex fs. *Anno Regni Regis & Reginæ Willielmi & Mariæ, nunc Angliæ, &c. quarto.*——

The jurors for our fovereign lord and lady the king and queen prefent, that Elizabeth How, wife of James How, of Ipfwich, in the county of Effex, the thirty-firft day of May, in the fourth year of the reign of our fovereign lord and lady William and Mary, by the grace of God, of England, Scotland, France and Ireland, king and queen, defenders of the faith, &c. and divers other days and times, as well before as after, certain deteftable arts, called witchcrafts and forceries, wickedly and felonioufly hath ufed, practifed and exercifed, at and within the townfhip of Salem, in the county of Effex, aforefaid, in, upon and againft one Mary Wolcott, of Salem Village, in the county aforefaid, fingle woman ; by which faid wicked arts the faid Mary Wolcott, the faid thirty-firft day of May, in the fourth year abovefaid, and divers other days and times, as well before as after, was and is tortured, afflicted, pined, confumed, wafted and tormented; and alfo for fundry other acts of witchcrafts, by faid Elizabeth How committed and done before and fince that time, againft the peace of our fovereign lord and lady, the king and queen, and againft the form of the ftatute in that cafe made and provided.

Witneffes— *Mary Wolcott, Ann Putman, Abigail Williams, Samuel Pearly and his wife Ruth, Jofeph Andrews, and wife Sarah, John Sherrin, Jofeph Safford, Francis Lane Lydia Fofter, Ifaac Cummins,* junior.

There was alfo a fecond indictment for afflicting *Mercy Lewis.* Witneffes — Mercy Lewis,
Mary Wolcott, Ann Putman, Samuel Pearly
and wife, Jofeph Andrews and wife, John Sherrin, Jofeph Safford, Francis Lane, Lydia Fofter.

The Trial of Elizabeth How, *June* 30, 1692;
*as is printed in Wonders of the Invifible World,
from p.* 126 *to p.* 132, *inclufively.*

1. Elizabeth How, pleading not guilty to the
indictment of witchcrafts then charged upon
her, the court, according to the ufual proceeding
of the courts in England in fuch cafes, began
with hearing the depofition of feveral afflicted
people, who were grievoufly tormented by fenfible and evident witchcrafts, and all complained
of the prifoner as the caufe of their trouble. It
was alfo found that the fufferers were not able to
bear her look; as likewife that in their greateft
fwoons they diftinguifhed her touch from other
people's, being thereby raifed out of them. And
there was other teftimony of people, to whom
the fhape of this How gave trouble nine or ten
years ago.

2. It has been a moft ufual thing for the bewitched perfons, at the fame time that the fpectres,
reprefenting the witches troubled them, to be
vifited with apparitions of ghofts, pretending to
have been murdered by the witches then repre-

fented. And fometimes the confeffions of the witches afterwards acknowledged thofe very murders, which thefe apparitions charged upon them, although they had never heard what information had been given by the fufferers. There were fuch apparitions of ghofts teftified by fome of the prefent fufferers, and the ghofts affirmed that this How had murdered them: which things were feared, but not proved.

3. This How had made fome attempts of joining to the church at Ipfwich, feveral years ago; but fhe was denied an admiffion into that holy fociety, partly through a fufpicion of witchcraft, then urged againft her. And there now came in teftimony of preternatural mifchiefs prefently befalling fome that had been inftrumental to debar her from the communion whereupon fhe was intruding.

4. There was a particular depofition of Jofeph Safford, that his wife had conceived an extreme averfion to this How, on the reports of her witchcrafts; but How one day taking her by the hand, and faying, *I believe you are not ignorant of the great fcandal that I lie under by an evil report raifed upon me*, fhe immediately, unreafonably, and unperfuadably, even like one enchanted, began to take this woman's part. How being foon after propounded, as defiring an admiffion to the table of the Lord, fome of

the pious brethren were unsatisfied about her. The elders appointed a meeting, to hear matters objected against her; and no arguments in the world could hinder this goodwife Safford from going to the lecture. She did indeed promise, with much ado, that she would not go to the church-meeting; yet she could not refrain going thither also. How's affairs were so canvassed, that she came off rather guilty than cleared; nevertheless goodwife Safford could not forbear taking her by the hand, and saying, *Though you are condemned before men, you are justified before God.* She was quickly taken in a very strange manner; frantic, raving, raging, and crying out, *Goody How must come into the church; she is a precious saint; and though she be condemned before men, she is justified before God.* So she continued for the space of two or three hours, and then fell into a trance. But coming to herself, she cried out, *Ha! I was mistaken!* afterwards again repeated, *Ha! I was mistaken!* Being asked by a stander-by wherein, she replied, *I thought goody How had been a precious saint of God, but now I see she is a witch: she has bewitched me and my child, and we shall never be well till there be testimony for her, that she may be taken into the church.*

And How said, afterwards, *That she was very sorry to see Safford at the church-meeting mentioned.* Safford, after this, *declared herself to be afflicted* by the shape of How, and that from that shape she endured many miseries.

5. John How, brother to the husband of the prisoner, testified, that he refusing to accompany the prisoner unto her examination as was by her desired, immediately some of his cattle were bewitched to death, leaping three or four feet high, turning about, squeaking, falling and dying at once; and going to cut off an ear, for an use that might as well perhaps have been omitted, the hand wherein he held his knife was taken very numb; and so it remained, and full of pain, for several days, being not well at this very time. And he suspected this prisoner for the author of it.

6. Nehemiah Abbot testified, that unusual and mischievous accidents would befall his cattle, whenever he had any difference with this prisoner. Once particularly she wished his ox choked; and within a little while that ox was choked with a turnip in his throat. At another time, refusing to lend his horse at the request of her daughter, the horse was in a preternatural manner abused. And several other odd things of that kind were testified.

7. There came in testimony, that one goodwife Sherwin, upon some difference with How, was bewitched, and that she died charging this How of having an hand in her death; and that other people had their barrels of drink unaccount-

ably mifchiefed, fpoilt and fpilt, upon their difpleafing her.

The things in themfelves were trivial; but there being fuch a courfe of them, it made them the more to be confidered. Among others, Martha Wood gave her teftimony, that a little after her father had been employed in gathering an account of this How's converfation, they once and again loft great quantities of drink out of their veffels, in fuch a manner as they could afcribe to nothing but witchcraft; as alfo that How giving her fome apples, when fhe had eaten of them fhe was taken with a very ftrange kind of a maze, infomuch that fhe knew not what fhe faid or did.

8. There was likewife a clufter of depofitions, that one Ifaac Cummins refufing to lend his mare to the hufband of this How, the mare was within a day or two taken in a ftrange condition. The beaft feemed much abufed, being bruifed, as if fhe had been running over the rocks, and marked where the bridle went, as if burnt with a red hot bridle. Moreover, one ufing a pipe of tobacco for the cure of the beaft, a blue flame iffued out of her, took hold of her hair, and not only fpread and burnt on her, but it alfo flew upwards towards the roof of the barn, and had like to have fet the barn on fire. And the mare died very fuddenly.

9. Timothy Pearly and his wife teftified, not only that unaccountable mifchiefs befel their cattle upon their having differences with this prifoner, but alfo that they had a daughter deftroyed by witchcrafts; which daughter ftill charged How as the caufe of her affliction; and it was noted that fhe would be ftruck down whenever How was fpoken of. She was often endeavoured to be thrown into the fire, and into the water, in her ftrange fits; though her father had corrected her for charging How with bewitching her, yet (as was teftified by others alfo) fhe faid fhe was fure of it, and muft die ftanding to it. Accordingly fhe charged How to the very death; and faid, *Though How could afflict and torment her body, yet fhe could not hurt her foul, and that the truth of this matter would appear when fhe fhould be dead and gone.*

10. Francis Lane teftified, that being hired by the hufband of this How to get him a parcel of pofts and rails, this Lane hired John Pearly to affift him. This prifoner then told Lane, that fhe believed the pofts and rails would not do, becaufe John Pearly helped him; but that if he had gotten them alone without John Pearly's help, they might have done well enough. When James How came to receive his pofts and rails of Lane, How taking them up by the ends, they, though good and found, yet unaccountably broke

off, so that Lane was forced to get thirty or forty more. And this prisoner being informed of it, she said, *she told him so before, because Pearly helped about them.*

11. Afterwards there came in the confessions of several other (penitent) witches, which affirmed this How to be one of those who with them had been baptised by the devil in the river, at Newbury-falls; before which, he made them there kneel down by the brink of the river, and worship him.

The Indictment of Martha Carrier.

Essex ss.   *Anno Regni Regis & Reginæ Willielmi & Mariæ, nunc Angliæ, &c. quarto.*——

The jurors for our sovereign lord and lady the king and queen present, that Martha Carrier, wife of Thomas Carrier, of Andover, in the county of Essex, husbandman, the thirty-first day of May, in the fourth year of the reign of our sovereign lord and lady William and Mary, by the grace of God, of England, Scotland, France and Ireland, king and queen, defenders of the faith, &c. and divers other days and times, as well before as after, certain detestable arts, called witchcrafts and sorceries, wickedly and feloniously hath used, practised and exercised, at and within the township of Salem, in the county of Essex, aforesaid, in, upon and against one Mary Wolcott, of Salem Village, in the county of Essex, single woman; by which said wicked arts the said Mary Wolcott, the thirty-first day of May, in the fourth year aforesaid, and at divers other days and times, as well before as after, was and is tortured, afflicted, pined, consumed, wasted and tormented; against the peace of our sovereign lord and lady, William and Mary, king and queen of England, their crown and dignity, and against the form of the statute, in that case made and provided.

Witnesses — *Mary Wolcott, Elizabeth Hubbard, Ann Putman.*

There was also a second indictment for afflicting *Elizabeth Hubbard*, by witchcraft. Witnesses — Elizabeth Hubbard, Mary Wolcott, Ann Putman, Mary Warren.

The Trial of Martha Carrier, *August* 2, 1692; *as may be seen in Wonders of the Invisible World, from p.* 132, *to p.* 138.

1. Martha Carrier was indicted for the bewitching of certain persons, according to the form usual in such cases. Pleading not guilty to her indictment, there were first brought in a considerable number of the bewitched persons; who not only made the court sensible of an horrid witchcraft committed upon them, but also deposed, that it was Martha Carrier, or her shape, that grievously tormented them, by biting, pricking, pinching and choking them. It was further deposed, that while this Carrier was on her examination before the magistrates, the poor people were so tortured, that every one expected their death upon the very spot; but that upon the binding of Carrier they were eased. Moreover the looks of Carrier then laid the afflicted people for dead; and her touch, if her eyes at the same time were off them, raised them again. Which things were also now seen upon her trial. And it was testified, that upon the mention of some having their necks twisted almost round by

the shape of this Carrier, she replied, *Its no matter, though their necks had been twisted quite off.*

2. Before the trial of this prisoner, several of her own children had frankly and fully confessed, not only that they were witches themselves, but that their mother had made them so. This confession they made with great shows of repentance, and with much demonstration of truth. They related place, time and occasion; they gave an account of journeys, meetings and mischiefs by them performed, and were very credible in what they said. Nevertheless, this evidence was not produced against the prisoner at the bar, in as much as there was other evidence enough to proceed upon.

3. Benjamin Abbot gave in his testimony, that, last March was a twelve-month, this Carrier was very angry with him, upon laying out some land near her husband's. Her expressions in this anger were, that she would stick as close to Abbot as the bark stuck to the tree; and that he should repent of it before seven years came to an end, so as doctor Prescot should never cure him. These words were heard by others besides Abbot himself, who also heard her say, she would hold his nose as close to the grindstone as ever it was held since his name was Abbot. Presently after this he was taken with a swelling in his foot, and then with a pain in his side, and ex-

ceedingly tormented. It bred a fore, which was lanced by Dr. Prefcot, and feveral gallons of corruption ran out of it. For fix weeks it continued very bad; and then another fore bred in his groin, which was alfo lanced by Dr. Prefcot. Another fore bred in his groin, which was likewife cut, and put him to very great mifery. He was brought to death's door, and fo remained until Carrier was taken and carried away by the conftable; from which very day he began to mend, and fo grew better every day, and is well ever fince.

Sarah Abbot alfo, his wife, teftified, that her hufband was not only all this while afflicted in his body, but alfo that ftrange, extraordinary and unaccountable calamities befel his cattle; their death being fuch as they could guefs no natural reafon for.

4. Allin Toothaker teftified, that Richard, the fon of Martha Carrier, having fome difference with him, pulled him down by the hair of the head; when he rofe again, he was going to ftrike at Richard Carrier, but fell down flat on his back to the ground, and had not power to ftir hand or foot, until he told Carrier he yielded; and then he faw the fhape of Martha Carrier go off his breaft.

This Toothaker had received a wound in the wars; and he now teftified, that Martha Carrier told him, he fhould never be cured. Juft before the apprehending of Carrier, he could thruft a knitting-needle into his wound four inches deep; but prefently after her being feized, he was thoroughly healed.

He further teftified, that when Carrier and he fometimes were at variance, fhe would clap her hands at him, and fay, *he fhould get nothing by it*. Whereupon he feveral times loft his cattle by ftrange deaths, whereof no natural caufes could be given.

5. John Roger alfo teftified, that, upon the threatening words of this malicious Carrier, his cattle would be ftrangely bewitched; as was more particularly then defcribed.

6. Samuel Prefton teftified, that about two years ago, having fome difference with Martha Carrier, he loft a cow in a ftrange, preternatural, unufual manner; and about a month after this, the faid Carrier having again fome difference with him, fhe told him he had lately loft a cow, and it fhould not be long before he loft another; which accordingly came to pafs; for he had a thriving and well-kept cow, which without any known caufe quickly fell down and died.

7. Phebe Chandler teftified, that about a fortnight before the apprehenfion of Martha Carrier, on a Lord's-day, while the pfalm was finging in the church, this Carrier then took her by the

shoulder, and shaking her, asked her where she lived: she made her no answer, although, as Carrier lived next door to her father's house, she could not in reason but know who she was. Quickly after this, as she was at several times crossing the fields, she heard a voice that she took to be Martha Carrier's, and it seemed as if it were over her head. The voice told her, *she should within two or three days be poisoned:* accordingly, within such a little time, one half of her right hand became greatly swollen and very painful, as also part of her face; whereof she can give no account how it came. It continued very bad for some days; and several times since she has had a great pain in her breast; and been so seized on her legs, that she has hardly been able to go. She added, that lately going well to the house of God, Richard, the son of Martha Carrier, looked very earnestly upon her, and immediately her hand, which had formerly been poisoned, as is abovesaid, began to pain her greatly, and she had a strange burning at her stomach; but was then struck deaf, so that she could not hear any of the prayer, or singing, till the two or three last words of the psalm.

8. One Foster, who confessed her own share in the witchcraft, for which the prisoner stood indicted, affirmed, that she had seen the prisoner at some of their witch-meetings, and that it was

this Carrier who perfuaded her to be a witch. She confeffed that the devil carried them on a pole to a witch-meeting; but the pole broke, and fhe hanging about Carrier's neck, they both fell down, and fhe then received an hurt by the fall, whereof fhe was not at this very time recovered.

9. One Lacy, who likewife confeffed her fhare in this witchcraft, now teftified, that fhe and the prifoner were once bodily prefent at a witch-meeting in Salem Village, and that fhe knew the prifoner to be a witch, and to have been at a diabolical facrament, and that the prifoner was the undoing of her and her children, by enticing them into the fnare of the devil.

10. Another Lacy, who alfo confeffed her fhare in this witchcraft, now teftified, that the prifoner was at the witch-meeting in Salem Village, where they had bread and wine adminiftered to them.

11. In the time of this prifoner's trial, one Sufanna Shelden, in open court, had her hands unaccountably tied together with a wheel-band fo faft that without cutting it could not be loofened. It was done by a fpectre; and the fufferer affirmed it was the prifoner's.

Memorandum. This *rampant hag*, Martha Carrier, was the perfon of whom the confeffions of the witches, and of her own children among the reſt, agreed that the devil had promiſed her ſhe ſhould be queen of hell.

Thus far the account given in *Wonders of the Inviſible World;* in which (ſetting aſide ſuch words as theſe, in the trial of G. B. viz. " They, i. e. the witneſſes, were enough to fix the character of a witch upon him"— in the trial of Biſhop, theſe words, " But there was no need of them," i. e. of further teſtimony — in the trial of How, where it is ſaid, " And there came in teſtimony of preternatural miſchiefs preſently befalling ſome that had been inſtrumental to debar her from the communion, whereupon ſhe was intruding,") Martin is called one of the moſt impudent, ſcurrilous, wicked creatures in the world; in his account of Martha Carrier, he is pleaſed to call her a *rampant hag,* &c.

Theſe expreſſions, as they manifeſt that he wrote more like an advocate than an hiſtorian, ſo alſo that thoſe that were his employers were not miſtaken in their choice of him for that work, however he may have miſſed it in other things: as, in his owning (in the trial of G. B.) that the *teſtimony of the bewitched, and confeſſors, was not enough againſt t'e accuſed;* for it is known that not only in New-England ſuch evidence has been taken for ſufficient, but alſo in England, as himself there owns, and will also hold true of Scotland, &c. they having proceeded upon such evidence, to the taking away of the lives of many. To assert that this is not enough, is to tell the world that such executions were but so many bloody murders; which surely was not his intent to say.

His telling that the court began to think that Burroughs stept aside to put on invisibility, is a rendering them so mean philosophers, and such weak christians, as to be fit to be imposed upon by any silly pretender.

His calling the evidence against How trivial, and others against Burroughs he accounts no part of his conviction, and that of lifting a gun with one finger, its being not made use of as evidence, renders the whole but the more perplext. (Not to mention the many mistakes therein contained.)

Yet all this (and more that might have been hinted at) does not hinder, but that his account of the manner of trials of those for witchcraft is as faithfully related as any trials of that kind, that were ever yet made public; and it may also be reasonably thought that there was as careful a scrutiny, and as unquestioned evidences improved, as had been formerly used in the trials of others, for such crimes, in other places. Though indeed a second part might be very useful, to set forth which was the evidence convictive in these trials; for it is not supposed that romantic or ridiculous stories should have any influence; such as biting a spectre's finger so that the blood flowed out; or such as Shattock's story of twelve years standing, which yet was presently eighteen years or more, and yet a man of so excellent memory as to be able to recall a small difference his wife had with another woman when eighteen years were past.

As it is not to be supposed that such as these could influence any judge or jury, so not unkindness to relations, or God's having given to one man more strength than to some others; the oversetting of carts, or the death of cattle; nor yet excrescences (called teats) nor little bits of rags tied together (called poppets;) much less any person's illness, or having their clothes rent, when a spectre has been well hanged; much less the burning the mare's fart, mentioned in the trial of How.

None of these being in the least capable of proving the indictment, the supposed criminals were indicted for afflicting, &c. such and such particular persons by witchcraft, to which none of these evidences have one word to say; and the afflicted and confessors being declared not enough, the matter needs yet further explaining.

But to proceed. The general court having

set and enacted laws, particularly one against witchcraft, assigning the penalty of death to any that shall feed, reward or employ, &c. evil spirits, though it has not yet been explained what is intended thereby, or what it is to feed, reward or employ devils, &c. yet some of the legislators have given this, instead of an explanation, that they had therein but copied the law of another country.

January 3. By virtue of an act of the general court, the first superior court was held at Salem, for the county of Essex; the judges appointed were mr. William Stoughton (the lieutenant governor), Thomas Danforth, John Richards, Wait Winthrop, and Samuel Sewall, esquires; where *ignoramus* was found upon the several bills of indictment against thirty, and *billa vera* against twenty-six more; of all these, three only were found guilty by the jury upon trial, two of which were (as appears by their behaviour) the most senseless and ignorant creatures that could be found; besides which, it does not appear what came in against those more than against the rest that were acquitted.

The third was the wife of Wardwell, who was one of the twenty executed, and it seems they had both confessed themselves guilty; but he, retracting his said confession, was tried and executed. It is supposed that this woman, fearing her husband's fate, was not so stiff in her denials of her former confession, such as it was. These three received sentence of death.

At these trials some of the jury made inquiry of the court, what account they ought to make of the spectre evidence; and received for answer, *As much as of chips in wort.*

January 31, 1692--3. The superior court began at Charlestown, for the county of Middlesex, mr. Stoughton, mr. Danforth, mr. Winthrop, and mr. Sewall, judges; where several had *ignoramus* returned upon their bills of indictment, and *billa vera* upon others.

In the time the court sat, word was brought in, that a reprieve was sent to Salem, and had prevented the execution of seven of those that were there condemned; which so moved the chief judge, that he said to this effect, *We were in a way to have cleared the land of these, &c. Who it is obstructs the course of justice, I know not; the Lord be merciful to the country;* and so went off the bench, and came no more that court.

The most remarkable of the trials, was of Sarah Daston. She was a woman of about seventy or eighty years of age. To usher her in to her trial, a report went before, that if there were a witch in the world she was one, as having been so accounted of for twenty or thirty years; which drew many people from Boston, &c. to hear her trial. There were a multitude of witnesses produced against her; but what testimony they gave in seemed wholly foreign, as of accidents, illness, &c. befalling them, or theirs, after some quarrel; what these testified was much of it of actions said to be done twenty years before that time. The spectre evidence was not made use of in these trials, so that the jury soon brought her in not guilty. Her daughter and granddaughter, and the rest that were then tried, were also acquitted. After she was cleared, judge Danforth admonished her in these words, *Woman, woman, repent; there are shrewd things come in against you.* She was remanded to prison for her fees, and there in a short time expired. One of Boston, that had been at the trial of Daston, being the same evening in company with one of the judges in a public place, acquainted him that some, that had been both at the trials at Salem and at this at Charlestown, had asserted, *That there was more evidence against the said Daston than against any at Salem;* to which the said judge conceded, saying, *that it was so.* It was replied by that person, *That he dare give it under his hand, that there was not enough come in against her to bear a just reproof.*

April 25, 1693. The first superior court was held at Boston, for the county of Suffolk; the judges were the lieutenant Governor, mr. Danforth, mr. Richards, and mr. Sewall, efquires; where (befides the acquitting mr. John Aldin by proclamation) the moft remarkable was, what related to Mary Watkins, who had been a fervant, and lived about feven miles from Bofton, having formerly accufed her miftrefs of witchcraft, and was fuppofed to be diftracted; fhe was threatened, if fhe perfifted in fuch accufations, to be punifhed. This, with the neceffary care to recover her health, had that good effect, that fhe not only had her health reftored, but alfo wholly acquitted her miftrefs of any fuch crimes, and continued in health till the return of the year, and then again falling into melancholy humours, fhe was found ftrangling herfelf; her life being hereby prolonged, fhe immediately accufed herfelf of being a witch; was carried before a magiftrate, and committed. At this court a bill of indictment was brought to the grand jury againft her, and her confeffion upon her examination given in as evidence; but thefe, not wholly fatisfied herewith, fent for her, who gave fuch account of herfelf, that they, (after they had returned into the court to afk fome queftions) twelve of them agreed to find *ignoramus*, but the court was pleafed to fend them out again, who again at coming in returned it as before. She was continued for fome time in prifon, &c. and at length was fold to Virginia. About this time the prifoners in all the prifons were releafed.

To omit here the mentioning of several wenches in Boston, &c. who pretended to be afflicted, and accused several, the ministers often visiting them, and praying with them, concerning whose affliction narratives are in being, in manuscript; not only these, but the generality of those accusers, may have since convinced the ministers, by their vicious courses, that they might err in extending too much charity to them.

The conclusion of the whole in the Massachusetts colony was, sir William Phips, governor, being called home, before he went he pardoned such as had been condemned, for which they gave about thirty shillings each to the king's attorney.

In August, 1697, the superior court sat at Hartford, in the colony of Connecticut, where one mistress Benom was tried for witchcraft. She had been accused by some children that pretended to the spectral sight; they searched her several times for teats; they tried the experiment of casting her into the water, and after this she was excommunicated by the minister of Wallinsford. Upon her trial nothing material appeared against her, save spectre evidence. She was acquitted, as also her daughter, a girl of twelve or thirteen years old, who had been likewise accused; but upon renewed complaints against them, they both flew into New-York government.

Before this, the government iffued forth the following proclamation:

By the honourable the lieutenant governor, council and affembly of his majefty's province of the Maffachufetts-bay, in general court affembled.

Whereas, the anger of God is not yet turned away, but his hand is ftill ftretched out againft his people in manifold judgments, particularly in drawing out to fuch a length the troubles of Europe, by a perplexing war; and more efpecially refpecting ourfelves in this province, in that God is pleafed ftill to go on in diminifhing our fubftance, cutting fhort our harveft, blafting our moft promifing undertakings more ways than one, unfettling us, and by his more immediate hand fnatching away many out of our embraces by fudden and violent deaths, even at this time when the fword is devouring fo many both at home and abroad, and that after many days of public and folemn addreffing him: and although, confidering the many fins prevailing in the midft of us, we cannot but wonder at the patience and mercy moderating thefe rebukes, yet we cannot but alfo fear that there is fomething ftill wanting to accompany our fupplications; and doubtlefs there are fome particular fins, which God is angry with our Ifrael for, that have not been duly feen and refented by us, about which God expects to be sought, if ever he turn again our captivity:

Wherefore it is commanded and appointed, that Thursday, the fourteenth of January next, be observed as a day of prayer, with fasting, throughout this province; strictly forbidding all servile labour thereon; that so all God's people may offer up fervent supplications unto him, for the preservation and prosperity of his majesty's royal person and government, and success to attend his affairs both at home and abroad; that all iniquity may be put away, which hath stirred God's holy jealousy against this land; that he would shew us what we know not, and help us wherein we have done amiss to do so no more; and especially that whatever mistakes on either hand have been fallen into, either by the body of this people, or any orders of men, referring to the late tragedy, raised among us by satan and his instruments, through the awful judgment of God, he would humble us therefor, and pardon all the errors of his servants and people, that desire to love his name; that he would remove the rod of the wicked from off the lot of the righteous; that he would bring in the American heathen, and cause them to hear and obey his voice.

Given at Boston, December 17, 1696, *in the eighth year of his Majesty's reign.*

Isaac Addington, *Secretary.*

OF FACT, &c. 339

Upon the day of the faft, in the full affembly at the fouth meeting-houfe in Bofton, one of the honourable judges, who had fat, in judicature in Salem, delivered in a paper, and while it was in reading, ftood up ; but the copy being not to be obtained at prefent, it can only be reported by memory to this effect, viz. It was to defire the prayers of God's people for him and his; and that God having vifited his family, &c. he was apprehenfive that he might have fallen into fome errors in the matters at Salem, and pray that the guilt of fuch mifcarriages may not be imputed either to the country in general, or to him or his family in particular.

Some, that had been of feveral juries, have given forth a paper, figned with their own hands, in thefe words :

"We, whofe names are under written, being in the year 1692 called to ferve as jurors in court at Salem on trial of many, who were by fome fufpected guilty of doing acts of witchcraft upon the bodies of fundry perfons :

"We confefs that we ourfelves were not capable to underftand, nor able to withftand, the myfterious delufions of the powers of darknefs, and prince of the air ; but were, for want of knowledge in ourfelves, and better information from others, prevailed with to take up with fuch evidence against the accused, as, on further consideration and better information, we justly fear was insufficient for the touching the lives of any, (*Deut.* xvii. 6) whereby we fear we have been instrumental, with others, though ignorantly and unwittingly, to bring upon ourselves and this people of the Lord the guilt of innocent blood; which sin the Lord saith, in scripture, he would not pardon, (2 *Kings*, xxiv. 4) that is, we suppose, in regard of his temporal judgments. We do therefore hereby signify to all in general (and to the surviving sufferers in special) our deep sense of, and sorrow for, our errors, in acting on such evidence to the condemning of any person; and do hereby declare, that we justly fear that we were sadly deluded and mistaken; for which we are much disquieted and distressed in our minds; and do therefore humbly beg forgiveness, first of God for Christ's sake, for this our error; and pray that God would not impute the guilt of it to ourselves, nor others; and we also pray that we may be considered candidly, and aright, by the living sufferers, as being then under the power of a strong and general delusion, utterly unacquainted with, and not experienced in, matters of that nature.

"We do heartily ask forgiveness of you all, whom we have justly offended; and do declare, according to our present minds, we would none of us do such things again on such grounds for the whole world; praying you to accept of this in way of satisfaction for our offence, and that you would bless the inheritance of the Lord, that he may be entreated for the land.

Foreman, *Thomas Fisk*,
William Fisk,
John Bacheler,
Thomas Fisk, jun.
John Dane,
Joseph Evelith,
Th. Pearly, sen.
John Peabody,
Thomas Perkins,
Samuel Sayer,
Andrew Eliot,
Henry Herrick, sen."

POSTSCRIPT.

INCE making the foregoing collections of letters, to the rev. mr. Cotton Mather, and others, &c. (which as yet remain unanswered) a book is come to hand intitled, "THE LIFE OF SIR WILLIAM PHIPS," printed in London, 1697: which book, though it bears not the author's name, yet the style, manner, and matter are such, that, were there no other demonstration or token to know him by, it were no witchcraft to determine that the said mr. Cotton Mather is the author of it. But that he, who has *encountered enchantments*, and gone through the *Wonders of the Invisible World*, and *discovered the devil*— that he should step aside into a remote country to put on invisibility, though the reason of this be not so manifest, yet it may be thought to be to gratify some peculiar fancies. And why may not this be one, that he might with the better grace extol the actions of mr. Increase Mather, as agent in England, or as president of Harvard college, not forgetting his own?

As to ſir William, it will be generally acknowledged, that notwithſtanding the meanneſs of his parentage and education, he attained to be maſter of a ſhip, and that he had the good hap to find a Spaniſh wreck, not only ſufficient to repair his fortunes, but to raiſe him to a conſiderable figure; which king James ſo far aſſiſted, as to make him a knight; and that after this, in the reign of his preſent majeſty, he took up with thoſe of the agents, that were for accepting the new charter, whereby himſelf became governor.

It is not doubted, but that he aimed at the good of the people; and great pity it is that his government was ſo ſullied (for want of better information and advice from thoſe whoſe duty it was to have given it) by that hobgoblin monſter, witchcraft, whereby this country was nightmared, and haraſſed, at ſuch a rate as is not eaſily imagined.

After which, ſome complaints going to England about mal-adminiſtration, in the leaſt matters comparatively, yet were ſuch, that he was called home to give account thereof, where he ſoon after expired, ſo finiſhing his life and government together.

Death having thus drawn the curtain, forbidding any further ſcene, it might have been prudent to let his duſt remain without diſturbance.

But the ſaid book endeavouring to raiſe a

ftatue to him, i. e. to afcribe to him fuch achievements as either were never performed by him, or elfe unduly aggravated, this has opened the mouth, both of friends and enemies, to recount the miftakes in the faid book; as alfo thofe mifcarriages wherewith fir William was chargeable; fuch as, had it not been for this book, would have been buried with him.

In page 3, fearch is made over the world, to whom to compare him in his advancement; and moft unhappily Pizarro is pitched upon, as a match for him; who was a baftard, dropt in a church-porch, put to fuck a fow, and, being grown, ran away, and fhipt himfelf for America; there fo profpered as to command an army; and therewith did mighty things, particularly took Atabalipa, one of the kings of Peru, prifoner; and, having received for his ranfom, in gold and filver, to the value of ten millions, perfidioufly put him to death; and was the death of no man knows how many thoufands of innocents, and is certainly one of the worft that could have been pitched upon for fuch comparifon. Though this, together with the rhetorical flourifhes and affected ftrains therein, are inftances of the author's variety of learning; for which he is recommended by thefe three venerable perfons in the entrance to the faid book; yet the integrity, prudence and veracity thereof are not fo manifestly to be seen. Passing over a multitude of misrepresentations that are therein, relating to the acts of sir William, as not designing to rake in the grave of the dead, who is it can see the veracity of those words? p. 40. "He lay within pistol-shot of the enemy's cannon, and beat them from thence, and much battered the town, having his ship shot through in an hundred places, with four and twenty pounders;" when, in the judgment of those present, they were not nearer to the enemy than about half or three quarters of a mile; that there might be in all about seven shot that struck the hull of the vessel, none of them known to be bigger than 18 pounders, the enemy having but one gun that would carry an eighteen pound ball.

It were a folly, after such assertions, to take any notice of this bedecked statue, when there was so much the less need of erecting one (as is asserted p. 108) having already been done so well, that even this author himself despairs of doing it better; and that by a man of such diffused and embalmed a reputation, as that his commendations are asserted to be enough to immortalize the reputation of sir William, or whomsoever else he should please to bestow them upon, viz. that reverend person who was the president of the only university then in the English America, p. 109. Which by the way is a much fairer statue, in honour of the prefident of the univerfity, than that erected for fir William.

For, notwithftanding all this noife of erecting ftatues, and the great danger in plucking them down, &c. yet, in p. 89, it is faid that even fir William fhewed choler enough, leaving it open for others thereby to underftand, that he was wholly given over to paffion and choler. And, in p. 92, it is faid he did not affect any mighty fhew of devotion. Thefe expreffions, with others, may prevail with the unbiaffed reader to think that thefe builders of ftatues had fome further defign in it, than to blazon the achievements of fir William Phips, viz. to fet forth mr. I. Mather's negotiation in England, his procuring the new charter, and fir William to be governor, and himfelf eftablifhed prefident of the college, are the things principally driven at in the book.

Another principal thing is, to fet forth the fuppofed witchcrafts in New England, and how well mr. Mather the younger therein acquitted himfelf.

As to the new charter, for the right underftanding that affair, it will be needful to fay, that the people that afterwards fettled in New-England, being about to leave their native foil, and to feek (as the providence of God fhould direct them) a fettlement in remote regions, wherein they might beſt ſecure their civil and religious intereſts, before they entered upon this, conſidering it might be needful on many accounts for their future well-being, they obtained a charter to be in the nature of a prime agreement, ſetting forth the ſovereign's prerogative, and the people's privileges; in the enjoyment whereof they long continued, after having purchaſed the title to their lands of the natives of their country, and ſettled themſelves therein, without any charge to the crown.

That clauſe in their charter for this country, viz. "Provided that no other chriſtian prince be prepoſſeſſed of it," being a tacit acknowledgment, that before ſettlement, no one chriſtian prince had any right thereto more than another. During this time of New-England's proſperity, the government here were very ſparing of granting freedoms, except to ſuch as were ſo and ſo qualified: whereby the number of non-freemen being much increaſed, they were very uneaſy, by their being ſhut out from any ſhare in the government, or having any votes for their repreſentatives, &c. It rendered many of them ready to join with ſuch as were undermining the government; not duly conſidering that it had been far more ſafe to have endeavoured to prevail with the legiſlators for an enlargement.

So that it will not be wondered at, that in the

latter end of the reign of king Charles II, and of king James, (when moſt of the charters in England were vacated) this was *quo warranto'd*, and finally judgment entered up againſt it, and the country was put into ſuch a form of government as was moſt agreeable to thoſe times, viz. a legiſlative power was lodged in the governor (or preſident) and ſome few appointed to be of his council, without any regard therein either to the laws of England, or thoſe formerly of this colony: thus rendering the circumſtances of this country beyond compariſon worſe than thoſe of any corporation in England; the people of thoſe corporations being acknowledged ſtill to have a right to *magna charta*, when their particular charters were made void; but here, when *magna charta* has been pleaded, the people have been anſwered, that they muſt not expect that *magna charta* would follow them to the end of the world; not only their eſtates, but their lives, being thereby rendered wholly precarious. And judge Palmer has ſet forth in print, that the king has power to grant ſuch a commiſſion over his people.

It is not hard to imagine, that under ſuch a commiſſion, not only the people were liable to be oppreſſed by taxes, but alſo by confiſcations, and ſeizing of lands, unleſs patents were purchaſed at exceſſive prices, with many other exorbitant innovations.

The firſt that accepted this commiſſion was mr. Dudley, a gentleman born in this country, who did but prepare the way for ſir Edmond Andros; in whoſe time things had grown to ſuch extremities, not only here, but in England, as rendered the ſucceeding revolution abſolutely neceſſary; the revolution here being no other than an acting according to the precedent given by England.

During the time of ſir Edmond's government, mr. Increaſe Mather, teacher of the north church in Boſton, having undergone ſome trouble by fobb-actions laid upon him, &c. (though with ſome difficulty) he made his eſcape, and got paſſage for England, being therein aſſiſted by ſome particular friends; where being arrived, he applied himſelf to king James for redreſs of thoſe evils the country then groaned under; and meeting with a ſeeming kind reception, and ſome promiſes, it was as much as might at that time be reaſonably expected.

Upon the day of the revolution here, though the greateſt part of the people were for reaſſuming their ancient government, purſuant to his royal highneſs's proclamation, yet matters were ſo clogged, that the people were diſmiſſed without it, who did not in the leaſt miſtruſt but that thoſe, who were put out of the government by mr. Dudley, would reaſſume; mr. Bradſtreet, who had been then governor, being heard to say that evening, when returned home, that had not he thought they would have reaffumed, he would not have ftirred out of his houfe that day. But after this, fome that were driving at other matters, had opportunities by threats and other ways not only to prevail with that good old gentleman, but with the reft of the government, wholly to decline it; which fome few obferving, they took the opportunity to call themfelves a committee of fafety, and fo undertook to govern fuch as would be governed by them.

It has been an obfervation of long continuance, that matters of ftate feldom profper, when managed by the clergy. Among the oppofers of the reaffuming, few were fo ftrenuous as fome of the minifters; and among the minifters, none more vehement than mr. Cotton Mather, paftor of the north church in Bofton, who has charged them, as they would anfwer it another day, not to reaffume. Among his arguments againft it, one was, that it would be to put a flight upon his father, who, he faid, was in England, labouring for a complete reftoration of charter privileges, not doubting but they would be fpeedily obtained. Any man that knows New-England cannot but be fenfible, that fuch difcourfes, from fuch men, have always been very prevalent. And hence it was, that even thofe that would think themfelves wronged, if they were not numbered among the beft friends to New-England, and to its charter, would not fo much as ftoop to take it up, when there was really nothing to hinder them from the enjoyment thereof.

After the committee of fafety had continued about feven weeks, or rather after anarchy had been fo long triumphant, an affembly having been called came to this refolution, and laid it before thofe gentlemen that had been of the government,—that if they would not act upon the foundation of the charter, that, purfuant to it, the affembly would appoint fome others in that ftation. The anfwer to which was, that they would accept, &c. And when a declaration, fignifying fuch a reaffuming, was prepared, with the good liking of the deputies, in order to be publifhed, fome, that were oppofers, fo terrified thofe gentlemen, that, before publifhing, it was underwritten that they would not have it underftood that they did reaffume charter-government, to the no fmall amazement of the people, and difappointment of the deputies, who, if thefe had not promifed fo to act, had taken other care, and put in thofe that would.

The next principal thing done was, they chofe two of their members, viz. one of the upper houfe, the other of the lower, both of them gentlemen of known integrity as well as ability, to go to England, in order to obtain their refettlement; and in regard mr. I. Mather was already there, they joined him, as alfo a certain gentleman in London, with thefe other two. Thofe from hence being arrived in London, they all united for the common intereft of the country, though without the defired effect. They were in doubt whether it were beft to improve their utmoft for a reverfal of the judgment in a courfe of law, or to obtain it in a parliamentary way, or to petition his majefty for a new grant of former privileges; and, confidering that the two firft might prove dilatory and expenfive, as well as for other reafons, they refolved upon the latter, and petitioned his majefty for the country's refettlement, with former privileges, and what further additions his majefty in his princely wifdom fhould think fit. Accordingly it pleafed his majefty to declare in council his determination, viz. That there fhould be a charter granted to New-England. But the minutes then taken thereof, and a draught of the new charter, being feen, it was the opinion of the two gentlemen fent from hence, that it were beft to tarry his majefty's return from Flanders, in hopes then to obtain eafe in fuch things as might be any ways deemed grievous. And this was the refult of the advice of fuch as were beft able to give it, that they could meet with; and accordingly they wholly defifted taking it out of the offices.

But mr. Mather and that other gentleman had, as it is faid, other advice given them, which they ftrenuoufly purfued; and his majefty having left it (as is afferted in the life of fir William, p. 57) to them to nominate a governor, they pitched upon fir William Phips, who was then in England, as the moft likely and able to ferve the king's interefts among the people there, under the changes, in fome things unacceptable, now brought upon them, p. 62; and, without tarrying for the concurrence of thofe other agents, the charter was taken out, &c.

But mr. Mather, perhaps fearing he fhould have but fmall thanks here for his having fo far an hand in bringing upon them thofe unacceptable changes, wrote, and caufed to be printed, an account of his negotiation; but, furely by fome error in the conception, it proved only an embryo, and was ftifled as foon as born. One indeed, defigned to be as it were a pofthumous, was left with mr. Bailey, formerly of Bofton, and a member of the north church, with a charge not to fuffer it to be feen till he were gone to New-England; yet it feems fome other perfon got a fight of it, which was the occafion of mr. Mather's fending him that minatory epiftle, by fome called a bull. But befides this, for fear of the worst, mr. Mather got several non-con. ministers to give him a testimonial, or letters of commendation, for his great service herein.

In the mean time, mr. Cotton Mather, being in some doubt of the same thing, handed about a paper of fables; wherein his father, under the name of Mercurius, and himself under the name of Orpheus, are extolled, and the great actions of Mercurius magnified; the present charter exalted, by trampling on the former, as being very defective, and all those called unreasonable that did not readily agree with the new one. And indeed the whole country are compared to no better than beasts, except Mercurius and Orpheus; the governor himself must not escape being termed an elephant, though as good as he was great; and the inferiors told by Orpheus, that for the quiet enjoyment of their land, &c. they were beholding to Mercurius. Though this paper was judged not convenient to be printed, yet some copies were taken, the author having shewn variety of heathen learning in it.

This is in short that eminent service for which the said mr. I. M. is in the present book so highly extolled, in so many pages, that to repeat them, were to transcribe a considerable part of the said book.

And no doubt he deserves as much thanks as dr. Sharp did, when he was sent by the presbytery of Scotland to procure the settlement of their kirk by king Charles II at his restoration.

Not but that the present charter of New-England is indeed truly valuable, as containing in it peculiar privileges, which abundantly engages this people to pay the tribute of thankfulness to his majesty, and all due subjection to whom it shall please him to substitute as governor over us; and to pray that the King of kings would pour out his richest blessings upon him, giving him a long and prosperous reign over the nations, under the benign influences whereof oppression and tyranny may flee away.

And if his majesty hath put this people into the present form of government, that they might be in the better condition of defence in a time of war, or that they might better understand the privilege of choosing their own governor by the want of it, and should be graciously pleased (the war being over) to restore to these, as has been already granted to the rest of his majesty's subjects, the full enjoyment of their ancient privileges, it would be such an obligation upon them to thankfulness and duty, as could never be forgotten, nor sufficiently exprest, and would rather abate than increase charge to the crown.

As to the supposed witchcrafts in New-England, having already said so much thereof, there is the less remains to be added.

In the times of fir Edmond Androf's government, goody Glover, a defpifed, crazy, ill-conditioned old woman, an Irifh Roman Catholic, was tried for afflicting Goodwin's children; by the account of which trial, taken in fhort hand for the ufe of the jury, it may appear that the generality of her anfwers were nonfenfe, and her behaviour like that of one diftracted. Yet the doctors, finding her as fhe had been for many years, brought her in *compos mentis*; and fetting afide her crazy anfwers to fome enfnaring queftions, the proof againft her was wholly deficient. The jury brought her in guilty.

Mr. Cotton Mather was the moft active and forward of any minifter in the country in thofe matters, taking home one of the children, and managing fuch intrigues with that child, and printing fuch an account of the whole in his *Memorable Providences*, as conduced much to the kindling of thofe flames, that in fir William's time threatened the deftruction of this country.

King Saul in deftroying the witches out of Ifrael is thought by many to have exceeded, and in his zeal to have flain the Gibeonites wrongfully under that notion; yet went after this to a witch to know his fortune. For his wrongfully deftroying the Gibeonites (befides the judgments of God upon the land) his fons were hanged; and for his going to the witch, himſelf was cut off. Our ſir William Phips did not do this; but, as appears by this book, had firſt his fortune told him, (by ſuch as the author counts no better) and though he put it off (to his paſtor, who he knew approved not thereof) as if it were brought to him in writing, without his ſeeking, &c. yet by his bringing it ſo far, and ſafe keeping it ſo many years, it appears he made ſome account of it; for which he gave the writer, after he had found the wreck, as a reward, more than two hundred pounds. His telling his wife, (p. 6) that he ſhould be a commander, ſhould have a brick houſe in Green-lane, &c. might be in confidence of ſome ſuch prediction; and that he could foretel to him (p. 90) that he ſhould be governor of New-England, was probably ſuch an one, the ſcriptures not having revealed it. Such predictions would have been counted, at Salem, pregnant proofs of witchcraft, and much better than what were againſt ſeveral that ſuffered there. But ſir William, when the witchcrafts at Salem began (in his eſteem) to look formidable, that he might act ſafely in this affair, aſked the advice of the miniſters in and near Boſton. The whole of their advice and anſwer is printed in *Caſes of Conſcience*, the laſt pages. But leſt the world ſhould be ignorant who it was that drew the faid advice, in this book of the life of fir William Phips, p. 77, are thefe words, *The minifters made to his excellency and the council a return, drawn up at their defire, by mr. Mather the younger, as I have been informed.* Mr. C. M. therein intending to beguile the world, and make them think that another, and not himfelf, had taken that notice of his (fuppofed) good fervice done therein, which otherwife would have been afcribed to thofe minifters in general; though indeed the advice then given looks moft like a thing of his compofing, as carrying both fire to increafe, and water to quench, the conflagration; particularly after the devil's teftimony, by the fuppofed afflicted, had fo prevailed, as to take away the life of one, and the liberty of an hundred, and the whole country fet into a moft dreadful confternation, then this advice is given, ufhered in with thanks for what was already done, and in conclufion putting the government upon a fpeedy and vigorous profecution, according to the laws of God, and the wholefome ftatutes of the Englifh nation; fo adding oil, rather than water, to the flame: for who fo little acquainted with the proceedings of England, as not to know that they have taken fome methods, with thofe here ufed, to difcover who were witches? The reft of the advice, confifting of cautions and directions, is inserted in this book of the life of sir William: so that if sir William, looking upon the thanks for what was past, and exhortation to proceed, went on to take away the lives of nineteen more, this is according to the advice said to be given him by the ministers; and if the devil, after those executions, be affronted, by disbelieving his testimony, and by clearing and pardoning all the rest of the accused, yet this also is, according to that advice, but to cast the scale. The same that drew this advice saith, in *Wonders of the Invisible World, Enchantments Encountered*, that to have a hand in any thing that may stifle or obstruct a regular detection of that witchcraft, is what we may well with a holy fear avoid: their majesties' good subjects must not every day be torn to pieces by horrid witchcraft, and those bloody felons be wholly left unprosecuted; the witchcraft is a business that will not be shammed. The pastor of that church, of which sir William was a member, being of this principle, and thus declaring it, after the former advice, no wonder though it cast the scale against those cautions. It is rather a wonder that no more blood was shed; for if that advice of his pastor could still have prevailed with the governor, witchcraft had not been so shammed off as it was. Yet now, in this book of the life of sir William, the pardoning the prisoners when condemned, and clearing the gaols, is called (p. 82) a vanquishing the devil; adding this conquest to the rest of the noble achievements of sir William, though performed not only without, but directly against, his pastor's advice. But this is not all; though this book pretends to raise a statue in honour of sir William, yet it appears it was the least part of the design of the author to honour him, but it was rather to honour himself, and the ministers; it being so unjust to sir William, as to give a full account of the cautions given him, but designedly hiding from the reader the encouragements and exhortations to proceed, that were laid before him, (under the name of the ministers' advice;) in effect telling the world that those executions at Salem were without and against the advice of the ministers, exprest in those cautions, purposely hiding their giving thanks for what was already done, and exhorting to proceed; thereby rendering sir William of so sanguinary a complexion, that the ministers had such cause to fear his going on with the tragedy, though against their advice, that they desired the president to write his *Cases of Conscience*, &c. To plead misinformation will not salve here, however it may seem to palliate other things, but is a manifest, designed travesty, or misrepresentation, of the minister's advice to sir William, a hiding the truth, and a wronging the dead, whom the author so much pretends to honour; for which the acknowledgments ought to be as universal as the offence. But though the ministers' advice, or rather mr. Cotton Mather's, was perfectly ambidexter, giving as great or greater encouragement to proceed in those dark methods, than cautions against them; yet many eminent persons being accused, there was a necessity of a stop to be put to it. If it be true, what was said at the council-board in answer to the commendations of sir William for his stopping the proceedings about witchcraft, viz. that it was high time for him to stop it, his own lady being accused; if that assertion were a truth, then New-England may seem to be more beholden to the accusers for accusing her, and thereby necessitating a stop, than to sir William, or to the advice that was given him by his pastor.

Mr. Cotton Mather, having been very forward to write books of witchcraft, has not been so forward either to explain or to defend the doctrinal part thereof; and his belief (which he had a year's time to compose) he durst not venture, so as to be copied. Yet in this book of the life of sir William he sufficiently testifies his retaining that heterodox belief, seeking by frightful stories of the sufferings of some, and the refined fight of others, &c. (p. 69) to obtrude upon the world, and confirm it in such a belief as hitherto he either cannot or will not defend, as if the blood already shed thereby were not sufficient.

Mr. I. Mather, in his *Cases of Conscience*, p. 25, tells of a bewitched eye, and that such can see more than others. They were certainly bewitched eyes, that could see as well shut as open, and that could see what never was; that could see the prisoners upon the afflicted, harming them, when those whose eyes were not bewitched could have sworn that they did not stir from the bar. The accusers are said to have suffered much by biting, (p. 73) and the prints of just such a set of teeth, as those they accused had, would be seen on their flesh; but such as had not such bewitched eyes have seen the accusers bite themselves, and then complain of the accused. It has also been seen, when the accused, instead of having just such a set of teeth, has not had one in his head. They were such bewitched eyes, that could see the poisonous powder (brought by spectres, p. 70) and that could see in the ashes the print of the brand, there invisibly heating to torment the pretended sufferers with, &c.

These, with the rest of such legends, have this direct tendency, viz. to tell the world that the devil is more ready to ferve his votaries, by his doing for them things above or againſt the courſe of nature, ſhewing himſelf to them and making explicit contracts with them, &c. than the Divine Being is to his faithful ſervants; and that as he is willing, ſo alſo able, to perform their deſires. The way whereby theſe people are believed to arrive at a power to afflict their neighbours, is by a compact with the devil, and that they have a power to commiſſion him to thoſe evils, p. 72. However irrational, or un-ſcriptural, ſuch aſſertions are, yet they ſeem a neceſſary part of the *faith* of ſuch as maintain the belief of ſuch a ſort of witches.

As the ſcriptures know nothing of a cove-nanting or commiſſioning witch, ſo reaſon cannot conceive how mortals ſhould by their wickedneſs arrive at a power to commiſſion angels, fallen angels, againſt their innocent neighbours. But the ſcriptures are full in it, and the inſtances numerous, that the Almighty Divine Being has this prerogative, to make uſe of what inſtruments he pleaſeth, in afflicting any, and conſequently to commiſſion devils: and though this word, *commiſſioning*, in the author's former books, might be thought to be by inadvertency, yet now, after he hath been cautioned of it, ſtill to perſiſt in it ſeems highly criminal; and therefore, in the name of God, I here charge such belief as guilty of sacrilege in the highest nature, and so much worse than stealing church plate, &c. as it is a higher offence to steal any of the glorious attributes of the Almighty, to bestow them upon mortals, than it is to steal the utensils appropriated to his service. And whether to ascribe such power of commissioning devils to the worst of men, be not direct blasphemy, I leave to others better able to determine. When the Pharisees were so wicked as to ascribe to Beelzebub the mighty works of Christ (whereby he did manifestly shew forth his power and godhead) then it was that our Saviour declared the sin against the Holy Ghost to be unpardonable.

When the righteous God is contending with apostate sinners for their departures from him, by his judgments, as plagues, earthquakes, storms and tempests, sicknesses and diseases, wars, loss of cattle, &c. then not only to ascribe this to the devil, but to charge one another with sending or commissioning those devils to do these things, is so abominable and so wicked, that it requires a better judgment than mine to give it its just denomination.

But that christians, so called, should not only charge their fellow christians therewith, but proceed to trials and executions; crediting that enemy to all goodness, and accuser of the brethren, rather than believe their neighbours in their own defence; this is so diabolical a wickedness, as cannot proceed but from a doctrine of devils; how far damnable it is, let others discuss. Though such things were acting in this country in sir William's time, yet (p. 65) there is a discourse of a guardian angel, as then overseeing it: which notion, however it may suit the faith of Ethnicks, or the fancies of Trithemius, it is certain that the Omnipresent Being stands not in need, as earthly potentates do, of governing the world by vicegerents. And if sir William had such an invisible pattern to imitate, no wonder though some of his actions were unaccountable, especially those relating to witchcraft: for if there was in those actions an angel superintending, there is little reason to think it was Gabriel, or the spirit of Mercury; nor Hanael, the angel or spirit of Venus; nor yet Samuel, the angel or spirit of Mars; names feigned by the said Trithemius, &c. It may rather be thought to be Apollyon, or Abaddon.

Objection. But here it will be said, What, are there no witches? Does not the law of God command that they should be extirpated? Is the command vain and unintelligible?

Sol. For any to say that a witch is one that makes a compact with, and commissions devils,

&c. is indeed to render the law of God vain and unintelligible, as having provided no way whereby they might be detected, and proved to be such; and how the Jews waded through this difficulty for so many ages, without the supplement of mr. Perkins and Bernard thereto, would be very mysterious. But to him that can read the scriptures without prejudice from education, &c. it will manifestly appear that the scripture is full and intelligible, both as to the crime, and means to detect the culpable. He that shall hereafter see any person, who, to confirm people in a false belief about the power of witches and devils, pretending to a sign to confirm it; such as knocking off of invisible chains with the hand, driving away devils by brushing, striking with a sword or stick, to wound a person at a great distance, &c. may (according to that head of mr. Gaule's, quoted by mr. C. M. and so often herein before recited, and so well-proved by scripture) conclude that he has *seen witchcraft performed.*

If Balaam became a sorcerer by sacrificing and praying to the true God against his visible people, then he that shall pray that the afflicted (by their *spectral* sight) may accuse some other persons (whereby their reputations and lives may be endangered) such will justly deserve the name of a *sorcerer.* If any person pretends to know more than can be known by human means, and professeth at the same time that they have it from the *black man, i. e. the devil*, and shall from hence give testimony against the lives of others, they are manifestly such as have a familiar spirit; and if any, knowing them to have their information from the *black man*, shall be inquisitive of them for their testimony against others, they therein are dealing with such as have a *familiar spirit*.

And if these shall pretend to *see the dead* by their *spectral sight*, and others shall be inquisitive of them, and receive their answers what it is the *dead say*, and who it is they accuse, both the one and the other are by scripture *guilty of necromancy*.

These are all of them crimes as easily proved as any whatsoever, and that by such proof as the law of God requires, so that it is *no unintelligible law*.

But if the iniquity of the times be such that these criminals not only escape, being indemnified, but are encouraged in their wickedness, and made use of to take away the lives of others, this is worse than a making the law of God *vain*, it being a rendering of it *dangerous*, against the lives of innocents, and without all hopes of better, so long as these bloody principles remain.

As long as christians do esteem the *law of*

God to be imperfect, as not defcribing that crime that it requires to be punifhed by death:

As long as men fuffer themfelves to be poifoned in their education, and be grounded in a *falfe belief by the books of the heathen:*

As long as the *devil* fhall be believed to have *a natural power to act above and againft the courfe of nature:*

As long as the *witches* fhall be believed to have a power to *commiffion him:*

As long as the *devil's teftimony*, by the pretended afflicted, fhall be received as *more valid to condemn*, than their plea of *not guilty* to acquit:

As long as the *accused* fhall have their *lives and liberties* confirmed and reftored to them *upon their confeffing themfelves guilty:*

As long as the *accufed* fhall be forced to *undergo hardfhips and torments* for their not confeffing:

As long as *teats* for the *devil to fuck* are fearched for upon the bodies of the accufed, as a token of guilt:

As long as the *Lord's prayer* fhall be profaned, by being made a teft, who are culpable:

As long as *witchcraft, forcery, familiarf pirits,* and *necromancy*, fhall be improved to difcover who are witches, &c.

24

So long it may be expected that innocents will suffer as witches:

So long God will be daily dishonoured, and so long his judgments must be expected to be continued.

GILES CORY.

The files of office contain numerous documents of the abfurd and ridiculous proceedings and teftimonies, by which the victims of a pretended witchcraft were driven on to their tragical end: of which the following will ferve as a fpecimen.

The examination of GILES CORY, at a Court at Salem Village, held by John Hathorn and Jona. Curwin, Efqrs. April 19, 1692.

Giles Cory, you are brought before authority upon high fufpicion of fundry acts of witchcraft ; now tell us the truth in this matter.

I hope through the goodnefs of God I fhall, for that matter I never had no hand in, in my life.

Which of you have feen this man hurt you ?

Mary Wolcott, Mercy Lewis, Ann Putman, jr. and Abigail Williams affirmed he had hurt them.

Hath he hurt you too ? fpeaking to Elizabeth Hubbard. She going to anfwer was prevented by a fit.

Benjamin Gold, hath he hurt you ?

I have feen him feveral times, and been hurt after it, but cannot affirm that it was he.

Hath he brought the book to any of you?

Mary Wolcott and Abigail Williams and others affirmed he had brought the book to them.

Giles Cory, they accufe you, or your appearance, of hurting them, and bringing the book to them. What do you fay ? Why do you hurt them ? Tell us the truth.

I never did hurt them.

It is your appearance hurts them, they charge you; tell us what have you done.

I have done nothing to damage them.

Have you never entered into contract with the devil ?

I never did.

What temptations have you had ?

I never had temptations in my life.

What, have you done it without temptations ?

What was the reafon (faid goodwife Bibber) that you were frighted in the cow-houfe? and then the queftionift was fuddenly feized with a violent fit.

Samuel Braybrook, goodman Bibber, and his daughter, teftified that he had told them this morning that he was frighted in the cow-houfe.

Cory denied it.

This was not your appearance but your perfon, and you told them fo this morning: why do you deny it?

What did you fee in the cow-houfe?

I never faw nothing but my cattle.

Divers witneffed that he told them he was frighted.

Well, what do you fay to thefe witneffes? What was it frighted you?

I do not know that ever I fpoke the word in my life.

Tell the truth, what was it frighted you?

I do not know any thing that frighted me.

All the afflicted were feized now with fits, and troubled with pinches. Then the court ordered his hands to be tied.

What, is it not enough to act witchcraft at other times, but muft you do it now in the face of authority?

I am a poor creature, and cannot help it.

Upon the motion of his head again, they had their heads and necks afflicted.

Why do you tell fuch wicked lies againft witneffes, that heard you fpeak after this manner, this very morning?

I never faw any thing but a black hog.

You faid that you were ftopt once in prayer; what ftopt you?

I cannot tell; my wife came towards me and found fault with me for faying living to God and dying to fin.

What was it frighted you in the barn?

I know nothing frighted me there.

Why here are three witneffes that heard you fay fo to-day.

I do not remember it.

Thomas Gold teftified that he heard him fay, that he knew enough againft his wife, that would do her bufinefs.

What was that you knew againft your wife?

Why that of living to God, and dying to fin.

The Marfhall and Bibber's daughter confirmed the fame, that he faid he could fay that that would do his wife's bufinefs.

I have said what I can say to that.

What was that about your ox?

I thought he was hipt.

What ointment was that your wife had when she was seized? You said it was ointment she made by major Gidney's direction.

He denied it, and said she had it of goody Bibber, or from her direction.

Goody Bibber said it is not like that ointment.

You said you knew, upon your own knowledge, that she had it of major Gidney.

He denied it.

Did not you say, when you went to the ferry with your wife, you would not go over to Boston now, for you should come yourself the next week?

I would not go over, because I had not money.

The Marshal testified he said as before.

One of his hands was let go, and several were afflicted. He held his head on one side, and then the heads of several of the afflicted were held on one side. He drew in his cheeks, and the cheeks of some of the afflicted were suckt in.

John Bibber and his wife gave in testimony concerning some temptations he had to make away with himself.

How doth this agree with what you said, that you had no temptations?

I meant temptations to witchcraft.

If you can give way to self murther, that will make way to temptation to witchcraft.

Note. There was witness by several, that he said he would make away with himself, and charge his death upon his son.

Goody Bibber testified that the said Cory called said Bibber's husband, damn'd, devilish rogue.

Other vile expressions testified in open court by several others.

Salem Village, April 19, 1692.
Mr. Samuel Parris being desired to take in writing the examination of Giles Cory, delivered it in; and upon hearing the same, and seeing what we did see at the time of his examination, together with the charge of the afflicted persons against him, we committed him to their majesties' gaol.

JOHN HATHORN.

The Wonders of the Invisible World:

Being an Account of the

TRYALS
OF

Several Witches

Lately Executed in

NEW-ENGLAND:
And of several Remarkable Curiosities
therein Occurring.

By *COTTON MATHER*.

Published by the Special Command of his **EX-CELLENCY** the Governour of the Province of the *Massachusetts-Bay* in *New-England*.

The Third Edition.

Printed first at *Boston* in *New England*, and reprinted at *London*, for *John Dunton*, at the *Raven* in the *Poultrey*. 1693.

THE AUTHOR'S DEFENCE.

'TIS, as I remember, the Learned *Scribonius*, who reports, That one of his Acquaintance, devoutly making his Prayers on the behalf of a Perſon moleſted by *Evil Spirits*, received from thoſe *Evil Spirits* an horrible blow over the Face: And I myſelf expect not few or ſmall Buffetings from Evil Spirits, for the Endeavours wherewith I am now going to Encounter them. I am far from inſenſible, that at this extraordinary Time of the *Devils coming down in great wrath upon us*, there are too many Tongues and Hearts thereby *ſet on fire of Hell*; that the various Opinions about the witchcrafts which of later time have troubled us, are maintained by ſome with ſo much cloudy Fury, as if they could never be ſufficiently ſtated, unleſs written in the Liquor wherewith Witches uſe to write their Covenants; and that he who becomes an Author at ſuch a time, had need be *Fenced with Iron, and the ſtaff of a Spear*. The unaccountable Forwardneſs, Aſperity, Un-

treatableness, and Inconsistency of many Persons, every Day gives a visible Exposition of that passage, *An evil spirit from the Lord came upon Saul;* and Illustration of that Story, *There met him two possessed with Devils, exceeding fierce, so that no man might pass that way.* To send abroad a Book, among such Readers, were a very unadvised thing, if a Man had not such Reasons to give, as I can bring, for such an Undertaking. Briefly, I hope it cannot be said, *They are all so:* No, I hope the Body of this People, are yet in such a Temper, as to be capable of applying their Thoughts, to make a *Right Use* of the Stupendious and Prodigious Things that are happening among us; And because I was concern'd, when I saw that no abler Hand emitted any Essays to engage the Minds of this People, in such holy, pious, fruitful Improvements, as God would have to be made of his amazing Dispensations now upon us; THEREFORE it is, that One of the Least among the Children of *New England*, has here done, what is done. None, but the *Father, who sees in Secret,* knows the Heart breaking Exercises, wherewith I have composed what is now going to be exposed, lest I should in any one thing miss of doing my designed Service for his Glory, and for his People; but I am now somewhat comfortably assured of his favourable acceptance; and, *I will not fear; what can a Satan do unto me?*

Having performed something of what God required, in labouring to suit his Words unto his Works, at this day among us, and therewithal handled a Theme that has been sometimes counted not unworthy the Pen, even of a King, it will easily be perceived, that some subordinate Ends have been considered in these Endeavours.

I have indeed set myself to countermine the whole PLOT of the *Devil*, against *New England* in every Branch of it, as far as one of my darkness, can comprehend such a *work of Darkness*. I may add, that I have herein also aimed at the Information and Satisfaction of Good Men in another Country, a thousand Leagues off, where I have it may be, more, or however, more considerable Friends, than in my own: And I do what I can to have that Country, now, as well as always, in the best terms with my own. But while I am doing these things, I have been driven a little to do something likewise for myself; I mean, by taking off the false Reports, and hard Censures about my Opinion in these Matters, the *Parter's Portions* which my *Pursuit of Peace* has procured me among the *Keen*. My hitherto *unvaried Thoughts* are here published; and I believe, they will be owned by most of the Ministers of God in these Colonies; nor can amends be well made me, for the wrong done me, by other sorts of *Representations*.

In fine: For the Dogmatical part of my Discourse, I want no Defence; for the Historical part of it, I have a very Great One; the Lieutenant-Governour of *New England* having perused it, has done me the Honour of giving me a Shield, under the umbrage whereof I now dare to walk abroad.

Reverend and Dear SIR,

You *very much gratify'd me, as well as put a kind Respect upon me, when you put into my hands your elaborate and most* seasonable *Discourse, entitled*, The Wonders of the Invisible World, *and having now perused so fruitful and happy a Composure, upon such a Subject, at this Juncture of Time; and* considering *the place that I hold in the Court of* Oyer and Terminer, *still* labouring and proceeding *in the Trial of the* persons accused and convicted for Witchcraft, *I find that I am more* nearly *and* highly concerned *than as a mere ordinary Reader, to express my* Obligation and Thankfulness *to you for so great* pains; *and* cannot but hold myself many ways bound even to the utmost of what is proper for me, in my present publick Capacity *to* declare my singular Appro-

bation *thereof*. *Such is your* Defign *moſt plainly expreſſed throughout the whole;* ſuch *your Zeal for* God, *your* Enmity to Satan and his Kingdom, *your* Faithfulneſs and Compaſſion *to this poor* People; *ſuch the Vigour, but yet great Temper of your Spirit; ſuch your* Inſtruction and Counſel, *your Care of Truth, your Wiſdom and Dexterity in* allaying and moderating *that among us which needs it; ſuch your clear* difcerning of Divine Providences and Periods, *now* running on *apace towards their Glorious Iſſues in the World; and* finally, *ſuch your* good News *of* the Shortneſs of the Devils Time, *that all* good men *muſt needs deſire the making of this your Diſcourſe publick to the World; and will* greatly rejoyce, *that the* Spirit of the Lord *has thus* enabled you to lift up a ſtandard *againſt the* Infernal Enemy, *that hath been* coming in like a flood upon us. *I do therefore make it* my particular and earneſt Requeſt unto you, *that as ſoon as may be, you will commit the ſame unto the* Preſs *accordingly*. I am,
Your aſſured Friend,
WILLIAM STROUGHTON.

I live by *Neighbours* that force me to produce theſe undeſerved Lines. But now, as when Mr. *Wilſon* beholding a great Muſter of Soldiers, had it by a Gentleman then preſent, ſaid unto him, *Sir, I'll tell you a great thing:* Here is a *mighty Body of People; and there is not* Seven *of them all, but what loves* Mr. Wilson. That gracious Man presently and pleasantly reply'd; *Sir, I'll tell you as good a thing as that; here is a mighty Body of People, and there is not so much as* One *among them all, but* Mr. Wilson *loves him.* Somewhat so: 'Tis possible, that among this Body of People, there may be few that love the Writer of this Book; but give me leave to boast so far, there is not one among all this Body of People, whom this *Mather* would not study to serve, as well as to love. With such a *Spirit of Love*, is the Book now before us written: I appeal to all this *World;* and if *this* World will deny me the Right of acknowledging so much, I appeal to the *other*, that it is *not written with an Evil Spirit:* for which cause, I shall not wonder, if *Evil Spirits* be exasperated by what is written, as the Sadduces doubtless were with what was discoursed in the Days of our Saviour. I only demand the *Justice*, that others read it, with the same Spirit wherewith I writ it.

ENCHANTMENTS ENCOUNTERED.

IT was as long ago as the Year 1637, that a Faithful Minister of the Church of *England*, whose Name was Mr. *Edward Symons*, did in a Sermon, afterwards Printed, thus express himself; *At* New-England, *now the Sun of Comfort begins to appear, and the glorious Day-Star to show it self,*—Sed Venient Annis Sæculæ Seris, *there will come Times in after Ages, when the* Clouds *will overshadow and darken the Sky there. Many now promise to themselves nothing but successive Happiness there, which for a time through God's Mercy they may enjoy; and I pray God they may a long time: but in this World there is no happiness perpetual.* An *Observation*, or I had almost said, an *Inspiration*, very dismally now verify'd upon us! It has been Affirm'd by some who best knew *New-England*, That the World will do *New-England* a great piece of Injustice, if it acknowledg not a measure of Religion, Loyalty, Honesty and Industry, in the people there, beyond what is to be found

with any other People for the number of them.
When I did a few years ago, Publifh a Book,
which mentioned a few memorable Witchcrafts,
committed in this Country; the excellent *Baxter*, graced the Second Edition of that Book,
with a kind Preface, wherein he fees caufe to
fay, *If any are Scandalized, that* New-England,
*a place of as ferious Piety, as any I can hear of,
under Heaven, fhould be troubled fo much with
Witckes; I think, 'tis no wonder: Where will the
Devil fhew moft Malice, but where he is hated, and
hateth moft:* And I hope, the Country will ftill
deferve and anfwer the Charity fo expreffed by
that Reverend Man of God. Whofoever travels
over this Wildernefs, will fee it richly befpan-
gled with Evangelical Churches, whofe Paftors
are holy, able, and painful Overfeers of their
Flocks, lively Preachers, and vertuous Livers:
and fuch as in their feveral Neighbourly Affo-
ciations, have had their Meetings whereat Ecclefiaftical Matters of common Concernment are
confidered: *Churches*, whofe Communicants have
been ferioufly examined about their Experiences of Regeneration, as well as about their
Knowledg, and Belief, and blamelefs Converfation, before their admiffion to the Sacred Communion; altho others of lefs but hopeful Attainments in Chriftianity are not ordinarily deny'd
Baptifm for themfelves and theirs; Churches,

which are shye of using anything in the Worship of God, for which they cannot see a Warrant of God; but with whom yet the Names of *Congregational,Presbyterian, Episcopalian,* or *Antipædobaptist,* are swallowed up in that of *Christian;* Persons of all those Perswasions being taken into our Fellowship, when visible Godliness has recommended them; Churches which usually do within themselves manage their own Discipline under the Conduct of their Elders; but yet call in the help of *Synods* upon Emergencies, or Aggrievancies: *Churches,* Lastly, wherein Multitudes are growing ripe for Heaven every day; and as fast as these are taken off, others are daily rising up. And by the Presence and Power of the Divine Institutions thus maintained in the Country. We are still so happy, that I suppose there is no Land in the Universe more free from the debauching, and the debasing Vices of Ungodliness. The Body of the People are hitherto so disposed, that *Swearing, Sabbath-breaking, Whoring, Drunkenness,* and the like, do not make a Gentleman, but a Monster, or a Goblin, in the vulgar Estimation. All this notwithstanding, we must humbly confess to our God, that we are miserably degenerated from the first Love of our Predecessors; however we boast ourselves a little, when Men would go to trample upon us, and we venture to say,

Whereinsoever any is bold (we speak foolishly) we are bold also. The first Planters of these Colonies were a chosen Generation of Men, who were first so pure, as to disrelish many things which they thought wanted Reformation elsewhere, and yet withal so peaceable, that they embraced a voluntary Exile in a squalid, horrid *American* Desart, rather than to live in Contentions with their Brethren. Those good Men imagined that they should never see the Inroads of Profanity, or superstition: And a famous Person returning hence, could in a Sermon before the Parliament, profess, *I have now been seven Years in a Country, where I never saw one Man drunk, or heard one Oath sworn, or beheld one Beggar in the Streets all the while.* Such great Persons as *Budæus*, and others, who mistook Sir *Thomas Moor's* UTOPIA; for a Country really existent, and stirr'd up some Divines charitably to undertake a Voyage thither, might now have certainly found a Truth in their Mistake; *New-England* was a true *Utopia*. But, alas, the Children and Servants of those old Planters must needs afford many degenerate Plants, and there is now risen up a Number of People, otherwise inclined than our *Joshua's*, and the Elders that out-liv'd them. Those two things our holy Progenitors, and our happy Advantages make Omissions of Duty, and such Spiritual Disorders as the whole World abroad is overwhelmed with, to be as provoking in us, as the moſt flagitious Wickedneſs committed in other places; and the Miniſters of God are accordingly ſevere in their Teſtimonies: But in ſhort, thoſe Intereſts of the Goſpel, which were the Errand of our Fathers into theſe Ends of the Earth, have been too much neglected and poſtponed, and the Attainments of an handſome Education, have been too much undervalued, by Multitudes that have not fallen into Exorbitances of wickedneſs; and ſome, eſpecially of our young Ones, when they have got abroad from under the Reſtraints here laid upon them, have become extravagantly and abominably Vicicious. Hence 'tis that the Happineſs of *New-England* has been but for a time, as it was foretold, and not for a long time, as has been defir'd for us. A Variety of Calamity has long follow'd this Plantation; and we have all the Reaſon imaginable to aſcribe it unto the Rebuke of Heaven upon us for our manifold *Apoſtacies;* we make no right uſe of our Diſaſters. If we do not, *Remember whence we are fallen, and repent, and do the firſt Works.* But yet our Afflictions may come under a further Conſideration with us: There is a further Cauſe of our Afflictions, whoſe due muſt be given him.

§ II. The *New-Englanders* are a People of

God settled in those which were once the *Devils* Territories; and it may easily be supposed that the *Devil* was exceedingly disturbed, when he perceived such a People here accomplishing the Promise of old made unto our Blessed Jesus, *That he should have the utmost parts of the Earth for his Possession.* There was not a greater Uproar among the *Ephesians*, when the Gospel was first brought among them, than there was among *The Powers of the Air* (after whom those *Ephesians* walked) when first the *Silver Trumpets* of the Gospel here made the *Joyful Sound.* The Devil thus Irritated, immediately try'd all sorts of Methods to overturn this poor Plantation: and so much of the Church, as was *Fled into this Wilderness*, immediately found, *The Serpent cast out of his Mouth a Flood for the carrying of it away.* I believe, that never were more *Satanical Devices* used for the Unsettling of any People under the Sun, than what have been Employed for the Extirpation of the *Vine* which God has here *Planted, Casting out the Heathen, and preparing a Room before it, and causing it to take deep Root, and fill the Land, so that it sent its Boughs unto the* Atlantic *Sea* Eastward, *and its Branches unto the* Connecticut *River* Westward, *and the Hills were covered with the shadow thereof.* But, All those Attempts of Hell have hitherto been Abortive, many an *Ebenezer* has been Erected unto the Praife of God, by his Poor People here; and *Having obtained Help from God, we continue to this Day:* Wherefore the Devil is now making one Attempt more upon us; an Attempt more Difficult, more Surprizing, more fnarl'd with unintelligible Circumftances than any that we have hitherto Encountred; an Attempt fo *Critical*, that if we get well through, we fhall foon Enjoy *Halcyon* Days, with all the *Vultures of Hell Trodden under our Feet.* He has wanted his *Incarnate Legions* to Perfecute us, as the People of God have in the other Hemifphere been perfecuted; he has therefore drawn forth his more *Spiritual* ones to make an Attacque upon us. We have been advifed by fome Credible Chriftians yet alive, that a Malefactor, accufed of *Witchcraft* as well as *Murder*, and Executed in this place more than Forty Years ago, did then give Notice of, *An Horrible PLOT againft the Country by* WITCH- CRAFT *and a Foundation of* WITCHCRAFT *then laid, which if it were not feafonably difcovered, would probably Blow up, and pull down all the Churches in the Country.* And we have now with Horror feen the *Difcovery* of fuch a *Witchcraft!* An Army of *Devils* is horribly broke in upon the place which is the *Center*, and after a fort, the *Firft born* of our *Englifh* Settlements: and the Houfes of the Good People there are filled with the doleful Shrieks of their Children and Servants, Tormented by Invisible Hands, with Tortures altogether preternatural. After the Mischiefs there Endeavoured, and since in part Conquered, the terrible Plague, of *Evil Angels*, hath made its Progress into some other places, where other Persons have been in like manner Diabolically handled. These our poor Afflicted Neighbours, quickly after they become *Infected* and *Infested* with these *Dæmons*, arrive to a Capacity of Discerning those which they conceive the *Shapes* of their Troubles; and notwithstanding the Great and Just Suspicion, that the *Dæmons* might Impose the *Shapes* of Innocent Persons in their *Spectral Exhibitions* upon the Sufferers, (which may perhaps prove no small part of the *Witch-Plot* in the issue) yet many of the Persons thus Represented, being Examined, several of them have been Convicted of a very Damnable *Witchcraft:* Yea, more than One. *Twenty* have *Confessed*, that they have Signed unto a *Book*, which the Devil show'd them, and Engaged in his Hellish Design of *Bewitching*, and *Ruining* our Land. *We* know not, at least I know not, how far the Delusions of Satan may be Interwoven into some Circumstances of the Confessions; but one would think all the Rules of Understanding Humane Affairs are at an End, If after so many most Voluntary

Harmonious Confeffions, made by Intelligent Perfons of all Ages in fundry Towns, at feveral Times, we muft not Believe the main ftrokes wherein thofe Confeffions agree: Efpecially when we have a Thoufand preternatural Things every day before our Eyes, wherein the Confeffors do acknowledg their Concernment, and give Demonftration of their being fo Concerned. If the Devils now can ftrike the Minds of Men with any Poyfons of fo fine a Compofition and Operation, that fcores of Innocent People fhall Unite, in Confeffions of a Crime, which we fee actually Committed, it is a thing prodigious beyond the Wonders of the former Ages, and it threatens no lefs than a fort of a Diffolution upon the World. Now, by thefe Confeffions 'tis Agreed, That the Devil has made a dreadful Knot of Witches in the Country, and by the help of Witches has dreadfully increafed that Knot: That thefe Witches have driven a Trade of Commiffioning their Confederate Spirits, to do all forts of Mifchiefs to the Neighbours, whereupon there have enfued fuch Mifchievous Confequences upon the Bodies and Eftates of the Neighbourhood, as could not otherwife be accounted for: Yea, That at prodigious Witch-Meetings, the Wretches have proceeded fo far, as to Concert and Confult the Methods of Rooting out the Chriftian Religion from this Countrey, and setting up instead of it, perhaps a more gross Diabolism, that ever the World saw before. And yet it will be a thing little short of Miracle, if in so spread a business as this the Devil should not get in some of his Judges, to confound the Discovery of all the rest.

§ III. Doubtless, the Thoughts of many will receive a great Scandal against *New-England*, from the Number of Persons that have been Accused, or Suspected, for *Witchcraft*, in this Country: But it were easie to offer many things, that may Answer and Abate the Scandal. If the holy Ghost should any where permit the Devils to hook two or three wicked *Scholars* into *Witchcraft*, and then by their Assistance to Range with their *Poisonous Insinuations* among Ignorant, Envious, Discontented People, till they have cunningly decoy'd them into some sudden *Act*, whereby the Toyls of Hell shall be perhaps inextricably cast over them: what Country in the World would not afford *Witches*, numerous to a Prodigy? Accordingly, The Kingdoms of *Sweden*, *Denmark*, *Scotland*, yea, and *England* it self, as well as the Province of *New-England*, have had their Storms of *Witchcrafts* breaking upon them, which have made most Lamentable Devastations: which also I wish, may be *the Last*. And it is not uneasie to be imagined, That God has not brought out all the *Witchcrafts* in many other Lands, with fuch a fpeedy, dreadful, deftroying *Jealoufie*, as burns forth upon fuch *High Treafons*, committed here in *A Land of uprightnefs:* Tranfgreffors may more quickly here than elfewhere become a Prey to the Vengeance of him, *Who has Eyes like a Flame of Fire,* and, *who walks in the midft of the Golden Candlefticks.* Moreover, There are many parts of the World, who if they do upon this Occafion infult over this People of God, need only to be told the Story of what happened at *Loim*, in the Dutchy of *Gulic*, where a Popifh Curate having ineffectually try'd many Charms to Eject the Devil out of a Damfel there poffeffed, he paffionately bid the Devil come out of her into himfelf; but the anfwered him, *Quid mihi Opus, eft eum centare, quem Noviffimo die, Jure Optimo fum poffeffurus?* That is, *What need I meddle with one whom I am fure to have, and hold at the Laft-day as my own for ever.*

An Hortatory and Necessary Address, *To a Country now Extraordinarily Alarum'd by the* Wrath *of the* Devil. *'Tis this.*

LET us now make a good and right use of the prodigious *Descent* which the *Devil* in Great *Wrath* is at this day making upon our Land. Upon the Death of a Great Man once, an Orator call'd the Town together, crying out, *Concurrite Cives, Dilapsa sunt vestra Mœnia!* that is *Come together, Neighbours, your Town Walls are fallen down!* But such is the Descent of the Devil at this day upon our selves, that I may truly tell you, *The Walls of the whole World are broken down!* The usual *Walls* of Defence about Mankind have such a Gap made in them, that the very *Devils* are broke in upon us, to seduce the *Souls*, torment the *Bodies*, sully the *Credits*, and consume the *Estates* of our Neighbours, with Impressions both as *real* and as *furious*, as if the *Invisible* World were becoming *Incarnate*, on purpose for the vexing of us. And what use ought now to be made of so tremendous a Dispensation? We are engaged in a *Fast* this day; but shall we try to fetch *Meat out of the Eater*, and make the *Lion* to afford some *Honey* for our *Souls*?

That the Devil is *come down unto us with*

great Wrath, we find, we feel, we now deplore. In many ways, for many years hath the Devil been affaying to extirpate the Kingdom of our Lord Jefus here. *New England* may complain of the Devil, as in *Pfal.* 129. 1, 2. *Many a time have they afflicted me, from my Youth,* may New England *now fay; many a time have they afflicted me from my Youth, yet they have not prevailed againſt me.* But now there is a more than ordinary *Affliction* with which the *Devil* is Galling of us; and fuch an one as is indeed Unparallelable. The things confeffed by *Witches*, and the things endured by *Others*, laid together, amount unto this account of our affliction. The *Devil*, exhibiting himfelf ordinarily as a fmall *Black Man*, has decoy'd a fearful knot of proud, froward, ignorant, envious and malicious Creatures, to lift themfelves in his horrid Service, by entring their Names in a Book by him tendered unto them. Thefe *Witches*, whereof above a Score have now *Confeffed and fhown their Deeds*, and fome are now tormented by the Devils for *Confeffing*, have met in Hellifh *Randezvouzes*, wherein the Confeffors do fay, they have had their Diabolical Sacraments, imitating the *Baptifm* and the *Supper* of our Lord. In thefe hellifh Meetings, thefe Monfters have affociated themfelves to do no lefs a thing than *to deſtroy the Kingdom of our Lord Jeſus Chriſt in theſe parts of the World;* and in order hereunto, First, they each of them have their *Spectres* or Devils, commission'd by them, and representing of them, to be the Engines of their Malice. By these wicked *Spectres* they sieze poor People about the Country, with various and bloody *Torments;* and of those evidently preternatural Torments there are some have dy'd. They have bewitched some, even so far as to make *Self-destroyers:* And others are in many Towns here and there languishing under their *Evil hands.* The People thus afflicted, are miserably scratched and bitten, so that the Marks are most visible to all the World, but the Causes utterly invisible: And the same invisible Furies do most visibly stick Pins into the Bodies of the Afflicted, and *scale* them, and hideously distort and disjoint all their Members, besides a thousand others of Plagues beyond these, of any natural Diseases which they give unto them. Yea, they sometimes drag the poor People out of their Chambers, and carry them over Trees and Hills for divers Miles together. A large part of the Persons tortured by these Diabolical *Spectres,* are horribly tempted by them, sometimes with fair Promises, and sometimes with hard Threatnings, but always with felt Miseries to sign the *Devils Laws* in a Spectral Book laid before them; which two or three of these poor Sufferers, being by their tirefome Sufferings overcome to do, they have immediately been releafed from all their Miferies, and they appeared in *Spectre* then to torture thofe that were before their Fellow-Sufferers. The *Witches*, which by their Covenant with the Devil, are become Owners of *Spectres*, are often-times by their own *Spectres* required and compelled to give their Confent, for the moleftation of fome, which they had no mind otherwife to fall upon; and cruel Depradations are then made upon the Vicinage. In the Profecution of thefe Witchcrafts, among a thoufand other unaccountable things, the *Spectres* have an odd faculty of cloathing the moft fubftantial and corporeal Inftruments of Torture with Invifibility, while the Wounds thereby given have been the moft palpable things in the World; fo that the Sufferers affaulted with Inftruments of Iron, wholly unfeen by the Standers-by, though, to their Coft, feen by themfelves, have, upon fnatching, wrefted the Inftruments out of the *Spectres* hands, and every one has then immediately not only *beheld*, but *handled* an Iron Inftrument taken by a Devil from a Neighbour. Thefe wicked *Spectres* have proceeded fo far, as to fteal feveral quantities of Money from divers People, part of which Money has, before fufficient Spectators, been dropt out of the Air into the hand of the

Sufferers, while the *Spectres* have been urging them to subscribe their *Covenant with Death.* In such extravagant ways have these Wretches propounded the *Dragooning* of as many as they can in their own Combination, and the *Destroying* of others, with lingring, spreading, deadly Diseases, till our Countrey should at last become to hot for us. Among the Ghastly Instances of the *Success* which those Bloody Witches have had, we have seen even some of their own Children so dedicated unto the Devil, that in their Infancy it is found the *Imps* have sucked them, and rendred them venemous to a Prodegy. We have also seen the Devils first Batteries upon the Town, where the first church of our Lord in this Colony was gathered, producing those distractions, which have almost ruin'd the Town. We have seen likewise the Plague reaching afterwards into other Towns far and near, where the Houses of good Men have the Devils filling of them with terrible Vexations!

This is the Descent, which it seems, the Devil has now made upon us. But that which makes this Descent the more formidable, is, The *multitude* and *quality* of Persons accused of an Interest in this *Witchcraft*, by the Efficacy of the *Spectres* which take their Name and Shape upon them; causing very many good and wise Men to fear, That many *innocent*, yea, and some *ver-*

tuous Perfons, are by the Devils in this matter impofed upon; That the Devils have obtained the Power, to take on them the likenefs of harmlefs People, and in that likenefs to afflict other people, and be fo abufed by Preftigious *Dæmons*, that upon their look or touch the afflicted fhall be odly affected. Arguments from the *Providence of God*, on the one fide, and from our *Charity* towards *Man* on the other fide, have made this now to become a moft agitated Controverfie among us. There is an *Agony* produced in the minds of Men, left the Devil fhould fham us with *Devices*, of perhaps a finer Thred, than was ever yet practifed upon the World. The whole bufinefs is become hereupon fo *fnarled*, and the determination of the Queftion one way or another, fo *difmal*, that our Honourable Judges have a room for *Jehofhaphat's* Exclamation, *We know not what to do!* They have ufed, as Judges have heretofore done, the *Spectral Evidences*, to introduce their further Enquiries into the *Lives* of the perfons accufed; and they have thereupon, by the wonderful Providence of God, been fo ftrengthened with *other Evidences*, that fome of the *Witch Gang* have been fairly executed. But what fhall be done, as to thofe againft whom the *Evidence* is chiefly founded in the *dark World*? Here they do folemnly demand our Addreffes to the

Father of Lights on their behalf. But in the mean time, the Devil improves the *Darkness* of this Affair, to push us into a *Blind mans Buffet*, and we are even ready to be *sinfully*, yea, hotly and madly, mauling one another in the dark.

The consequence of these things every *considerate man* trembles at, and the more, because the frequent cheats of Passion and Rumour, do precipitate so many, that I wish I could say, The most were *considerate*.

But that which carries on the formidableness of our Trials, unto that which may be called, *A wrath unto the uttermost*, is this: It is not without the *wrath* of the Almighty *God* himself, that the *Devil* is permitted thus to come down upon us in *wrath*. It was said in *Isa*. 9. 19. *Through the wrath of the Lord of Hosts the Land is darkned*. Our Land is *darkned* indeed, since the *Powers of Darkness* are turned in upon us: 'Tis a dark time, yea, a black night indeed, now the *Ty-dogs* of the Pit are abroad among us: but, *it is through the wrath of the Lord of Hosts!* Inasmuch as the *Firebrands* of *Hell* it self are used for the scorching of us with cause enough may we cry out, *What means the heat of this Anger?* Blessed Lord! Are all the other Instruments of thy Vengeance too good for the chastisement of such Transgressors as we are? Must the very *Devils* be sent out of *their own place*, to be our

Troublers? Muſt we be laſh'd with *Scorpions*, fetch'd from the *Place of Torment*? Muſt this *Wilderneſs* be made a Receptacle for the *Dragons of the Wilderneſs*? If a *Lapland* ſhould nouriſh in it vaſt numbers, the Succeſſors of the old *Biarmi*, who can with looks or words bewitch other people, or ſell Winds to Mariners, and have their *Familiar Spirits* which they bequeath to their Children when they die, and by their enchanted Kettle-drums can learn things done a thouſand Leagues off. If a *Swedeland* ſhould afford a Village, where ſome Score of Haggs may not only have their Meetings with *Familiar Spirits*, but alſo by their Enchantments drag many ſcores of poor Children out of their Bed-chambers, to be ſpoiled at thoſe Meetings; This, were not altogether a matter of ſo much wonder! But that *New-England* ſhould this way be haraſſed! They are not *Chaldeans*, that *Bitter and Haſty Nation*, but they are *Bitter and Burning Devils:* They are not *Swarthy Indians*, but they are *Sooty Devils*; that are let looſe upon us. Ah, poor *New-England!* muſt the Plague of *Old Egypt* come upon thee? Whereof we read in Pſ. 78. 49. *He caſt upon them the fierceneſs of his Anger, Wrath and Indignation, and Trouble, by ſending Evil Angels among them.* What, O what muſt next be looked for? Muſt that which is there next mentioned be next encountred? *He spared not their Soul from Death, but gave their Life over to the Pestilence.* For my part, when I consider what *Melancton* says, in one of his Epistles, *That these Diabolical Spectacles are often Prodigies;* and when I consider, how often People have been by *Spectres* called upon, just before their Deaths, I am verily afraid, lest some wasting *Mortality* be among the things, which this Plague is the *Forerunner* of. I pray God prevent it!

But now, *What shall we do?*

I. Let the Devils *coming down in great wrath* upon us, cause us to *come down in great grief* before the Lord. We may truly and sadly say, *We are brought very low! Low* indeed, when the Serpents of the Dust are crawling and coyling about us, and insulting over us. May we not say, *We are all in the Belly of Hell,* when *Hell it self* is feeding upon us? But how *low* is that! O let us then most penitently lay our selves very Low before the God of Heaven who has thus abased us. When a truculent *Nero,* a *Devil of a Man,* was turned in upon the *World,* it was said in 1 Pet. 5. 6. *Humble your selves under the mighty hand of God.* How much more now ought we to *humble our selves* under that *Mighty Hand of that God,* who indeed has the *Devil* in a *Chain,* but has horribly lengthened out the *Chain?* When the old People of God heard any *Blas-*

phemies, tearing of his ever-blessed Name to pieces, they were to rend their *Cloaths* at what they heard. I am sure that we have cause to *rend our hearts this day*, when we see what an high Treason has been committed against the most High God, by the Witchcrafts in our Neighbourhood. We may say; and shall we not be *humbled* when we say it? *We have seen an horrible thing done in our Land!* O 'tis a most humble thing to think, that ever there should be such an Abomination among us, as for a Crew of Humane Race to Renounce their *Maker*, and to unite with the *Devil*, for the troubling of Mankind; and for People to be (as is by some confess'd) *Baptised by a Fiend* using this Form upon them, *Thou art mine, and I have a full power over thee!* afterwards communicating in an Hellish *Bread* and *Wine*, by that Fiend administred to them. It was said in *Deut*. 18. 10, 11, 12. *There shall not be found among you an Inchanter, or a Witch, or a Charmer, or a Consulter with Familiar Spirits, or a Wizzard, or a Necromancer; For all that do these things are an Abomination to the Lord, and because of these Abominations, the Lord thy God doth drive them out before thee.* That *New England* now should have these *Abominations* in it, yea, that some of no mean *Profession*, should be found guilty of them: Alas, what *Humiliations* are we all hereby obliged unto? O 'tis a defiled Land wherein we live; Let us be humbled for thefe *Defiled Abominations*, left we be driven out of our Land. It's very *humbling* thing to think, what Reproaches will be caft upon us for this matter among *the Daughters of the Philiftins*. Indeed, enough might eafily be faid for the *Vindication* of this Country from the *Singularity* of this Matter, by ripping up what has been difcovered in others. *Great Brittain* alone, and this alfo in our days of *Greateft Light*, has had that in it, which may divert the Calumnies of an ill-Natured World, from centring here. They are Words of the devout Bifhop *Hall*, *Satans prevalency in this Age is moft clear, in the marvellous number of Witches abounding in all places. Now hundreds are difcovered in one Shire; and, if Fame deceives us not, in a Village of Fourteen Houfes in the North, are found fo many of this damned Brood; yea, and thofe of both Sexes, who have profeffed much Knowledg, Holinefs and Devotion, are drawn into this damnable Practice.* I fuppofe the Doctor in the firft of thofe Paffages, may refer to what happened in the year 1645, when fo many Vaffals of the Devil were detected, that there was *Thirty* try'd at one time, whereas about *Fourteen* were hanged, and an hundred more detained in the Prifons of *Suffolk* and *Effex*. Among other things which many of thefe acknowledged; one was, That they were to undergo certain Punifhments, if they did not fuch and fuch Hurts as were appointed them. And, amongft the reft that were then Executed, there was an old Perfon called *Lowis*, who confeffed, That he had a couple of Imps, whereof one was always putting him upon the doing of Mifchief. Once particularly, that *Imp* calling for his confent fo to do, went immediately and funk a Ship, then under Sail. I pray, let not *New-England* become of an unfavoury and fulphurous Refentment in the Opinion of the World abroad, for the doleful things which are now fallen out among us, while there are fuch Hiftories of other places abroad in the World. Neverthelefs, I am fure that we, the People of *New-England*, have caufe enough to *humble* our felves under our moft *humbling* Circumftances. We muft no more be *haughty, becaufe of the Lord's holy Mountain among us*. No, it becomes us rather to be *humbled, becaufe we have been fuch an Habitation of unholy Devils*.

II. Since the Devil is *come down in great wrath upon us*, let not us in our *great wrath* againft one another provide a *Lodging* for him. It was a moft wholefome Caution, in *Eph*. 4. 26, 27, *Let not the Sun go down upon your wrath. Neither give place to the Devil*. The Devil is come down to fee what *Quarter* he fhall find among us: And if his coming down do now fill us with *wrath* against one another; and if betwixt the Cause of the Sufferers on one hand, and the Cause of the Suspected on the other, we carry things to such Extreams of *Passion* as are now gaining upon us, the Devil will bless himself to find such a convenient Lodging as we shall therein afford unto him. And it may be that the *wrath* which we have had against one another, has had more than a little Influence upon the coming down of the Devil in that *wrath* which now amazes us. Have not many of us been Devils one unto another for Sladerings, for Back-bitings, for Animosities? For this, among other Causes, perhaps, God has permitted the Devils to be worrying, as they now are, among us. But it is high time to leave off all *Devilism*, when the *Devil* himself is falling upon us: And it is *no time* for us to be censuring and reviling one another, with a *Divilish wrath*, when the *wrath* of the *Devil* is annoying us. The way for us to out-wit the Devil in the Wiles with which he now vexes us, would be for us to joyn as one Man in our Cries to God, for the directing and issuing of this Thorny Business; but if we do not *lift up* our Hands to Heaven *without wrath*, we cannot then do it *without doubt*, of speeding in it. I am ashamed when I read *French* Authors giving this Character of *English-men.* [*Ils se haissent Les uns les autres, & font en Division continuelle.*] They hate one another, and are always *Quarrelling* one with another. And I shall be much more ashamed, if it become the Character of *New-Englanders;* which is indeed what the Devil would have. *Satan* would make us *bruise* one another, by breaking of the Peace among us: But O let us disappoint them. We read of a thing that sometimes happens to the *Devil,* when he is foaming with his *wrath,* in *Matth.* 12. 43. *The unclean Spirit seeks rest, and finds none.* But we give *rest* unto the *Devil,* by *wrath* one against another. If we would lay aside all fierceness and keeness, in the Disputes which the Devil has raised among us; and if we would use to one another none but the *soft Answers, which turn away wrath;* I should hope that we might light upon such Counsels, as would quickly extricate us out of our *Labyrinths.* But the old Incendiary of the World is come from Hell, with Sparks of Hell-Fire flashing on every side of him; and we make ourselves Tynder to the Sparks. When the Emperor *Henry* III. kept the Feast of *Pentecost,* at the City of *Mentz,* there arose a Dissension among some of the *People* there, which came from *Words to Blows,* and at last it passed on to the *shedding of Blood.* After the *Tumult* was over, when they came to that

Clause in their Devotions, *Thou haſt made this Day glorious;* the Devil, to the inexpreſſible Terror of that vaſt Aſſembly, made the *Temple* ring with that Out-cry, *But I have made this Day Quarrelſome:* We are *truly* come into a day, which by being well managed, might be very *Glorious* for the Exterminating of thoſe *Accurſed Things*, which have hitherto been the Clogs of our Proſperity. But if we make this day quarrelſome, through any *Raging Confidences*, Alas, *O Lord, my fleſh trembles for fear of thee, and I am afraid of thy Judgments*. *Eraſmus*, among other Hiſtorians, tells us, that at a Town in *Germany*, a Witch, or Devil, *appear'd on the top of a Chimney*, threatening to ſet the Town on Fire: And at length, ſcattering a Pot of Aſhes abroad, the Town was preſently and horribly *burnt unto the Ground*. Methinks I ſee the Spectres from the *top of the Chimneys* to the Northward, threatening to ſcatter Fire about the *Country;* but let *us quench that Fire* by the moſt Amicable Correſpondencies; leſt, as the Spectres have, they ſay, already moſt literally *burnt ſome of our Dwellings*, there do come forth a *further fire* from the Brambles of Hell, which may terribly Devour us. Let *us* not be like a *Troubled Houſe*, altho we are ſo *much haunted by the Devils*. Let our *long ſuffering* be a *well placed piece of Armour about us*, againſt the Fiery Darts of the wicked ones. History informs us, That so *long ago* as the year 858: a certain *Pestilent and Malignant* sort of a *Dæmon*, molested *Chaumont* in *Germany*, with all sorts of Methods to stir up strife among the Citizens. He uttered Prophecies, he detected Villanies, he branded People with all kind of *Infamies*. He *incensed* the Neighbourhood against *One Man* particularly, as *the Cause of all the Mischiefs;* who yet proved himself *innocent.* He threw *Stones* at the *Inhabitants*, and at length burnt their Habitations, till the Commission of *the Dæmon* could go no further. I say, *let us be well aware lest such* Dæmons *do come hither also.*

III. Inasmuch as the Devil is come down in *great Wrath*, we had need labour with all the care and speed we can, to divert the great *Wrath of Heaven* from coming at the same time upon us. The God of Heaven has with long and loud Admonitions been calling us to *a Reformation of our provoking Evils*, as the only way to avoid that *Wrath* of his, which does not *only threaten*, but *consume us*. 'Tis because we have been Deaf to those Calls that we are now by a provoked God laid open to the *Wrath of the Devil himself*. It is said in *Prov.* 16. 7. *When a mans ways please the Lord, he maketh even his Enemies to be at peace with him.* The Devil is our grand Enemy; and tho we would not be at peace *with* him, yet we would be at peace from him; that is, we would have him unable to disquiet *our Peace*. But inasmuch as the *wrath* which we endure from this Enemy, will allow us no *peace*, we may be sure *our ways have not pleased the Lord*. It is because we have *broken the Hedge of God's Precepts*, that the Hedge of God's *Providence* is not so entire as it uses to be about us; but *Serpents* are *biting* of us. O let us then see our selves, to make our *peace* with our God, whom we have *displeased* by our Iniquities: And let us not imagine that we can encounter the *Wrath of the Devil*, while there is the *Wrath of God Almighty* to set that Mastiff upon us. REFORMATION, REFORMATION, has been the repeated Cry of all the Judgments that have hitherto been upon us; because we have been as *deaf Adders* thereunto; the *Adders* of the Infernal Pit are now hissing about us. At length, as it was of old said, Luke 60. 13. *If one went unto them from the dead, they will repent;* even so, there are some come unto us from the damned. The Great God has loosed the Bars of the Pit, so that many damned Spirits are come in among us, to make us repent of our Misdemeanors. The Means which the Lord had formerly employ'd for our awakening, were such, that he might well have said,

What could I have done more? And yet after all, he has done more, in some regards, than was ever done for the awakening of any People in the World. The things now done to awaken our Enquiries after our provoking Evils, and our Endeavours to reform those Evils, are most extraordinary things; for which cause I would freely speak it, if we now do not some extraordinary things in speedily returning to God, we are the most incurable; and I wish it be not quickly said, the most miserable People under the Sun. Believe me, 'tis a time for all People to do something *extraordinary, in searching and trying of their ways, and in turning to the Lord.* It is an extraordinary rate of *circumspection*, and *Spiritual mindedness*, that we should all now maintain a *walk with God.* At such a time as this, ought not Magistrates to do something extraordinary in promoting of what is laudable, and in restraining and chastising of *Evil doers?* At such a time as this, ought not *Ministers* to do something extraordinary in pulling the Souls of Men out of the Snares of the Devil, not only by publick *Preaching*, but by personal Visits and Counsels, *from house to house.* At such a time as this ought not *Churches* to do something extraordinary in renewing of their Covenants, and in remembring and reviving the Obligations of what they have renewed. Some admirable Designs about the Reformation of Manners, have lately been on foot in the *English* Nation, in pursuance of the most excellent Admonitions which have been given for it, by the Letters of their Majesties. Besides, the Vigorous Agreements of the *Justices* here and there in the Kingdom, assisted by godly Gentlemen and Informers, to *execute* the Laws upon prophane Offenders; there has been started a Proposal for the well affected People in every Parish, to enter into orderly Societies, whereof every Member shall bind himself, not only to avoid Prophaneness, in himself, but also according unto their Place, to do their *utmost* in first Reproving; and if it must be so, then Exposing, and so *Punishing*, as the Law directs, for others that shall be *guilty*. It has been observed, that the *English* Nation has had some of its great *Successes*, upon some special and signal Actions this way; and a *discouragement* given unto Legal Proceedings of this kind, must needs be very exercising to the *Wise that observe these things.* But O, why *should not New-England* be the most forward part of the *English* Nation *in such Reformation?* Methink I hear the Lord from Heaven saying over us, *O that my people had harkned unto me, then I should soon have subdued the Devils, as well as their other Enemies!* There have been some feeble Essays towards Reformation of late in *our*

Churches; but I pray what comes of them? Do we ſtay till the ſtorm of his Wrath be over? Nay, let *us* be doing what we can, as faſt as we can to divert the ſtorm. The Devils having broke in upon *our World*, there is great aſking, *Who is it that has brought them in?* And many do by *Spectral Exhibitions* come to be cryed *out upon*. I hope in Gods time it will be *found*, that among thoſe that are *thus cryed out upon*, there are Perſons yet *clear from the great Tranſgreſſion;* but indeed, all the Unreformed among us, may juſtly be *cryed out upon*, as having *too much* of an hand in letting of the Devils into *our Borders;* 'tis *our Worldlineſs, our Formality, our Senſuality*, and *our Iniquity*, that has helped this letting of the Devils in. O let *us* then at laſt, *conſider our ways*. 'Tis a ſtrange paſſage recorded by Mr. *Clark*, in the life of his Father, That the people of his Pariſh refuſing to be Reclaimed from their *Sabbath-breaking*, by all the Zealous Teſtimonies which that good Man bore againſt it; at laſt, on a Night after the People had retired home from a Revelling *prophanation of the Lord's Day*, there was heard a great Noiſe, with ratling of Chains up and down the Town, and an horrid Scent of Brimſtone fill'd the *Neighbourhood*. Upon which the *guilty Conſciences* of the Wretches told them, the Devil was come to fetch them away; and it ſo terrified them, that an Eminent Reformation followed the Sermons which that Man of God preached thereupon. Behold Sinners, behold and wonder, left *you perish;* the very Devils are *walking about our streets;* with lengthned Chains, making a *dreadful Noise in our Ears,* and *Brimstone* even *without a Metaphor,* is making an hellish and horrid stench in *our Nostrils.* I pray leave off all those things whereof *your guilty Consciences* may *now accuse you,* left the Devils do yet more *direfully fall upon you.* Reformation is at this time our only preservation.

HAVING thus discours'd on *Wonders of the Invisible World,* I shall now with God's help, go on to relate some Remarkable and Memorable Instances of Wonders which that World has given to *our selves.* And altho the chief Entertainment which my Readers do expect, and shall receive, will be a *true* History of what has occurred, respecting the 𝔚𝔦𝔱𝔠𝔥𝔠𝔯𝔞𝔣𝔱𝔰 wherewith we are at this day *persecuted;* yet I shall choose to Usher in the mention of those things, with,

A Narrative of an APPARITION *which a Gentleman in* Boston, *had of his Brother, just then Murthered in* London.

IT was on the 2*d of May*, in the year 1687, that a moſt ingenious accompliſhed and well diſpoſed Gentleman, Mr. *Joſeph Beacon* by Name, about five a Clock in the Morning, as he lay, whether Sleeping or Waking he could not ſay, (but judged the latter of them) had a View of his Brother then at *London*, altho he was now himſelf at our *Boſton*, diſtanced from him a *Thouſand Leagues*. This his Brother appear'd unto him in the Morning about five a Clock at *Boſton*, having on him a Bengal Gown, which he *uſually* wore, with a Napkin tyed about his Head; his *Countenance* was very Pale, Gaſtly, Deadly: and he had a *Bloody Wound* on one ſide of his Forehead. *Brother!* ſays the affrighted *Joſeph*. *Brother*, anſwered the Apparition. Said *Joſeph*, *What's the matter Brother? How came you here?* The Apparition replied, *Brother, I have been moſt* barbarouſly *and* injuriouſly *Butcher'd, by a Debauch'd, drunken Fellow, to whom I never did any wrong in my Life.* Whereupon he gave a particular deſcription of the Murderer; adding, *Brother, this Fellow changing his Name, is attempting to come over unto*

New-England, *in* Foy *or* Wild: *I would pray you on the first Arrival of either of these, to get an Order from the Governour, to Seize the Person whom I have now described; and then do you Indict him for the Murder of me your Brother: I'll stand by you and prove the Indictment.* And so he vanished. Mr. *Beacon* was extreamly astonished at what he had seen and heard; and the people of the Family not only observed an extraordinary Alteration upon him, for the week following, but have also given me under their hands a full Testimony, that he then gave them an Account of this Apparition.

All this while, Mr. *Beacon* had no advice of any thing amiss attending his Brother then in *England*; but about the latter end of *June* following, he understood by the common ways of Communication, that the *April* before, his Brother, going in haste by Night to call a Coach for a Lady, met a Fellow then in Drink, with his Doxy in his Hand: Some way or other the Fellow thought himself Affronted with the hasty passage of this *Beacon*, and immediately ran into the Fireside of a Neighbouring Tavern, from whence he fetch'd out a Fire-fork wherewith he grievously wounded *Beacon* in the Skull; even in that very part where the Apparition show'd his Wound. Of this Wound he Languished until he Dyed on the Second of *May*, about five of the Clock in the Morning at *London*. The Murderer it seems was endeavouring to Escape, as the Apparitoin affirmed, but the Friends of the Deceased *Beacon*, Seized him; and prosecuting him at Law, he found the help of such Friends as brought him off without the loss of his Life; since which there has no more been heard of the Business.

This History I received of Mr. *Joseph Beacon* himself, who a little before his own pious and hopeful Death, which follow'd not long after, gave me the Story written and signed with his own Hand, and attested with the Circumstances I have already mentioned.

BUT I shall no longer detain my Reader from his expected Entertainment, in a brief Account of the Tryals which have passed upon some of the Malefactors lately Executed at *Salem*, for the *Witchcrafts* whereof they stood Convicted. For my own part, I was not present at any of them; nor ever had I any Personal prejudice at the Persons thus brought upon the Stage; much less at the surviving Relations of those Persons, with and for whom I would be as hearty a Mourner as any Man living in the World: *The Lord Comfort them!* But having received a particular Command so to do, I can do no other than shortly relate the Chief *Matters of Fact*, which occurr'd in the Tryals of some that were Executed, in an Abridgment Collected out of the *Court Papers*, on this occasion put into my hands. You are to take the Truth just as it was; and the Truth will hurt no good man. There might have been more of these, if my Book would not thereby have swollen too big; and if some other worthy hands did not perhaps intend something further in these *Collections*; for which cause I have only singled out Four or Five, which may serve to illustrate the way of Dealing, wherein *Witchcrafts* use to be concerned; and I report matters not as an *Advocate*, but as an *Historian*.

They were some of the Gracious Words inserted in the Advice, which many of the Neighbouring Ministers did this Summer humbly lay before our Honourable Judges, *We cannot but with all thankfulness, acknowledge the success which the Merciful God has given unto the Sedulous and Assiduous endeavours of our Honourable Rulers, to detect the abominable Witchcrafts which have been committed in the Country; humbly Praying, that the discovery of these mysterious and mischievous wickednesses, may be perfected.* If in the midst of the many Dissatisfactions among us, the Publication of these Tryals, may promote such a pious Thankfulness unto God for Justice being so far executed among us, I shall Rejoyce that God is

Glorified; and pray that no wrong steps of ours may ever sully any of his Glorious Works. But we will begin with

A Modern Instance of Witches, Discovered and Condemned in a Tryal, before that Celebrated Judg, Sir Matthew Hale.

IT may cast some Light upon the Dark things now in *America*, if we just give a glance upon the *like things* lately happening in *Europe*. We may see the *Witchcrafts* here most exactly resemble the *Witchcrafts* there; and we may learn what sort of Devils do trouble the World.

The Venerable *Baxter* very truly says, *Judge* Hale *was a Person, than whom no man was more Backward to condemn a Witch, without full Evidence.*

Now, one of the latest Printed Accounts about a *Tryal of Witches*, is of what was before him, and it ran on this wise. [Printed in the Year 1682.] And it is here the rather mentioned, because it was a Tryal, much considered by the Judges of *New-England*.

I. *Rose Cullender* and *Amy Duny*, were severally Indicted, for Bewitching *Elizabeth Durent, Ann Durent, Jane Bocking, Susan Chandler, William Durent, Elizabeth and Deborah Pacy*, and the Evidence whereon they were Convicted, stood upon divers particular Circumstances.

II. *Ann Durent, Sufan Chandler,* and *Elizabeth Pacy,* when they came into the Hall, to give Inftructions for the drawing the Bills of Indictments, they fell into ftrange and violent Fits, fo that they were unable to give in their Depofitions, not only then, but alfo during the whole Affizes. *William Durent* being an Infant, his Mother fwore, That *Amy Duny* looking after her Child one Day in her abfence, did at her return confefs, that fhe had given fuck to the Child: (tho' fhe were an Old Woman:) Whereat, when *Durent* expreffed her difpleafure, *Duny* went away with Difcontents and Menaces.

The Night after, the Child fell into ftrange and fad Fits, wherein it continued for divers Weeks. One Dr. *Jacob* advifed her to hang up the Childs Blanket in the Chimney Corner all Day, and at Night when fhe went to put the Child into it, if fhe found any thing in it then to through it without fear into the Fire. Accordingly at Night, there fell a great Toad out of the Blanket, which ran up and down the Hearth. A boy catch't it, and held it in the Fire with the Tongs, where it made an horrible Noife and flafh'd like to Gun-Powder, with a report like that of a Piftol: Whereupon the Toade was no more to be feen. The next Day a Kinfwoman of *Duny's* told the Deponent, that her Aunt was all grievoufly fcorch'd with the

Fire, and the Deponent going to her House, found her in such a Condition. *Duny* told her, she might thank her for it; but she should live to see some of her Children Dead, and herself upon Crutches. But after the Burning of the Toad, this Child recovered.

This Deponent further testified, that her Daughter *Elizabeth*, being about the Age of ten Years, was taken in like manner as her first Child was, and in her Fits complained much of *Amy Duny*, and said that she did appear to her, and afflict her in such manner as the former. One day she found *Amy Duny* in her House, and thrusting her out of Doors, *Duny* said, *You need not be so angry, your Child won't live long.* And within three days the Child died. The Deponent added, that she herself, not long after was taken with such a Lameness in both her Legs, that she was forced to go upon Crutches, and she was now in Court upon them. [It was Remarkable, that immediately upon the Juries bringing in *Duny* Guilty, *Durent* was restored unto to the use of her Limbs, and went home without her Crutches.]

III. As for *Elizabeth* and *Deborah Pacy*, one Aged Eleven Years, the other Nine; the elder being in Court, was made utterly senseless, during all the time of the Trial, or at least speechless, by the direction of the Judge, *Duny* was privately brought to *Elizabeth Pacy*, and she touched her hand : whereupon the Child, without so much as seeing her, suddenly leap'd up and flew upon the Prisoner; the younger was too ill to be brought into the Assizes. But *Samuel Pacy*, their Father, testified, that his Daughter *Deborah* was taken with a sudden Lameness; and upon the grumbling of *Amy Duny*, for being denied something, where this Child was then sitting, the Child was taken with an extream pain in her stomach, like the pricking of Pins; and shrieking at a dreadful manner, like a Whelp, rather than a Rational Creature. The Physicians could not conjecture the cause of the Distemper, but *Amy Duny*, being a Woman of ill Frame, and the Child in Fits crying out of *Amy Duny*, as affrighting her with the Apparition of her Person, the Deponent suspected her, and procured her to be set in the Stocks. While she was there, she said in the hearing of two Witnesses, Mr. Pacy *keeps a great stir about his Child, but let him stay till he has done as much by his Children as I have done by mine*. And being asked what she had done to her Children, she answered, *She had been fain to open her Childs Mouth with a Tap to give it Victuals*. The Deponent added, that within two days the Fits of his Daughters were such, that they could not preserve either Life or Breath, without the help of a Tap. And that the Children cry'd out of *Amy Duny*, and of *Rose Cullender*, as afflicting them with her Apparition.

IV. The Fits of the Children were various. They would sometimes be Lame on one side, sometimes on t'other. Sometimes very sore, sometimes restored unto their Limbs, and then Deaf, or Blind, or Dumb, for a long while together. Upon the Recovery of their Speech, they would Cough extreamly, and with much Flegm, they would bring up crooked pins, and at one time, a Two-penny Nail, with a very broad Head. Commonly at the end of every Fit, they would cast up a Pin. When the Children Read, they could not pronounce the Name of *Lord*, or *Jesus*, or *Christ*, but would fall into Fits; and say, Amy Duny *says, I must not use that Name.* When they came to the Name of *Satan* or *Devil*, they would clap their Fingers upon the Book, crying out, *This bites, but it makes me speak right well!* The Children in their Fits would often Cry out, *There stands* Amy Duny, or *Rose Cullender;* and they would afterwards relate, *That these Witches appearing before them, threatned them, that if they told of what they saw or heard, they would Torment them more than ever they did before.*

V. *Margaret Arnold*, the Sister to Mr. *Pacy*, Testifi'd unto the like Sufferings being upon the Children, at her House, whither her Brother had removed them. And that sometimes, the Children (*only*) would see things like Mice, run about the House; and one of them suddenly snap'd one with the Tongs, and threw it into the Fire, where it screeched out like a Rat. At another time, a thing like a Bee flew at the Face of the younger Child, the Child fell into a Fit, and at last Vomited up a *Two-penny Nail*, with a broad Head; affirming, *That the Bee brought this Nail, and forced it into her Mouth.* The Child would in like manner be assaulted with Flies, which brought crooked Pins unto her, and made her first swallow them, and then Vomit them. She one day caught an Invisible Mouse, and throwing it into the Fire, it flash'd like to Gun-Powder. None besides the Child saw the Mouse, but every one saw the Flash. She also declared out of her Fits, that in them, *Amy Duny* much tempted her to destroy her self.

VI. As for *Ann Durent*, her Father testified, That upon a Discontent of *Rose Cullender*, his Daughter was taken with much Illness in her Stomach, and great and sore pains, like the pricking of Pins, and then Swooning Fits, from which recovering, she declared, *She had seen the Apparition of* Rose Cullender, *threatning to Torment her.* She likewise Vomited up divers Pins. The Maid was present at Court, but when *Cul-*

lender looked upon her, she fell into such Fits, as made her utterly unable to declare any thing.

Ann Baldwin deposed the same.

VII. *Jane Bockin*, who was too weak to be at the Assizes, but her Mother Testified, that her Daughter having formerly been Afflicted with Swooning Fits, and Recovered of them, was now taken with a great pain in her Stomach, and New Swooning Fits. That she took little Food, but every day Vomited Crooked Pins. In her first Fits, she would extend her Arms, and use postures as if she catched at something: and when her Clutched Hands were forced open, they would find several pins diversely Crooked, unaccountably lodged there. She would also maintain a Discourse with some that were invisibly present, when casting abroad her Arms, she would often say, *I will not have it!* but at last say, *Then I will have it!* and closing her hand, which when they presently after opened, a Lath Nail was found in it. But her great Complaints were of being visited by the shapes of *Amy Duny*, and *Rose Cullender*.

VIII. As for *Susan Chandler*, her Mother Testified, That being at the Search of *Rose Cullender*, they found on her Belly a thing like a Teat, of an Inch long; which the said *Rose* ascribed to a strain. But near her privy parts they found three more, that were smaller than the former. At the end of the long Teat there was a little hole, which appeared as if newly Sucked; and upon ſtraining it, a white Milky Matter iſſued out. The Deponent further ſaid, That her Daughter being one day concerned at *Roſe Cullenders* taking her by the hand ſhe fell very ſick, and at night cry'd out, *That* Roſe Cullender *would come to Bed unto her.* Her Fits grew violent, and in the Intervals of them, ſhe declared, *That ſhe ſaw* Roſe Cullender *in them, and once having a great Dog with her.* She alſo Vomited up crooked Pins; and when ſhe was brought into Court, ſhe fell into Fits. She recovered her ſelf in ſome time, and was aſked by the Court, whether ſhe was in a condition to take an Oath, and give Evidence. She ſaid ſhe could, but having been Sworn, ſhe fell into her Fits again, and *Burn her! Burn her!* were all the words that ſhe could find Power to ſpeak. Her Father likewiſe gave the ſame Teſtimony with her Mother, as to all but the Search.

IX. Here was the ſum of the Evidence: which was not thought ſufficient to Convict the Priſoners. For admitting the Children were Bewitched, yet, ſaid he, it can never be apply'd unto the Priſoners, upon the Imagination of the Parties only Afflicted; inaſmuch as no perſon whatſoever could then be in Safety.

Dr. *Brown*, a very Learned Perſon then preſent, gave his Opinion, that thefe Perfons were bewitched. He added, that in *Denmark*, there had been lately a great difcovery of Witches; who ufed the very fame way of afflicting people, by conveying Pins and Nails into them. His opinion was, that the Devil in Witchcrafts, did work upon the Bodys of Men and Women, upon a *Natural Foundation;* and that he did Extraordinarily afflict them, with fuch Diftempers as their Bodies were moft fubject unto.

X. The Experiment about the *Ufefulnefs*, yea, or *Lawfulnefs* whereof Good Men have fometimes difputed, was divers Times made, that though the afflicted were utterly deprived of all fenfe in their Fits, yet upon the *Touch* of the accufed, they would fo fcreech out, and fly up, as not upon any other Perfons. And yet it was alfo found that once upon the touch of an innocent perfon, the like effect followed, which put the whole Court unto a ftand! although a fmall Reafon was at length attempted to be given for it.

XI. However, to ftrengthen the Credit of what had been already produced againft the Prifoners, one *John Soam* teftifi'd, that bringing home his Hay in Three Carts, one of the Carts wrenched the Window of *Rofe Cullenders* Houfe, whereupon fhe flew out, with violent Threatnings againft the Deponent. The other two

Carts, paffed by twice, Loaded, that day afterwards; but the Cart which touched *Cullenders* Houfe, was twice or thrice that day overturned. Having again Loaded it, as they brought it thro' the Gate which leads out of the Field, the Cart ftruck fo faft in the Gates Head, that they could not poffibly get it thro', but were forced to cut down the Poft of the Gate, to make the Cart pafs thro', altho' they could not perceive that the Cart did of either fide touch the Gate-Poft. They afterwards did with much Difficulty get it home to the Yard; but could not for their Lives get the Cart near the place, where they fhould unload. They were fain to unload at a great Diftance; and when they were Tired, the Nofes of them that came to affift them, would burft forth a Bleeding; fo they were fain to give over till next morning; and then they unloaded without any difficulty.

XII. *Robert Sherringkam* alfo Teftified, that the Axle Tree of his Cart, happening in paffing, to break fome part of *Rofe Cullenders* Houfe, in her Anger, at it, fhe vehemently threatned him, *His Horfes fhould fuffer for it*. And within a fhort time all his Four Horfes dyed; after which he fuftained many other Loffes in the fudden dying of his Cattle. He was alfo taken with a Lamenefs in his Limbs; and fo vexed with Lice of an extraordinary Number and Bignefs, that no Art could hinder the Swarming of them, till he burnt up two Suits of Apparel.

XIII. As for *Amy Duny*, 'twas Teftifi'd by one *Richard Spencer* that he heard her fay, *That the Devil would not let her Reft, until fhe were Revenged on the Wife of* Cornelius Sandfwel. And that *Sandfwel* teftifi'd that her Poultry dy'd fuddainly, upon *Amy Dunys* threatning of them; and that her Hufbands Chimney fell, quickly after *Duny* had fpoken of fuch a difafter. And a Firkin of Fifh could not be kept from falling into the Water, upon fufpicious words of *Dunys*.

XIV. The Judge told the Jury, they were to inquire now, firft, Whether thefe Children were Bewitched; and fecondly, Whether the Prifoners at the Bar were guilty of it. He made no doubt, there were fuch Creatures as Witches; for the Scriptures affirmed it; and the Wifdom of all Nations had provided Laws againft fuch Perfons. He prayed the God of Heaven to direct their Hearts in the weighty thing they had in hand; for *To condemn the Innocent, and let the Guilty go free, were both an Abomination to the Lord.*

The Jury in half an hour brought them in Guilty upon the feveral Indictments, which were Nineteen in Number.

The next Morning, the Children with their Parents, came to the Lodgings of the Lord

Chief Juſtice, and were in as good health as ever in their Lives; being reſtored within half an Hour after the Witches were Convicted.

The Witches were Executed, and *Confeſſed* nothing; which indeed will not be wondered by them, who Conſider and Entertain the Judgment of a Judicious Writer, *That the Unpardonable Sin, is moſt uſually Committed by Profeſſors of the Chriſtian Religion, falling into Witchcraft.*

We will now proceed unto ſeveral of the like Trials among our ſelves.

NOTE. — See Calef (pp. 278 to 329 of this volume), who has inſerted the account of the trials in the ſame words as Cotton Mather, prefixing alſo copies of the indictments.

Having thus far done the Service impos'd upon me; I will further purfue it, by relating a few of thofe matchlefs Curiofities, with which the Witchcraft now upon us has entertained us. And I fhall Report nothing but with good Authority and what I would invite all my Readers to examine, while 'tis yet frefh and new, that if there be found any miftake, it may be as willingly Retracted, as it was unwillingly committed.

The firft Curiofity.

I. 'Tis very Remarkable to fee what impious and impudent *Imitation* of Divine Things, is apifhly affected by the Devil, in feveral of thofe Matters, whereof the Confeffions of our *Witches*, and the Afflictions of our *Sufferers* have informed us.

That Reverend and Excellent Perfon, Mr. *John Higginfon*, in my Converfation with him, once invited me to this Reflection; that the *Indians* which come from far to fettle about *Mexico*, were in their Progrefs to that Settlement, under a Conduct of the *Devil*, were ftrangely Emulating what the Bleffed God gave to *Ifrael* in the Wildernefs.

Acofta, is our Author for it, that the Devil in their Idol *Vitzlipultzli*, governed that mighty

Nation. *He commanded them to leave their Country, promising to make them* Lords *over all the Provinces possessed by* Six *other Nations of* Indians, *and give them a Land abounding with all precious things.* They went forth, carrying their Idol with them, in a Coffer of Reeds, supported by four of their Principal Priests, with whom he still discoursed in secret, revealing to them the Successes, and Accidents of their way. He advised them when to March, and where to Stay, and without his Commandment they moved not. The first thing they did, wherever they came, was to erect a Tabernacle *for their false God;* which they set always in the midst of their Camp, and they placed the Ark *upon an* Altar. When they, tired with Pains, talked of proceeding no further in their Journey, than a certain pleasant Stage, whereto they were arrived, this Devil in one Night, horribly killed them that had started this Talk, by pulling out their Hearts. And so they passed on till they came to Mexico.

The Devil which *then* thus imitated what was in the Church of the *Old Testament*, now among *us* would imitate the Affairs of the Church in the *New*. The *Witches* do say, that they form themselves much after the manner of *Congregational Churches;* and that they have a *Baptism* and a *Supper* and *Officers* among them, abominably Resembling those of our Lord.

But there are many more of thefe Bloody *Imitations*, if the Confeffions of the *Witches* are to be received; which I confefs, ought to be but with very much Caution.

What is their ftriking down with a fierce *Look*? What is their making of the Afflicted *Rife*, with a touch of their *Hand*? What is their Tranfportation through the *Air*? What is their Travelling in *Spirit*, while their Body is caft into a Trance? What is their caufing of *Cattel* to run mad and perifh? What is their Entring their Names in a *Book*? What is their coming together from all parts, at the Sound of a *Trumpet*? What is their appearing fometimes clothed with *Light* or *Fire* upon them? What is their covering of themfelves and their Inftruments with *Invifibility*? But a blafphemous Imitation of certain things recorded about our Saviour or his Prophets, or the Saints in the Kingdom of God.

A Second Curiofity.

II. In all the *Witchcraft* which now grievoufly Vexes us, I know not whether any thing be more unaccountably, than the Trick which the Witches have to render themfelves, and their Tools *Invifible*. *Witchcraft* feems to be the Skill of Applying the *Plaftic Spirit* of the

World, unto some unlawful purposes, by means of a Confederacy with *Evil Spirits*. Yet one would wonder how the *Evil Spirits* themselves can do some things; especially at *Invisibilizing* of the grossest Bodies. I can tell the Name of an ancient Author, who pretends to shew the way, how a Man may come to walk about *Invisible*, and I can tell the Name of another ancient Author, who pretends to Explode that way. But I will not speak too plainly, lest I should unawares Poison some of my *Readers*, as the Pious *Hemingius* did one of his *Pupils*, when he only by way of Diversion recited a Spell, which, they had said, would cure *Agues*. Thus much I will say; The notion of procuring *Invisibility*, by any *Natural Expedient*, yet known, is, I believe, a meer PLINYISM; How far it may be obtained by a *Magical Sacrament*, is best known to the dangerous Knaves that have try'd it. But our *Witches* do seem to have got the knack; and this is one of the Things, that make me think, *Witchcraft* will not be fully understood, until the day when there shall not be one Witch in the World.

There are certain People very *Dogmatical* about these Matters; but I'll give them only these three Bones to pick.

First, One of our bewitched People, was cruelly assaulted by a *Spectre*, that, she said, ran at her with a *Spindle;* tho no body elfe in the Room, could fee either the *Spectre* or the *Spindle.* At laft, in her Miferies, giving a fnatch at the *Spectre,* fhe pull'd the *Spindle* away, and it was no fooner got into her Hand, but the other People then prefent, beheld, that it was indeed a real, proper, Iron *Spindle,* belonging they knew to whom; which when they lock'd up very fafe, it was neverthelefs by *Dæmons* unaccountably ftole away, to do further mifchief.

Secondly, Another of our Bewitch'd People, was haunted with a moft abufive *Spectre,* which came to her, fhe faid, with a *Sheet* about her. After fhe had undergone a deal of Teaze, from the Annoyance of the *Spectre,* fhe gave a violent fnatch at the Sheet, that was upon it; wherefrom fhe tore a Corner, which in her hand immediately became *Vifible* to a Room full of Spectators; a palpable Corner of a Sheet. Her Father, who was now holding her, catch'd that he might keep what his Daughter had fo ftrangely feifed, but the unfeen *Spectre* had like to have pull'd his hand off, by endeavouring to wreft it from him; however he ftill held it, and I fuppofe has it ftill to fhew; it being but a few hours ago, namely about the beginning of this *October,* that this Accident happened in the Family of one *Pitman,* at *Manchefter.*

Thirdly, A young Man, delaying to procure

Testimonials for his Parents, who being under confinement on Suspicion of *Witchcraft*, required him to do that service for them, was quickly pursued with odd Inconveniences. But once above the rest, an Officer going to put his *Brand* on the Horns of some *Cows*, belonging to these People, which tho he had seised for some of their Debts, yet he was willing to leave in their Possession, for the Subsistence of the poor Family: this young Man help'd in holding the Cows to be thus branded. The three first *Cows* he held well enough; but when the hot *Brand* was clap'd upon the Fourth, he *winc'd* and *shrunk* at such a Rate, as that he could hold the Cow no longer. Being afterwards Examined about it, he confessed, that at that very instant when the *Brand* entred the *Cows Horn*, exactly the like burning *Brand* was clap'd upon his own Thigh; where he has exposed the lasting Marks of it, unto such as asked to see them.

Unriddle these Things.——*Et Eris mihi magnus Apollo.*

A Third Curiosity.

III. If a drop of *Innocent Blood* should be shed, in the Prosecution of the *Witchcrafts* among us, how unhappy are we! For which cause, I cannot express my self in better terms, than thofe of a moft worthy Perfon, who lives near the prefent Center of these things. *The Mind of* God *in thefe Matters, is to be carefully lookt into, with due Circumfpection, that Satan deceive us not with his Devices, who transforms himfelf into an Angel of Light, and may pretend Juftice, and yet intend Mifchief.* But on the other fide, if the ftorm of Juftice do now fall only on the Heads of thofe guilty *Witches* and *Wretches* which have defiled our Land, *How Happy!*

The Execution of fome that have lately dyed, has been immediately attended, with a ftrange Deliverance of fome, that had lain for many years, in a moft fad Condition, under, they knew not whofe *evil hands*. As I am abundantly fatisfied, That many of the Self-Murders committed here, have been the effects of a cruel and bloody *Witchcraft*, letting fly *Dæmons* upon the miferable *Seneca's;* thus, it has been admirable unto me to fee, how a devilifh *Witchcraft*, sending Devils upon them, has driven many poor People to *Defpair*, and perfecuted their Minds, with fuch buzzes of *Atheifm* and *Blafphemy*, as has made them run *diftracted with Terrors:* And fome long *bow'd down* under fuch a *Spirit of Infirmity*, have been marvelloufly recovered upon the Death of the Witches.

One *Whetford* particularly ten years ago, challenging of *Bridget Bifhop* (whofe *Trial* you have had) with *stealing* of a *Spoon*, *Bishop* threatned her very *direfully:* presently after this, was *Whetford* in the Night, and in her Bed, visited by *Bishop*, with one *Parker*, who making the Room light at their coming in, there discoursed of several Mischiefs they would inflict upon her. At last they pull'd her out, and carried her unto the Sea-side, there to *drown* her; but she calling upon God, they left her, tho not without Expressions of their *Fury*. From that very time, this poor *Whetford* was *utterly spoilt*, and *grew a tempted, froward, crazed* sort of a *Woman*; a Vexation to her *self*, and all about *her*; and many *ways* unreasonable. In this *Distraction* she lay, till those *Women* were *Apprehended* by the *Authority; then* she began to *mend*, and upon their *Execution*, was *presently* and *perfectly recovered*, from the *ten years Madness* that had been upon her.

A Fourth Curiosity.

IV. 'Tis a thousand pities, that we should permit our Eyes to be so *Blood-shot* with *Passions*, as to lose the sight of many wonderful things, wherein the *Wisdom* and *Justice* of *God*, would be *glorified*. Some of those things, are the frequent 𝔄𝔭𝔭𝔞𝔯𝔦𝔱𝔦𝔬𝔫𝔰 of *Ghosts*, whereby many old 𝔐𝔲𝔯𝔡𝔢𝔯𝔰 among us, come to be *con-*

sidered. And, among many *Instances* of this *kind,* I will single out one, which concerned a *poor Man,* lately *prest* unto *Death,* because of his *refusing* to *Plead* for his Life. I shall make an Extract of a Letter, which was written to my Honourable Friend, *Samuel Sewal,* Esq; by Mr. *Putnam,* to this purpose;

"THE last Night my *Daughter Ann* was griev-
" ously tormented by Witches, threatning
" that we *should* be *Pressed* to Death, before *Giles*
" *Cory.* But through the Goodness of a Gra-
" cious God, she had at last a little Respite:
" Whereupon there appeared unto her (she said)
" a Man in a Winding sheet, who told her, that
" *Giles Cory* had Murdered him by *Pressing* him
" to *Death* with his Feet; but that the Devil
" there appeared unto him, and Covenanted with
" him, and promis'd him, *He should not be*
" *Hanged.* The Apparition said, God hardned
" his Heart, that he should not hearken to the
" Advice of the Court, and so die an easie
" Death; because as it said, *It must be done to*
" *him as he has done to me.* The Apparition also
" said, that *Giles Cory* was carried to the Court
" for this, and that the Jury had found the Mur-
" ther, and that her Father knew the Man, and
" the thing was done before she was Born. Now
" Sir, this is not a little strange to us, that no

"Body should remember these things all the
"while that *Giles Cory* was in Prison, and so
"often before the Court. For all People now
"remember very well, (and the Records of the
"Court also mention it) That about Seventeen
"Years ago, *Giles Cory* kept a Man in his House,
"that was almost a Natural Fool; which Man
"died Suddenly: A Jury was Impannel'd upon
"him, among whom was Dr. *Zerobbabel Endi-*
"*cot;* who found the Man bruiz'd to Death;
"and having clodders of Blood about his Heart.
"The Jury, whereof several are yet alive, brought
"in the Man Murdered; but as if some Enchant-
"ment had hindered the Prosecution of the Mat-
"ter, the Court proceeded not against *Giles Cory,*
"tho it cost him a great deal of Money to get
"off. Thus the Story.

THE *Reverend and Worthy Author, having at the Direction of his Excellency the Governour, so far obliged the Publick, as to give some Account of the Sufferings brought upon the Country by* Witchcraft; *and of the Tryals which have passed upon several Executed for the same.*

Upon *perusal whereof, we find the Matters of Fact and Evidence truly reported; and a Prospect given of the Methods of Conviction, used in the Proceedings of the Court at* Salem.

 Boston Octob. 11. William Stoughton,
   1692.   Samuel Sewall.

BUT is *New England* the only Chriftian Country, that hath undergone fuch Diabolical Moleftations? No, there are other good People, that have in this way been harraffed; but none in Circumftances more like to *Ours*, than the People of God in *Sweedland*. The Story is a very famous one, and it comes to fpeak *Englifh* by the acute Pen of the Excellent and Renowned Dr. *Horneck*. I fhall only fingle out a few of the more Memorable Paffages therein occurring; and where it agrees with what happened among our felves, my Reader fhall underftand, by my inferting a word of every fuch thing in 𝔅𝔩𝔞𝔠𝔨 𝔏𝔢𝔱𝔱𝔢𝔯.

I. It was in the Year 1669, and 1670. That at *Mobra*, in *Sweedland*, the 𝔇𝔢𝔳𝔦𝔩𝔰, by the help of 𝔚𝔦𝔱𝔠𝔥𝔢𝔰, committed a moft horrible Outrage. Among other Inftances of Hellifh Tyranny there exercifed, One was, that Hundreds of their Children were ufually in the Night fetch'd from their Lodgings, to a Diabolical Rendezvouz, at a place they call'd *Blockula*, where the Monfters that fo fpirited them, tempted them all manner of ways to 𝔄𝔰𝔰𝔬𝔠𝔦𝔞𝔱𝔢 with them. Yea, fuch were the perilous growth of this *Witchcraft*, that Perfons of Quality began to fend their Children into other Countries to avoid it.

II. The Inhabitants had earneftly fought God by **Prayer**, and **yet** their Affliction continued. Whereupon **Judges** had a fpecial **Commiffion** to find and root out the Hellifh Crew; and the rather, becaufe another County in the Kingdom, which had been fo molefted, was deliver'd upon the Execution of the *Witches*.

III. The **Examination** was begun with a day of **Humiliation** appointed by Authority. Whereupon the Commiffioners **Confulting** how they might refift fuch a dangerous Flood; the **Suffering Children** were firft Examined; and though they were Queftioned **One** by **One** apart, yet their **Declarations all agreed**. The **Witches** Accuf'd in thefe Declarations, were then Examined; and though at firft they obftinately **denied**, yet at length many of them ingenuoufly **Confeffed** the Truth of what the Children faid; owning, with Tears, that the **Devil**, whom they called *Locyta*, had **stopt** their **Mouths**; but he being now **gone** from them, they could **No longer Conceal** the Bufinefs. The things by them **acknowledged**, moft wonderfully agreed with what other Witches in other Places had confeffed.

IV. They confeffed, That they did ufe to **Call upon the Devil**, who thereupon would **carry** them away over the Tops of Houfes, to a Green Meadow, where they gave themfelves unto him. Only one of them faid, that fometimes the Devil only took away her **Strength**, leaving her **Body** on the Ground; but fhe went at other times in **Body** too.

V. Their manner was to come into the **Chambers** of People, and fetch away their Children upon Beafts of the Devil's providing; promifing **fine Clothes** and other fine Things unto them, to inveagle them. They faid, they never had power to do thus, till of late; but now the Devil did **Plague** and **Beat** them, if they did not gratifie him in this piece of Mifchief. They faid, they made ufe of all forts of **Instruments** in their Journeys! Of **Men**, of **Beasts**, of **Posts**; the Men they commonly laid afleep at the Place whereto they rode them, and if the Children mentioned the **Names** of them that ftole them away, they were miferably **Scurged** for it, until fome of them were killed. The **Judges** found the Marks of the Lafhes on fome of them; but the Witches faid, **They would quickly vanish**. Moreover, the Children would be in ftrange **Fits**, after they were brought home from thefe Tranfportations.

VI. The **first thing** they faid they were to do at *Blockula*, was to give themfelves unto the Devil, and **Vow** that they would ferve him. Hereupon they **cut their fingers**, and with Blood writ their **Names** in his **Book**. And he alfo caufed them to be **Baptized** by fuch **Priests** as he had in this Horrid Company. In some of them the *Mark* of the cut finger was to be found; they said, that the Devil gave *Meat* and *Drink*, as to *Them*, so to the Children they brought with them; that afterwards their custom was to *Dance* before him, and *Swear* and *Curse* most horribly. They said, that the Devil shewed them a great frightful cruel *Dragon*, telling them, *If they confessed any thing*, he would let loose that great Devil upon them: They added, that the Devil had a great *Church*, and that when the 𝔍𝔲𝔡𝔤𝔢 were coming, he told them, *He would kill them all*; and that that some of them had *attempted to murder the Judges, but could not*.

VII. Some of the Children talked much of a *white Angel*, which did use to forbid them what the Devil bid them to do, and assure them, that these doings would *not last long*; but that what had been done, was permitted for the Wickedness of the People. This *white Angel* would sometimes Rescue the Children from *Going* in with the Witches.

VIII. The Witches confess'd many Mischiefs done by them, declaring with what kind of 𝔈𝔫𝔠𝔥𝔞𝔫𝔱𝔢𝔡 𝔗𝔬𝔬𝔩𝔰 they did their Mischiefs: They thought especially to *Kill the Minister of Elfdala*, but could not. But some of them said, that such as they wounded, would be recovered, upon or before their Execution.

IX. The Judges would fain have had them fhow'd fome of their *Tricks;* but they unanimoufly declared, *That fince they had confeffed all, they found all their* Witchcraft *gone;* and the Devil then *appeared very terrible unto them, threatning with an Iron Fork to thruft them into a burning Pit, if they perfifted in their Confeffion.*

X. There were difcovered no lefs than *threefcore and ten* Witches in one Village; three and twenty of which *freely confeffing their Crimes,* were condemned to Die. The reft (one pretending fhe was with Child) were fent to *Fahluna,* where moft of them were afterwards executed. Fifteen Children, which confeffed themfelves engaged in this Witchery, died as the reft, Six and thirty of them between *Nine* and *Sixteen* Years of Age, who had been lefs guilty, were forced to run the Gantlet, and be lafhed on their Hands once a Week, for a Year together. Twenty more, who had lefs inclination to thefe Infernal Enterprizes, were lafhed with Rods upon their Hands for three *Sundays* together, at the Church-door. The Number of the Seduced Children, was about Three Hundred. This Courfe, together with Weekly Prayers in all the Churches through the Kingdom, iffued in the deliverance of the Country.

XI. The moft Accomplifh'd Dr. *Horneck* incerts a moft wife Caution in his Preface to this Narrative, fays he, *There is no Publick Calamity, but fome ill People will ferve themfelves of the fad Providence, and make ufe of it for their own ends ; as Thieves, when an Houfe or Town is on Fire, will Steal what they can.* And he mentions a remarkable Story of a young Woman at *Stockholm,* in the Year 1676, who accufed her own Mother of being a Witch; and fwore pofitively, that fhe had carried her away in the Night; the poor Woman was burnt upon it, profeffing her Innocency to the laft. But though fhe had been an ill Woman, yet it afterwards prov'd, that fhe was not fuch an one; for her Daughter came to the Judges, with hideous Lamentations, confeffing that fhe had wronged her, out of a wicked fpight againft her; whereupon the Judges gave order for her Execution too.

But fo much of thefe things. *And now, Lord, make thefe Labours of thy Servant profitable to thy People.*

FINIS.

Cambridge: Printed by H. O. Houghton.

APPENDIX.

THE following is a list of persons who lost their lives in the delusion of 1692, by the hand of the executioner, on Gallows Hill in Salem : —

Rev. George Burroughs of Wells; Wilmot Reed of Marblehead; Margaret Scot of Rowley; Susanna Martin of Amesbury; Elizabeth How of Ipswich; Sarah Wildes and Mary Easty of Topsfield; Samuel Wardwell, Martha Carrier, * and Mary Parker of Andover; John Proctor, George Jacobs sen., John Willard, Sarah Good, Rebecca Nurse, and Martha Cory of Salem Village; Ann Pudeater, Bridget Bishop, Alice Parker of Salem.

Giles Cory, of Salem Farms, was pressed to death.

The following persons were condemned to death, but did not suffer : —

Abigail Faulkner, Mary Lacy, Ann Foster, † Mary Post, Sarah Wardwell, and Elizabeth Johnson of Andover; Dorcas Hoar, Beverly; Mary Bradbury of Salisbury; Rebecca Eames of Boxford; Abigail Hobbs of Topsfield, and Elizabeth Proctor of Salem Farms.

The following list contains the names of all the persons who were accused of witchcraft, as far as we have been able to ascertain : —

Salem. — Philip English, Mary English, Ann Pudeater, Mrs. White, Sarah Pease, Alice Parker, Thomas Hardy, Mary De Riels, Sarah Cole, Candy, a slave.

Salem Village and Salem Farms. — Daniel Andrews, George Jacobs sen., George Jacobs, Rebecca Jacobs, Margaret Jacobs, Bridget Bishop, Edward Bishop, John Buxton, Sarah Bishop, Mary Black (negress), George Burroughs, Goodwife Bibber, Sarah Cloyce, John Proctor, Elizabeth Proctor, Rebecca Nourse, Mary Warren, Sarah Good, Tituba, John Indian, Martha Jacobs, John

---

* Martha Carrier had four of her children with her in prison.

† Ann Foster died in prison, and after her death, her son Abraham Foster was compelled to pay 2 pounds 10 shillings, to the keeper of the prison, to obtain her body.

Willard, Sarah Buckley, Mary Whittredge, Giles Cory, Martha Cory, Dorothy Good, Benjamin Proctor.

Topsfield and Ipswich. — Mary Easty, Abigail Hobbs, William Hobbs, Sarah Wildes, Deliverance Hobbs, Nehemiah Abbott jun., James How, Elizabeth How.

Lynn. — Wife of Isaac Hart, Thomas Farrar, Elizabeth Hart, Mary Ireson, Mary Derrick, Sarah Bassett, Sarah, wife of John Cole, widow Mary Derrill, widow Mary Rich.

Charlestown. — Elizabeth Carey, Elizabeth Payne.

Beverly. — Dorcas Hoar, Sarah Merrell, Susanna Roote, Sarah Bulkley, Sarah Riste, Job Tukey, John Wright, Rebecca Johnson, Sarah Morey.

Woburn. — Ann Seers, Bethiah Carter, Bethiah Carter jun.

Reading. — Elizabeth Colsen, Lydia Dustin, wife of Nicholas Rice.

Boxford. — Robert Eames, Rebecca Eames.

Haverhill. — Widow of Francis Hutchinson, Mary Green.

Rowley. — Margaret Scot, Mary Post.

Marblehead. — Wife of Samuel Reed, Wilmot Reed.

Boston. — Capt. John Alden, Capt. John Flood.

Billerica. — Mary Toothaker, Margaret Scot, ——— Abbott, Jason Toothaker, M. Andrews, Roger Toothaker.

Malden. — Elizabeth Fosdick.

Chelmsford. — Martha Sparks.

Gloucester. — Martha Prince, Mary Coffin, Ann Doliver, Abigail Somes.

Amesbury. — Susanna Martin.

Salisbury. — Mary Bradbury.

Andover. — Martha Carrier, Nehemiah Abbott, Deliverance Dane, Richard Carrier, Abigail Faulkner, Ann Foster, Mary Lacy, Samuel Wardwell, Elizabeth Carey, Mary Parker, Sarah Wilson, Sarah Wilson jun., Sarah Bridges, Stephen Johnson, Mary Osgood, Eunice Frye, Mary Marston, wife of Hope Tyler, wife of Ebenezer Baker, wife of Nathan Dane, Mary Wardwell, William Barry, ——— Harrington, William Barker, Hannah Tyler, Abigail Baker, John Laundry, William Barker jun., Mary Barker, Martha Tyler, Joanna Tyler, Sarah Cave, John Bradstreet.*

* John Bradstreet was accused of bewitching a dog, but made his escape, — the dog was hung as a witch.

APPENDIX. 449

Children accused of Witchcraft. — John Laundry, aged ten years; Deborah Faulkner, ten years; Abigail Faulkner, eight years; Mary Lacy jun., fourteen years; Stephen Johnson, thirteen years; Abigail Johnson, eleven years; Sarah Carrier, eight years; Mary Bridges, twelve years; Dorothy Good, five years.

As the Court Records for 1692, have been lost, we do not know the place where Giles Cory was executed. We have been able to gather but very little in regard to the witchcraft delusion from aged persons, resident in what was once Salem Village.

About forty years ago there lived within the bounds of that village, an aged man of nearly one hundred years, who would talk freely of the Indian Wars, but could be induced to say but little concerning witchcraft. He said it was a distressing and fearful subject to talk about. He however frequently expressed the belief, that the devil stole the church book from Mr. Parris, and had it in his possession during the whole of the summer of 1692, and that it was only after a severe struggle the church recovered it again. In 1830 we examined these ancient records, and while copying a portion of them, could not but notice they were in a state of good preservation, considering in whose keeping they had been. In regard to the origin of Salem Witchcraft there have been many opinions. The one most common, and we think the most correct is, that it originated with children, through their love for sport and mischief. The testimony of Daniel Elliott, given in at the trial of Elizabeth Proctor was that she heard one of the accusing girls say, that she cried out against Goody Proctor for sport. "The girls (she added) must have some sport." She expressed without doubt the feeling of the whole circle of these youthful accusers. For a remarkable letter upon the detection of three children engaged in a supposed case of witchcraft in the year 1720, the reader is referred to the sixth page of the tenth volume of the second series of Massachusetts Historical Collections. It should be noticed that all the pretended spiritual manifestations of any note that have ever occurred in this country, had their origin with children and young persons.

We will conclude our notes by mentioning the assertion of Rev. Samuel Mather, son of Dr. Cotton Mather, made in the year 1728, in respect to the first edition of " More Wonders of the Invisible World." He says, (referring to Calef,) "there was a certain disbeliever of Witchcraft, who wrote against his father's book the 'Wonders of the Invisible World,' but the *man* is dead, his book died long before him." Alas! for his hasty opinion. Mather's "Wonders of the Invisible World," and Calef's reply to it, are now printed in one volume together; Calef's work has been printed four times.

Danvers, Sept. 1860.   S. P. F.

www.ingramcontent.com/pod-product-compliance
Lightning Source LLC
Chambersburg PA
CBHW020217170426
43201CB00007B/238